Anthropology & Law

Anthropology &

General Editors: William O. Beeman and David Kertzer, Department of Anthropology, Brown University

Anthropology & Law
James M. Donovan and H. Edwin Anderson, III

Anthropology & Mass Communication
Mark Allen Peterson

ANTHROPOLOGY
&
LAW

James M. Donovan and H. Edwin Anderson, III

Berghahn Books
New York • Oxford

First published in 2003 by
Berghahn Books
www.BerghahnBooks.com

Library of Congress Cataloging-in-Publication Data
Donovan, James M.
Anthropology & law / James M. Donovan and H. Edwin Anderson, III.
   p. cm. — (Anthropology &)
Includes bibliographical references and index.
ISBN 1-57181-423 X (cl.: alk. paper)
   1. Law and anthropology I. Title: Anthropology and law. II. Anderson, H.
Edwin. III. Title IV. Series.

K487.A57D66 2003
340'.115-dc21   2003043674

British Library Cataloguing in Publication Data

A catalogue record for this book is available from the British Library

Printed in the United States on acid-free paper

CONTENTS

To my parents, Dennis and Dolly Donovan,
for their support and inspiration.
— J.M.D.

For my mother, Margaret Witherspoon Scott.
— H.E.A., III

PREFACE TO THE PAPERBACK EDITION

The release of ANTHROPOLOGY & LAW in paperback allows us a rare occasion to reflect on the text and its reception by its intended audiences. As perhaps all authors experience, we are able to identify sections that continue to read as we intended, as well as others that, in retrospect, we might have written otherwise. Those latter realizations are pleasingly few.

We can address most concerns that have come to our attention through clarification of a central theme of the book—the distinction between "anthropology and law" and "legal anthropology."

The backbone of the book, in terms of both content and structure, is what we have termed "balanced reciprocity," defined as a condition wherein "neither discipline is independent of, parasitic upon, or subordinate to, the other. Anthropology, to fully realize its own vision, needs a collateral discipline of jurisprudence; law, in order to achieve its goal of justice and social order, requires the theoretical grounding and empirical conclusions of anthropology" (p. 2). This thesis of balanced reciprocity perhaps formalizes the impression of other anthropologists who study legal institutions, among them Laura Nader who has argued "for separate but equal arenas: we do different things. We have much to learn from each other, but if we try to do each other's work, the work suffers from out naïveté and inexperience" (Laura Nader, THE LIFE OF THE LAW: ANTHROPOLOGICAL PROJECTS [2002]). To our knowledge no one has disputed the desirability of this respectful cooperation between the peer disciplines, although there has been reasonable disagreement over our book's success in realizing its own aspirations in this regard.

At the same time, some reviewers have criticized what appear to their eyes as a disconcerting lack of citation to, and discussion of, the fundamental literature of legal anthropology. We can concede that illustrative examples other than those we chose could have served our didactic purposes equally well, and might have incorporated more of the sources familiar to legal anthropologists. As explained in the Introduction, we chose our examples because they reflected our own expertise, not because they were uniquely required by the arguments asserted in the text (p. 20). The work of Nader and others in the field of alternative dispute resolution stands out particularly as a possible addition to Chapter Three, one that illuminates a further theoretical benefit of anthropology to law.

From our perspective, however, ours is not an incomplete work in legal anthropology, but rather an exercise in something somewhat different, anthropology and law. With the principle of balanced reciprocity as the philosophical and methodological touchstone for the book, it becomes clear why a field of legal anthropology would fall short for our present purposes: even the coordinate terms are not equal. Legal anthropology shows by its name that anthropology is the primary emphasis, with law assuming the subordinate status expected of a qualifying adjective. For our purposes, therefore, we needed to distinguish legal anthropology from the intellectual area we were marking out. That area we labeled "anthropology and law," which treats the fields as equals modeled by the conjunction of the two nouns. In contrast with the ethnographically centered legal anthropology, which asks questions about the place of law in society, and its use by group members, anthropology and law examines the intersection of the independent practices of law and anthropology: in what ways should legal processes recognize the findings of anthropology, and reciprocally, what benefits can the legal institution confer upon the discipline of anthropology, among other questions. There is a place for both, but this book was not intended as an introduction to the field of legal anthropology. That overview exists elsewhere (e.g., James M. Donovan, LEGAL ANTHROPOLOGY: AN INTRODUCTION [forthcoming]).

Are we here imposing a sterile distinction? We think not.

Our hypothesis—admittedly untested—is that the theoretical orientation of those working from a perspective of legal anthropology is discernible from those practicing from an anthropology and law orientation. For valid reasons legal anthropologists will give priority to problems of interest to the anthropologist. When studying law of a particular society the emphasis tends, for example, to be on the comparative sociological dimensions of the processes of disputing, such as differential access to the legal systems and factors influencing choices from among the culturally available options.

While such issues are of immeasurable interest to those specializing in anthropology and law, these practitioners do not eschew subject matter falling outside the ordinary concerns of today's legal anthropologists. For example, they share with practicing lawyers the assumption that law can be concerned with more than dispute settlement—which many American legal anthropologists in practice treat as the entire realm of law—as well as an interest in the deeper nature of the category of law itself. In other words, legal anthropologists tend to limit their inquiries into problems of how law is used, while "anthropology and law" anthropologists consider also what law is. Only if law "is" something in the same sense that anthropology "is" something, can the two meet as equals on the intellectual field. Balanced reciprocity, then, entails the irreducibility of law as a cultural category, at least to the extent that anthropology itself is a distinct discipline within the academy.

If "legal anthropology" and "anthropology and law" represent discrete interdisciplinary relationships, the divergence between them may arise out of the formal backgrounds of the anthropologists involved. Anthropology and law projects require expertise not always necessary to the practice of legal anthropology. Not least, anthropology and law applies a knowledge of law as deep as that of anthropology. The concluding chapter of ANTHROPOLOGY & LAW contains a strong recommendation that "neither field should consider itself healthy unless it has a cadre of persons formally trained in both" law and anthropology (p. 208). To routinely speak about law without actually knowing law (and vice versa), risks incorporating naive presumptions about the unstudied specialty as already happens when conclusions of folk anthropology receive the imprimatur of law. In part our rationale behind this conclusion has been that researchers, being only human, will tend to rely upon the conceptual categories they know best. Those trained in both law and anthropology have more law-related ways of thinking about social phenomena, and can speak to both disciplines as "insiders" to the professional practices and discourses.

These three topics—the thesis of balanced reciprocity, theoretical orientation of the practitioner, and the educational training received—can now be stated more systematically than was first offered in the book. Within a framework of balanced reciprocity, the research interests of legal anthropology proper, and of anthropology and law, diverge almost immediately. Correlated, but not entailed by this divergence is the educational background of the respective researchers, because this is a principle means by which most of us have been socialized into the paradigms of our respective disciplines.

We do not wish to make this distinction more marked than it needs to be to accomplish the intellectual work at hand. But those who expressed concern that we gave short shrift to the admirable accomplishments of legal anthropology were overlooking the intent of the authors to produce a work with a different orientation, one that we hope can make its own contribution to both theory and practice.

PREFACE TO THE
FIRST EDITION

This book arose from our experiences co-teaching a course in "Law and Anthropology" at the Tulane Law School. Rather than being a synopsis of the materials discussed, this manuscript better represents the major philosophical presumptions underlying the course design. When approaching any intellectual subject matter, the outcome can be heavily influenced by the initial assumptions of the inquiry. This rule holds true here as well, when considering the interfaces of—and often, the collisions between—anthropology and law.

The one point we emphasize throughout, is that anthropology and law both benefit when the two disciplines are approached as intellectual equals. This position contradicts the usual practice that one should dominate or even ignore the other. The evenhandedness upon which we design our argument derives from our own backgrounds. Of the two authors, the anthropologist has extensive professional experience as a law librarian and writes frequently for legal audiences; the lawyer, besides having earned an additional master's degree in Latin American Studies, pursues his own work on the development of legal concepts in early societies. While either anthropology or law may appropriately predominate any specific problem, on the whole, neither consistently trumps the other. This balance allows each discipline to benefit from the best of the other. We argue that this attitude of balanced reciprocity specially characterizes the relationship between anthropology and law, and, if ardently pursued, can yield rich benefits to both.

The effort to be evenhanded presented unique difficulties as we wrote this book. We hope (even expect) that this book will find an audience among both anthropologists and lawyers. Legal scholarship is notorious for its extensive footnotes, both exhaustive and exhausting.[1] Unless every fact, statement, and observation has a footnoted citation or elaboration, the lawyer will tend to think the scholarship is thin and

---

Notes for this section can be found on page xiii.

the opinions baseless, as common law requires precedent for authority. If law errs on the side of excess, some feel that anthropology documents its claims too sparsely. The classic ethnography particularly indulges in "general statements, without any information as to the source of the statements or evidence for them."[2]

We have tried to land somewhere between the lawyer's obsession with detail and the anthropologist's disdain of documentation. A quick flip through these pages will reveal what, to the anthropologist, appears to be an excessive quantity of footnotes following, with some modifications,[3] the legal citation style of the celebrated (and equally maligned) *Bluebook*.[4] All we can say is that there are actually less than would be routine had these chapters appeared in a law review. In the end, we thought it better to surprise anthropologists with too much information than to discourage lawyers with too little.

For those unfamiliar with the *Bluebook*, a few words of explanation may be useful. The *Bluebook* is a citation system devised and revised by a consortium of the leading law reviews, particularly that at Harvard Law School. Its major differences from the citation systems familiar to social scientists pertain to citations to court decisions and signals preceding citations. Citations to court decisions follow the following format: case name, Volume number • Case reporter title • first page of the opinion, [optional pin point cite to the specific quote] (court, date).

Much of the invective directed at the *Bluebook* pertains to its complicated rules regulating citation signals. We have used only the most important of them. If a point is either directly quoted or straightforwardly paraphrased, the citation is simply given. If, however, some inference is required to link the cited source to the point made in the text, the citation is preceded by "*see.*" A citation that supports the point without being precisely germane will be preceded by "*cf.*"

In most instances the *Bluebook* citation can be easily decoded. Any lingering doubt about an important source can be allayed by reference to the selected bibliography at the end of the book, which is composed in more traditional format. Beyond providing familiarity to readers with a legal background, our use of the *Bluebook* does provide at least one benefit to social scientists that their customary citation formats do not: if a work is repeatedly cited, the citation always identifies the location of the full bibliographic information with a "*supra*" note.

Notes

1. *See* Anthony Grafton, The Footnote: A Curious History 25-26 (1997).
2. Patricia M. Greenfield, *What Psychology Can Do for Anthropology, or Why Anthropology Took Postmodernism on the Chin*, 102(3) American Anthropologist 564, 565 (2000).
3. For example, we offer the reader the complete titles for periodicals, instead of providing only the approved format abbreviations. Also, we have used endnotes instead of the more traditional footnotes.
4. The Bluebook: A Uniform System of Citation (17th ed., 2000).

Introduction

THE THESIS OF
BALANCED RECIPROCITY

Anthropology and law interact in several contexts, formal and informal, practical and theoretical, and deliberate and accidental. One accidental collision occurred on a law school torts exam. The test hypothetical set the scene with Cain and Abel of Biblical fame. Cain pointed a blowgun at Abel's head, reasonably thinking him to be a statue of a Canaanite deity. Was Cain thereby liable to Abel for an intentional tort of assault?

The correct answer in the professor's mind was, "No." Assault is a tort against a *person*. Since Cain did not intend to assault a person, he lacked the requisite frame of mind required for culpability (he may, however, still be liable for negligence). Although the professor designed the hypothetical to be a straightforward exercise on the element of tortious intent, he spoiled it by identifying the deity as "Canaanite."

Canaanite religion was one of the ancient Semitic religions, the study of which is most notably associated with William Robertson Smith.[1] Smith concluded that the "savages" of that primitive society were unable

> to distinguish between phenomenal and noumenal existence, between organic and inorganic nature, and between animals and plants. Reasoning wholly by analogy, therefore, savages ascribed to all material objects a life similar to their own; and "the more incomprehensible any form of life seems to them, the more wonderful and worthy of reverence do they take it to be."[2]

Smith held that "the sacred object was the *embodiment* of the god himself," and not the temporary *habitation* of the god, as argued in the animistic theory of his friend and contemporary, James Frazer,[3] and very much less its mere *representation*. The statue of a Canaanite deity (of

---

Notes for this section begin on page 24.

which the biblical *Ba'al* is the best known example) was therefore more than an inanimate depiction of the god; to a Canaanite it would have been equivalent to the god himself. And since these "savages" failed to distinguish between the noumenal and the phenomenal, that means that the statue of a god was to Cain a person in the same sense that he would have recognized Abel to be a person.

Presumably the professor thought of the Canaanite statue only in terms of its representational significance because that is the customary attitude toward statues in our own culture. But by projecting this onto-logical assumption onto another culture he inadvertently undermined the elegance of his exam question. Contrary to the credited response, a plausible argument exists that a statue of a Canaanite deity was, for a member like Cain of the ancient Semitic culture, not merely "a" person, but the most vivid exemplar of personhood in his experience. By this reading, Cain *would* have been liable for an assault on Abel because he did intend an assault on a person, even if he did not intend to assault Abel. That he was mistaken in the identity of the person he intended to assault would, by established legal doctrine,[4] be no defense.

No doubt in the mind of the professor this hypothetical posed a very elementary question in nothing but colorful terms. The unexpected irruption of anthropological detail spoiled the elegance of his exam question. The same complication arises in other, more important con-texts where, similarly, the lawyer remains unaware of the anthropolog-ical import of what he or she says and does, and of the dynamics of the cases and issues he or she champions. Of course, the anthropologist can be similarly surprised by unanticipated legal implications incurred by the practice of his or her specialty. Our goal in this volume is to outline, we hope to the benefit of both, a few of the ways in which law and anthropology interact.

This volume differs from most of the existing works on anthropol-ogy and law in that we treat both disciplines as equals on the intellec-tual playing field. Our unifying thesis is that anthropology and law stand in a position of *balanced reciprocity*. Balanced reciprocity means that neither discipline is independent of, parasitic upon, or subordinate to, the other. Anthropology, to fully realize its own vision, needs a col-lateral discipline of jurisprudence; law, in order to achieve its goal of justice and social order, requires the theoretical grounding and empiri-cal conclusions of anthropology.[5]

Although it amounts to much the same thing, this point can be argued from the other direction in terms not of needs but of offers: Anthropology has refined many of the central terms of legal discourse, and accumulated factual findings relevant to ongoing legal disputes, and as such, it should make these available to the law. On the other hand, law has resources of its own—such as a higher social prestige and a unique entrée into the cultural round of a new social system—which would be beneficial to anthropology. Each discipline both needs from and offers to the other something of critical importance. This is the sense in which their relationship can be characterized as a balanced reciprocity. Although the legal or anthropological input on any particular problem need not be equal, in the main, neither discipline should or will be consistently privileged over the other.

The posited equality of a balanced reciprocity is not typical of the relationships either law or anthropology has had with its sister disciplines.[6] Michael Freeman characterizes law's search for a partner with the evocative image of a spinster desperate to become betrothed:

> What do other disciplines think of law? Since it dropped its pretence to discreteness, like a mendicant it has wandered round the corridors of academe seeking first succour here and there. It was nearly a century ago that it tried sociology, and since then it has sought support in a variety of disciplines including anthropology (this taught lawyers something about dispute resolution and may have helped spawn the ADR (Alternative Dispute Resolution) movement), political science, philosophy, literature, history, geography, and economics. Economics embraced law with open arms but, like a Victorian marriage, it was not a partnership of equals.[7]

If economics has traditionally subordinated law to its own interests, the same can be said of the typical relationship between law and anthropology. Rather than viewing law as an intellectual peer from whose input anthropology could benefit, the tendency has been to regard law strictly as an object of anthropological scrutiny. As a result, a discussion of "anthropology and law" can be confused with a summary of "legal anthropology," which subordinates legal perspectives to the theoretical schemes of anthropology. Without question, the cross-cultural comparative study of legal systems is a fascinating and meritorious undertaking.[8] Several works in this area are rightly considered classics in the field of anthropology generally. Sir Henry Sumner Maine's *Ancient Law*,[9] *The Cheyenne Way* by Karl N. Llewellyn and E. Adamson Hoebel,[10] and Bronislaw Malinowski's *Crime and Custom in Savage Society*[11] are outstanding examples. But our immediate interests move us in a different direction. Instead of looking at law as a focus of anthropological inquiry, we inspect the intersection of the practice of anthropology with the practice of law. When should the legal scholar or practitioner seek out the counsel of the anthropologist? Why is the anthropologist unschooled in legal ideas handicapped in the pursuit of even the most basic research endeavors?

We hope this book addresses these questions at least in a preliminary way. Balanced reciprocity stipulates that each discipline make important contributions to the other, contributions beyond the isolated interests of subject specialists. We will identify only a few of these.

Balanced reciprocity informs the structure of the book itself. The two main parts of the book are devoted to "Practical Benefits" and "Theoretical Benefits." Each part has two sections, highlighting the benefits of that kind from one discipline to the other. The practical benefit of anthropology to law that we examine is the wealth of cultural facts that can serve as a foundation for legal reasoning and policy. The practical benefit of law to anthropology is a heightened social visibility and influence that may lead to allocating greater respect, more resources, and even increased employment for anthropologists. The highlighted theoretical benefit of anthropology to law is the refinement of critical concepts. We discuss two such concepts: *religion* and *human rights*. Law's theoretical benefit to anthropology is its privileged perspective on the round of culture. Cultural analysis can begin from any point, but law provides an especially fruitful key.

Although these benefits themselves differ, the kind and value of these benefits are argued to be equivalent, enabling law and anthropology to stand as intellectual peers. A concluding section will suggest the preconditions that must exist before the mutual benefits we have identified can be more fully realized in the future practice of either discipline.

Our thesis will be better understood if the reader shares (at least for present purposes) some of our background assumptions and premises. While many of these will be introduced as needed, we should here clarify what we mean by "anthropology" and "law."

Specialists in these fields might judge as simplistic our description of their own discipline. The primary audience for these sections is persons who lack specialized background in that area. Although practitioners might be tempted to skip our description of their own field, we recommend that they resist this urge. Reading our short overview of their own field might seem unnecessary, but it establishes a uniform vocabulary and identifies our own working premises. Not everyone will agree with those premises. In this short and focused work, we are unable to defend and argue them all. By identifying them, however, we hope we can spare the reader much misunderstanding.

What is Anthropology?

The anthropologist of this partnership had never heard the term "anthropology" until after his undergraduate degree when he was laying the groundwork, only halfheartedly, for graduate studies in physics. "Why not," said a good friend who had participated in one of the "teach an orangutan sign language" projects that were much in vogue twenty years ago, "consider anthropology?" What, he wondered, was *that*? What he read in one college guide literally changed his life: Anthropology, it said, was "the ultimate liberal art."

The characterization of anthropology as the ultimate liberal art is largely true, and constitutes the discipline's major strength. The very scope that makes the claim accurate also makes it difficult to communicate just what anthropology is or does. Yet a conclusion any more specific betrays the field's protean nature and threatens to miss the point.

Perhaps it is easier to begin our inquiry by sketching the outlines of what the study of anthropology includes. When, during cocktail party chitchat, someone learns that their conversational partner is an anthropologist, either of two responses are common. Either he has no idea what that is, or, after thinking about it, his eyes light up as he proudly retrieves the datum that anthropologists are the ones who dig around for bones. In other words, people often confuse anthropology with archaeology.

This confusion is forgivable. In the United States all archaeologists are anthropologists, although not all anthropologists are archaeologists. This is because the formal study of the discipline has been structured according to the "four fields" approach. The anthropology doctoral candidate is expected to demonstrate competency in each of the four major subfields of the discipline: (1) *sociocultural anthropology,* (2) *linguistic anthropology,* (3) *physical anthropology,* and (4) *archaeology.* Specialization is encouraged only after competency is demonstrated in all four fields. The four-field approach is normative but not universal. Some programs in the United States do not require exposure to the full breadth of the discipline, and most European programs are restricted to one specialty or the other.

Each subfield has its particular problem and method. Sociocultural anthropology depends heavily upon participant-observation (living with the focus population for an extended period), with an ethnography[12] as its ultimate work product. The principle foci here are issues of social relationships, institutions, and behaviors among extant peoples. The anthropologist of this type best known to the general public was Margaret Mead, who roared onto the public stage with a provocative study on the adolescent members of a New Guinea tribe.[13] The recently deceased Marvin Harris also enjoyed his share of notoriety for his theories of cultural materialism.[14]

Linguistic anthropology focuses on languages and how they develop over time and space, and interact with other aspects of culture. This subfield can be further divided into three major divisions: (1) *descriptive linguistics,* which studies the properties of a particular language; (2) *historical linguistics,* which tries to relate one language to another, and to isolate features of the ancestor language that generated the daughter languages; and (3) *sociolinguistics*, which studies how social contexts can influence patterns of language use. Although some pure linguists have achieved general recognition (e.g., Noam Chomsky), Edward T. Hall may be the most popularly regarded linguistic anthropologist.[15] Other candidates would include Dell Hymes and William Labov.[16]

Physical (or biological) anthropology addresses two large problems, our own evolutionary ancestry and our relationship to extant primates. *Primatologists* have devoted their lives to the study of gorillas (Dian Fossey) and chimpanzees (Jane Goodall), among other primate species. These studies provide a baseline for claims about what is or is not unique to our own species, and what behaviors may have been typical of our evolutionary ancestors. The *paleoanthropologist* (such as the Leakey dynasty: Louis and Mary, and their son Richard and his wife, Meave) reads the fossil record or our own genetic code for indicators of our development into the species *Homo sapiens*.

The archaeologist, romantically portrayed by the dashing figure of Indiana Jones, concentrates on the material culture of prehistorical societies. He or she digs for potsherds or building remains, and after many analyses incorporating sophisticated classification systems, statistical techniques, and consultations with other disciplines such as geology and ecology, uses these bits of information to reach conclusions about human behaviors in antiquity or even more recent times.

The subdisciplines of the four-field method depend upon familiarity with all the others. The competent ethnographer must know the language of the group as well as its historical movements. Physical anthropology and archaeology both involve the study of bone fragments. Although archaeologists most often study prehistoric populations, they are well served by knowledge of the details of any surviving descendant groups. Each subdiscipline inevitably incorporates the others—providing, perhaps, the prototypical example of balanced reciprocity between coordinate fields.

Against this background we may productively return to the question about what anthropology is. What do all the specialties described above have in common that would warrant their being embraced by the single term, "anthropology"? Simplistically, they are all ultimately concerned with what it means to be "human." What are the differences and similarities between "us" and other cultures, between other species and our own, between ancestor and descendent? What is the range of variation permissible within a wider pattern of universality that makes us all of one piece?

Most other academic disciplines restrict their attentions to only a small segment of this very broad question. As one anthropologist puts it:

Most cultural anthropologists believe that the main difference between their discipline and other human sciences lies not so much in the subjects they investigate as in the approach they take to their studies. This approach involves analyzing human ways of life *holistically, comparatively,* and *relativistically.*[17]

One metaphor we find useful involves flowing streams.[18] Anthropology is not an independent stream running from its source to its end, parallel to all the other streams of the universe of knowledge embodied within other university departments. Rather, it is the confluence of all those other streams into one intellectual moment where they can be mutually informed, to the end that a multidimensional understanding is achieved of what it means to be what we are. In adopting this image, we echo David Hume, who believed "that all the sciences have a relation, greater or less, to human nature; and that however wide any of them may seem to run from it, they still return back by one passage or another."[19] One practitioner has captured the point this way: "our task is to study and debate exactly what the conditions of human life actually are, both in their cross-cultural multiplicity and also in their universal existential reality. It is a task that requires a willingness to argue about what it means to be a human being."[20] When one claims to be an anthropologist, one indeed aspires to be "the ultimate liberal artist." The goal of this book will be to articulate the relationship between this discipline and another of the humane sciences: the law.

What is Law?

"Law" can be a particularly slippery term to grasp for several reasons. First, the label applies both to an academic discipline and a cultural institution. Although our special focus will be on the former, it can be hard to consider them separately. One reason is because the study of law is not normally distinguished from the practice of law. A formal legal education can only be obtained in law schools, and these are unabashedly bastions of professional training rather than scholarly enclaves. This fact minimizes the likelihood that an independent academic legal tradition will emerge (in contrast, for example, to the way that academic biology is not subsumed by medical practice). In fact, in many law schools there is only one course offered in jurisprudence, the actual study of law *qua* law (as opposed to specific statutory studies), and this course is almost always an elective.

Still, at least a few words can be said about special features of law as an academic discipline. In the United States, law degrees are awarded after three years of study in a specialized graduate school of law. The first year is devoted to a standardized curriculum, with more opportunity to take electives of special interest in later years. Students have the option of pursuing either of two tracks of legal education: the *civil law* or the *common law*. Historically, civil law descends from the earlier Roman tradition; common law, from the English legal system. Common law typically develops from judicial decisions rather than statutory or constitutional formulations, whereas civil law finds its primary authority in the written code. In practice, the distinction today appears most markedly when courts are confronted with gaps in the law. A common law judge possesses recognized power to fill this gap: "[W]hen there is no decisive precedent [or law, the judge] must then fashion the law for the litigants before him."[21] When a civilian judge is confronted with a gap, however, she will dismiss the case for lacking a cause of action or an available remedy; she will not seek to "fashion" new law to fill the gap.

However strict these distinctions may have been in former times, today they are matters of degree and not of kind. The traditions might be distinguished by the ratio of legal rules to jurisprudential doctrines within court decisions, and not by their presence or absence. Of the fifty United States, only Louisiana follows the civil law tradition, along with much of Europe and Latin America. The other forty-nine states and the members of the former British Empire are common law jurisdictions.

A special feature of legal education is its reliance upon the casebook. The casebook method, introduced by Christopher C. Landell at Harvard Law School in 1869, is an "inductive system of teaching law in which students study specific cases to learn general legal principles."[22] This approach contrasts with the hornbook method more familiar to students in other disciplines. The hornbook outlines the major principles of the subject area, and is in many ways the mirror image of the casebook. In the hornbook method, the student is told the rule, and then challenged to apply it in specific circumstances, deducing the proper result; in the casebook method, the student is exposed to the details of specific cases from which she must infer the underlying rule.

The heavy reliance upon the casebook method by law schools has several unanticipated repercussions, not least among them the lesson that caselaw contains all that is necessary to speak competently about the law. "Classical legal theory [has] treated law as a closed system. The best evidence for this proposition is legal pedagogy's assumption, unchallenged until recently, that appellate cases are both a necessary and sufficient resource for learning law."[23] All in all, each subject area of law is taught as a self-contained system that does not interact with either other areas of law or other social institutions. Judicial decisions should not be faulted for this myopic perspective. They are written to resolve specific disputes, not to provide material for law school texts.

The oversight arises from the casebook's use of these practical documents to mark the theoretical boundaries of the discipline.

The end result is that the image of law absorbed by law students contains two erroneous elements: first, that it is nothing but a system of rules, and second, that the only necessary restraint upon these rules is that they be internally self-consistent. In law school, courses in specialized subject areas such as estate tax, copyrights and patents, or business organizations are taught with few, if any, references to any other area of law. For example, a criminal law professor was questioned by a student about the proper answer on a multiple-choice exam. Although the teacher intended one answer, another seemed better if the principles of property law were also taken into consideration. The teacher confessed that he did not know property law, and that if the student felt that recourse to any other specialty was needed, she was probably overcomplicating the problem. With the possible exception of a rare course in jurisprudence or legal history, the law school curriculum usually does not require courses that examine how law complements other institutions of society.[24]

This pedagogical method encourages intellectual compartmentalization, allowing a student to gain theoretical knowledge of particular areas of the law while discouraging investigation into the dependency of law on culture. To argue that this educational strategy precludes the formation of a substantive generic concept of the "law" only slightly exaggerates the reality. Consider the following definition of "law" from the authoritative legal dictionary, *Black's Law Dictionary*:

> The regime that orders human activities and relations through systematic application of the force of politically organized society, or through social pressure, backed by force, in such a society; the legal system.[25]

"Law" as a generic concept rarely if ever arises in legal studies, and this tendered definition proves no exception. Legal systems are always specific: Anglo-American law, canon law, military law, and so forth. "Law" is therefore necessarily conceived by lawyers in terms of its idiosyncratic context, a tendency encouraged by the method of their legal educations. Accordingly, and ironically, lawyers are not in the best position to answer the general question, What is law?[26]

Our brief description of legal education has resulted in the negative conclusion that lawyers are not well-positioned intellectually to articulate a generic concept of law. A more positive outcome can be had by considering what form such a concept might assume. Not surprisingly, we believe that anthropology is better equipped to construct a workable nonspecific definition of "law."

That said, we find various proposals by anthropologists over how best to characterize generic law. E. Adamson Hoebel's often-quoted definition is that a "social norm is legal if its neglect or infraction is regularly met in threat or fact, by the application of physical force by an individual or group possessing the socially recognized privilege of so acting."[27] This sounds like the dictionary definition quoted above, and since we rejected that one, we should expect to find difficulties here as well. Hoebel's reference to a "social norm" is clearly an improvement over the requirement of *Black's* "regime." But several kinds of actions uncontroversially regarded as legal, escape the net of Hoebel's definition. For one, actions that merit group shunning—an effective deterrent in many hunting and gathering societies as well as tightly knit agricultural societies such as the Amish—would not count as "legal norms" because they entail no threat of actual *physical* force. Even further, innumerable infractions incur no force of any kind, physical or otherwise, unless that idea is unhelpfully broadened to include fines, garnishment, and other monetary sanctions. Yet we would be surprised to learn that breaking the speed limit is not a violation of the law.

Also escaping Hoebel's definitional net are actual rules that we ordinarily classify as part of the law if for no other reason than that they were enacted by a competent rule-making entity such as a legislature or city council but whose infraction rarely incurs any repercussion whatsoever. Prime examples here are purely symbolic pronouncements that by design are to be enforced sporadically, if at all:

> Criminal law, and Good Samaritan laws in particular, serve a higher purpose apart from concerns of mere punishment. These laws provide some sort of "moral compass" that points society in its proper direction.
> Nowhere is this argument more relevant than in Minnesota .... Minnesota's Good Samaritan statute has been fallow since its enactment in 1983. An original sponsor of the bill indicates that its purpose was largely symbolic, consonant with Minnesota's vision of an ideal society. Regardless, the message is clear; what at first glance appears to be lack of enforcement might actually be manifestation of legislative intent.[28]

Other statutes become pure symbols in practice even if not by original design, as has happened with most jurisdictions' statutes criminalizing sodomy. So a jurisdiction may forbid both oral and anal sex,[29] but still officially recognize "Gay Pride Week." The greater social shock would not be the infraction of these laws, but instead their sudden enforcement, as was seen when another symbolic law was dusted off in Israel. A 1986 ban, "virtually unenforced" since its passage, forbade the public display of leavened goods during Passover. When inspectors arrived with warrants to enforce the law, one restaurant owner "thought it was a joke," and was fined $25.00.[30]

By Hoebel's definition, these symbolic statutes are not "legal" because their infractions are not *regularly* met "in threat or fact by the application of physical force." All told, Hoebel's definition results in so many counterintuitive conclusions about what is or is not the "law," that it must be discarded.

A different perspective derives from a view of culture as a series of restrictions that function to preserve society.[31] Bronislaw Malinowski, an architect of contemporary cultural anthropology, proposed that law reinforced these restrictions, and accordingly, law could be equated with "rules which protect the rights of one citizen against the concupiscence, cupidity or malice of the other; rules which pertain to sex, property and safety."[32] Whereas Hoebel's definition suffers the infirmity of being underinclusive, Malinowski's errs in the opposite direction by being overinclusive, including every "rule," whatever it may be, within the category of "law." For example, there are numerous cultural rules about sex, but not all of them warrant serious legal notice. Fornication is not a crime in most U.S. jurisdictions, although promiscuity continues to contravene idealized social behavior.[33] As one eminent lawyer-anthropologist noted, "[f]ollowing [Malinowski] down this road, one has not too little to talk about but far too much."[34]

Although these proposed definitions can be enumerated further, we have all we need to develop what we feel is the most productive strategy. Despite the differences between these two anthropologists, their conclusions could be said to be looking at the whole forest, in contrast to legal analysis's focus on the tree. They agree that law stands as only one institution among many within any given culture (although, as we shall later argue, a very special one). The parameters of and relationships between these cultural institutions are the proper focus of the inquiry. Any given rule will be of interest less for its own sake than for how it reflects, interacts with, and is otherwise generally entangled with other culture variables and ideas. Legal prohibitions against incest, for example, can tell us much about the background assumptions about family structure because such prohibitions vary not only between societies but even among factions within a single society. Incest in one American state is not always incest in another, and this variability can shed light on regional cultural differences.[35]

Malinowski's specific formulation is flawed, but we agree with his premise that an understanding of "law" should be grounded in the work expected of anything deserving of the label. This *functionalist* perspective labels a sociocultural institution, or some part thereof, "legal" if it performs a specific set of end-related behaviors (we will consider functional analysis more thoroughly in chapter 3). By contrast, Hoebel's definition might be termed *reactionist*: a legal norm is not recognized by the work it does, but by how people react to its infraction—for example, with threats or force. Just as anything that fulfills the legal function should be recognized as a "legal," to Hoebel, anything that provoked the legal response was a law.

Functionalism tells us how to identify the potential members of the set of social norms that are to be counted as "law": any set of behaviors that performs the function identified as legal is thereby necessarily part of the law. This is as far as Malinowski got. As we saw, however, this premise leads to conceptual trouble, so something more is needed. The suggestion we make distinguishes between "the Law" as it is identified functionally and which is a sociocultural universal, and "the law" as it exists as a formal cultural construct, and which is not universally present in all societies.[36] A universal law against murder must be analytically differentiated from a law requires shops to close on Sunday.

A consequence of functional analysis is that the (generic) "Law" is distinguishable from the aggregate of the (specific) "law." They are different levels of analysis, and require distinct but interrelated justifications. Moreover, it is possible that they do not describe identical data. In theory, the set of all norms fulfilling the legal function is not equivalent to the set of all norms contained within legal codes. Some true (function-fulfilling) Law may lie outside the formal codes. Any nuanced consideration of the law in this general sense must allow for this distinction. Much of the difficulty in Malinowski's definition arises because he conflates these two levels of analysis, resulting in a statement that fails to accurately capture neither.

While we cannot digress so far as to exhaustively consider what are the legal functions,[37] we can sketch out a few observations. First, granting that culture is a series of restrictions, Law acts as a mechanism for the enforcement of only *some* of those restrictions (thus avoiding the overinclusiveness of Malinowski's definition). Other, nonlegal enforcement can take many forms. Religion, for instance, enforces some cultural restrictions. Although religion and law can overlap significantly, they are not interchangeable and must be kept conceptually distinct. Even further, some restrictions require no enforcement at all because the socialization process makes their breach unthinkable: no law is required, for example, to discourage the vast majority of people from acts of cannibalism or incest. Consequently, to identify the restrictions necessary for culture is not necessarily to have identified those properly accorded legal status.

Second, the fulfillment of the legal function does not require that Law become embodied in formal rules of law or specialized legal structures. In less specialized societies, Law may not exist as an independent institution. Hunting and gathering societies do not have a legal institution in the sense that these duties are delegated to specialists. Instead, the legal elements are more uniformly distributed throughout the society: "In a small co-operative group no individual would want the job either of passing judgment or of administering punishment, so like everything else in Pygmy life the maintenance of law was a co-operative affair."[38] In hunting and gathering societies, almost every individual is at times a legitimate judge, jury, and perhaps even executioner of other individuals, recalling to mind the state of nature as Locke imagined it, wherein natural law and justice are executable by each person.[39] This diffuse assignment of functions is, in the opinion of some, superior to our own hyperspecialized structure:

> The extension of the sphere and importance of observable law in the more highly developed societies is not in itself an index of social progress. It is merely an index of a greater complexity of the society and hence of the norms or imperatives to be observed, and hence, finally, of an increasing difficulty in obtaining universal adherence to such norms. Conversely, this means that the less call there is for law as law, and upon law as law (relative to the degree of complexity of a society), the more successful is that society in attaining a smooth social functioning.[40]

As an institution, the Law may include (as does our own) a court system, a legislature, and an enforcement branch. Even if this triad legitimately parses the legal function, it does not thereby also identify necessary social entities. Roman civilization, for example, never had an independent judiciary. A characterization of Law in only these terms will ring false, and not merely because of its blatant ethnocentricity.

A complete idea of the Law would take into account both the *formal* and the *informal* dimensions of the system. Overemphasis upon the legal structures can obscure the equally important actions of legal entities. If the president of the United States limited his acts only to those specified in the U.S. Constitution, he would fail to do many things we require of successful politicians generally and expect of presidents specifically. The Constitution does not bestow upon the president a "bully pulpit," but we think him a failure if he declines to use it. As recent history has shown, a president who has fulfilled his formal duties well can still be regarded with contempt for his inability to effectively accomplish his informal obligations, such as being a "role model." Anyone interested in understanding the structural position of the president within our society must therefore consider both the formal grants of power as well as the informal expectations. So, too, an understanding of Law that overemphasizes the formal elements over the informal ones will be unable to fully account for the range of phenomena we need to include within its scope.

The immediate lesson is that our own society is perhaps not the best specimen from which to abstract general conclusions about Law. It is too specialized and too fragmented to discern the essential links from the accidental ones or to ascertain what is idiosyncratic in our law from what is essential about the Law. In many ways, it could be said that our law has been overthought and has become too self-conscious to provide a suitable subject for this particular study. To invoke a cinematic image, it plays to the camera of our inquiry, when what we really need is a more naturalistic subject. If we are correct, we must look toward less complex societies for an elucidation of general Law. And this, of course, is the special genius of anthropology, and of legal anthropology particularly.

We earlier concluded that lawyers, by consequence of their educations, are poorly positioned to consider "law" in the abstract. We may now assert the more positive conclusion that anthropologists are in a position to do what lawyers cannot, that is, to extract from all the legal particulars the generic idea of "law," one that transcends any singular instantiation. By remaining aware of the distinction between the capital "L" Law and the little "l" law, anthropologists are less likely to confuse the necessary with the merely contingent. The idea of a generic institution of law is the primary gift to law from anthropology.

The Historical Interactions between Anthropology and Law

From what has been said thus far, one might think that the symbiotic relationship between anthropology and law would have been easily recognized and early encouraged.[41] And, indeed, earlier this century, anthropology and law enjoyed much friendlier relations than is currently the case. At one time, anthropological discussions and field reports would have been comfortable reading for the legally trained mind in terms of both style and content, fostering their warm reception.

As sciences go, anthropology is a young discipline, no more than 150 years old. Necessarily, the progenitors of the field had their formal educations in other areas. People are usually surprised to learn that Franz Boas, the father of American anthropology, received his doctorate in physics (as did Malinowski) for a dissertation on the perception of the color of water.[42] From among the assorted trainings of these early founders, none "had a greater influence on the birth and growth of anthropology than law."[43]

This result emerged from three converging influences. First, the study of law naturally segues into anthropological method. Much of the Anglo-American legal tradition can find its elemental precursors in earlier systems such as Roman law or canon law.[44] A competent analysis of such precursors requires that the legal rules be contextualized into their original cultural settings so that their intended scope and significance can be accurately reconstructed, with the goal of extrapolating to current applications. This project requires that one delve into historical reconstructions of earlier societies, cross-cultural comparisons, and evolutionary development of legal concepts as they moved from the precursor to current form. In retrospect, a student of the history of law would have found himself in the midst of the disparate but as yet unconnected elements of an anthropological inquiry. This innate disciplinary tendency needed only to be pushed a bit further before lawyers began doing true anthropology (or at least ethnohistory).

Just as important is the reverse process. Any discipline, especially a relatively new one such as anthropology, must find an audience outside its inner circle of initiated specialists. To thrive, the field must garner the benefits of public support in terms of funding and endowments, not to mention recruitment of new students by piquing their interest. This chore was eased for anthropology in that it had a ready-made audience of potential supporters. If their own interests encouraged attorneys to consider questions in anthropological ways, so too did they facilitate the consumption of anthropological materials even when not on legal subjects. Early anthropology texts (such as Sir Henry Sumner Maine's *Ancient Law*) were, by dint of training and simple interest, intellectually compatible to lawyers.

This link between the two fields is noticeably weaker today. Legal education is not as broad as it previously was. An attorney can no longer be presumed to be interested in, or even to have been seriously exposed to, the issues that originally brought the disciplines together, particularly legal history and legal philosophy, not to mention classic languages such as Latin and the associated studies of ancient societies. In consequence, anthropological inquiry does not resonate with the modern lawyer as once it did.

The unequaled impact of law on the formation of anthropology goes beyond the parallels of method. The second converging influence was that, by virtue of their training, lawyers were also predisposed to ask what would later become typical anthropological questions. Besides the exploration of the development of legal systems, nonlegal subjects that would later become synonymous with the pursuit of anthropology include kinship particularly and social structure generally. Analyzing a case of intestacy (dying without a will) requires the same triangle-and-circle kinship diagrams known to all anthropology students.

This influence has fared no better than the first. Simply put, the core legal curriculum no longer requires the contemplation of anthropological questions. Whereas in times past, mastery of a wide-ranging treatise such as Francis Lieber's *Manual of Political Ethics*[45] was de rigueur for the aspiring attorney, today's pedagogical approach, described above, restricts itself almost exclusively to the reading of prior case decisions from appellate courts. Because the law is now treated as a set of rules with tricky exceptions whose only evaluative standard is self-consistency, rather than as an institution interacting with other sociocultural systems, the lawyer is less inclined than before to frame an anthropological question.

Finally, even nonlegal topics were approached from a viewpoint that the lawyer would find familiar. Much of becoming enculturated into the legal profession is learning how to think, argue—and most important—to write like a lawyer. At least one semester in law school includes a required course on this skill. Two features that characterize legal writing are its form of argument and its minimalist language.

The form of a typical legal argument is called "IRAC," which stands for "Issue, Rule, Analysis, Conclusion."[46] IRAC is a recursive style of argument, meaning that the main IRAC can have embedded within it any number of "mini-IRACs" addressing each element of the argument individually. While not making a legal document a creative read, it does impose a tight logical structure upon the argument. From the internal memorandum to the expansive law review article, all kinds of legal writing can be distilled into its component IRACs.

Legal language is typically devoid of any of the flourishes that might be expected in other writing styles, indicative of its primary function to convey information rather than to communicate ideas, relegating the work of persuading the judge or jury to the oral components of legal work. Whereas most writing discourages the use of the same word or phrase over and over, the opposite is true of legal writing, which prefers a highly restricted vocabulary. So while an anthropological text might have as one of its goals to evoke the experiences and perspectives of the informants, legal writing strives only to convey and interpret "the facts" à la television's *Dragnet* of the 1960s. The net effect is that legal writing can be dry, but in its favor it also minimizes the potential for misunderstandings by eliminating colorful but possibly confounding language.

The point is that a theory presented in a format familiar and comfortable to its audience is more readily accepted than even the best theory in an unfamiliar style. Much of the early anthropological materials, written as they were by lawyers, were framed in a writing style reminiscent of the traditional legal mode of argument. Although this would not have been sufficient to gain the argument's immediate acceptance, it would have significantly facilitated its being read and considered. The presentation, in other words, would not have been an obstacle to understanding.

That a prior legal education should deeply influence the style of presentation of later work in other areas is a claim not restricted to anthropology. Charles Darwin was profoundly inspired by Charles Lyell's three-volume *Principles of Geology* (1830-1833). In that work, Lyell demonstrated that the natural forces seen to operate today are the very ones responsible for geologic formations of the earth. This insight was formalized into his principle of uniformitarianism: "physical and chemical laws are invariant and their products change only in distribution, abundance, and configuration."[47] Part of what made Lyell's presentation so convincing was that he applied his training in law to frame the issue into analogous legal arguments. This tactic enabled him, like any good attorney, successfully to corral his audience into accepting the desired conclusion.[48]

Early anthropologists shared with their contemporaries in law a methodological preference, a topical focus, and a style of presentation. For these and perhaps other reasons, law and anthropology were predisposed to form an early and formative relationship. A short review of some of these transitional personalities should help reveal just how important this collaboration was to anthropology.

The years from 1860 to 1865 were "an astounding period vital to the foundations of anthropology [for in them] came the major works of Darwin, Lubbock, Bachofen, Maine, McLennan, Waitz, and Tylor."[49] Several names on this list were originally lawyers. Sir Henry Sumner Maine, author of *Ancient Law* (1861), is an obvious example. A lawyer who served in India, he is most famous for his division of the evolutionary development of law into two major periods: "the movement of the progressive societies has hitherto been a movement *from Status to Contract.*"[50] Maine is closely followed in both time and importance by Lewis Henry Morgan, a lawyer from New York. The author of *Ancient Society*, Morgan is best remembered for his division of human cultural history into seven stages, normally collapsed into the three stages of savagery, barbarism, and civilization.[51] Although forgotten by their original legal professions, both Maine and Morgan continue to be seminal figures of early anthropology.

Writing at this same time was Adolf Bastian, whose formal training was in both law and medicine.[52] Klaus-Peter Koepping credits Bastian with the elevation of ethnology above the haphazard practices then prevalent. Bastian's vision for this enterprise was ambitious:

[F]irst, the new science was to proceed inductively; *secondly*, ethnology is to provide raw-materials for a scientific psychology, those raw-materials being the *collective representations* of all ethnic groups, and this collective consciousness and its manifestations should, where possible, be grounded in principles of physiology and the notion of the average or mean; *thirdly*, the collective representations in their variety are called *folk ideas*; and *fourthly*, the general similarity of folk ideas points to certain underlying primary principles or *elementary ideas*, which seem to be the same for

all mankind and point to the validity of the notion of the *psychic unity of mankind.*[53]

The principle of psychic unity is perhaps Bastian's most enduring contribution to anthropology, one that we will employ in chapter 3 as a complement to the idea of human nature. Psychic unity remains a contentious category of thought within anthropological circles,[54] but one that we believe has been undervalued.

Around this foundation of thought and application arose other persons, both earlier and later. Karl von Savigny, a German law professor, published *History of Roman Law in the Middle Ages* from 1814 through 1834. He argued "that law had no 'rational' or 'natural' basis but arose from the patterns of life of the people," drawing comparisons between law and language.[55] An early proponent of the comparative method, he would later be the teacher of the Brothers Grimm, the renowned folklorists and linguists.

J.J. Bachofen studied law at the University of Berlin for three years beginning in 1835. His most influential work contributed to early theories about kinship and social organization.[56] John Fergusen McLennan "was admitted to the Scottish bar in 1857."[57] His research distinguished "two types of marriage rules: rules of *exogamy* ('out-marriage') and rules of *endogamy* ('in-marriage')."[58]

Any list of later anthropologists of major influence would have to include Max Weber. His best-known volume is *The Protestant Ethic and the Spirit of Capitalism.*[59] First published in 1904, Weber's book theorized that the Calvinistic Protestant theology centering on an Elect of God made possible the rise of capitalism and the creation of a middle class.

The number of law-trained anthropologists declined after the first generation. As anthropology became an established discipline in its own right, it became possible for new students to enroll in the new degree programs offered at the major universities. Future anthropology could draw upon its own, specially trained students, no longer needing to convert those from other departments. Fewer anthropologists of stature subsequently came to the field after first training in law. We note three exceptions to this generalization.

If any of his books reflect Claude Lévi-Strauss's law degree, it would be *The Elementary Structures of Kinship.*[60] Like all of his tomes, this is a ponderous and difficult (even painful) read, dedicated to his fellow lawyer-turned-anthropologist, Lewis Morgan.

> The main concern of *Elementary Structures* is described in three different ways: to "show that marriage, rules, nomenclature, and the system of rights and prohibitions are indissociable aspects of one and the same reality, viz., the structure of the system under consideration"; to provide "an

introduction to the general theory of kinship systems"; and to answer the question "where does nature end and culture begin?"[61]

He pursues these sundry goals through an exhausting analysis of exogamous cross-cousin marriage systems among Australian aborigines. Lévi-Strauss further champions his theoretical structuralism via his analyses of transformation of myths, in which he attempts to unveil the natural tendency of the human mind to think in terms of dichotomously opposed concepts: Young/Old, Male/Female, and, serving as the title of his first volume on this topic, *The Raw and the Cooked*.[62] These works reveal his "ultimate concern … to establish facts which are true about 'the human mind' rather than about the organization of any particular society or class of societies."[63]

Max Gluckman also had legal training,[64] which found application in his analysis of the legal system of the Barotse of southern Africa.[65] He is perhaps best remembered by students of anthropology for his formulations regarding "rituals of rebellion." These rituals were open expressions "of social tensions: women have to assert license and dominance as against their formal subordination to men, princes have to behave to the king as if they covet the throne, and subjects openly state their resentment of authority."[66] This annual purging of pent-up resentments purportedly strengthened the group's social unity.

Our final example of a modern lawyer-turned-anthropologist is Robert Redfield.[67] A central theme of his research was the contrasts between rural and urban life, such as the face-to-face basis for social relations in the former as compared with impersonality of the latter.[68] Redfield was perhaps the first anthropologist to provide expert testimony against segregation in the public schools.[69]

Although the early relationship between law and anthropology may have been in many ways superior to today's, it was not characterized by the balanced reciprocity we advocate here. If "law had a lasting impact on anthropology's origin, early anthropology has exerted little influence on legal scholarship."[70] There was little significant flow in the opposite direction, from anthropology to law, of either persons or ideas.[71] We could identify no example of a professional anthropologist who later went on to enter the upper echelons of the law, either as practitioner or scholar, either then or now. Although such individuals surely exist, their rarity indicates that the possession of anthropological training does not translate into success in law with sufficient regularity as to cause this path to be taken more often. Any documentable migration from anthropology to law usually signifies an *abandonment* of anthropology in favor of legal practice,[72] rather than an *expansion* of their anthropological expertise into a new area.

The conclusion we reach is that law was disproportionately influential in the formative years of the new discipline of anthropology. As time passed, and anthropology attained an independent recognized status among the academic disciplines, the factors that favored law's influence waned, never again to be equaled in later years. In its turn, anthropology has yet to influence law to a degree commensurate with what might be expected given the invaluable intellectual resources it has to offer. Although we will argue that the ideal relationship between law and anthropology is balanced and reciprocal, that condition has never actually pertained.

Limitations of the Argument

The reader is entitled to a few warnings about the style and structure of the argument we present. First, cultural anthropology predominates the examples we offer. When we teach our course on the interface between anthropology and law, we are careful to present examples from each of the four fields of anthropological study. For purposes of this book, however, we felt most comfortable remaining within the areas of our surest expertise. The admitted underrepresentation of the other subfields should be taken only as a comment upon our own limitations, and not upon the applicability of our argument to anthropology as a whole. We are not, in other words, treating "anthropology" and "cultural anthropology" as synonyms. Where we are aware of pertinent issues from other subfields, we shall indicate them to the reader.

Second, many of the claims and statements imputed to anthropology in the following chapters are technically about the social sciences generally and not about anthropology specifically. We justify this practice with the assertion that anthropology is a social science. Members of the overarching category "social science" are sufficiently similar, so that many claims for one—claims that are not about particular subject matter but rather about philosophical foundations or epistemological features—are equally true of the others.

For example, the social sciences are distinguishable from the physical sciences less by their subject matter than by their inherently inexact conclusions. If any science can in theory aim toward complete predictability, it will be a "physical" or "hard" science.[73] By contrast, the social or "soft" sciences cannot, even theoretically, aspire to such complete knowledge of their subject matter. Conclusions here will *always* be probabilistic, never deterministic, even in a perfect world.[74] This is not a failing of social scientific method. No future procedural refinements can abolish this limit. The most that can be hoped for is that they may effectively minimize this constraint in most practical applications. This limit of the social sciences generally also applies to anthropology.

This venue is not the one for us to further defend this view of the social sciences generally, or anthropology specifically, a position we are aware is not shared by all anthropologists.[75] We present these points not to persuade the reader but to identify the authors' premises. Essentially, we understand anthropology to be a *science*. Exactly what this honorific entails can be elusive, and any discussion quickly becomes a highly technical exposition. For our purposes, easily digestible criteria are offered by physicist Robert Park: "How well the template [of science] fits comes down to two questions: Is it possible to devise an experimental test? Does it make the world more predictable? If the answer is no to either of these questions, it isn't science."[76] Good anthropological research, in the main, strives to respond affirmatively to these two concerns, and thereby qualifies as science. Much of the resistance we might expect can be avoided by noticing that Park requires only that it be *possible* to devise an experimental test. Anthropologists are not required, by this standard, to actually conduct such testing themselves; the claim that anthropology is a science is not an insistence that all anthropologists become experimentalists. Classic ethnography continues to play an irreplaceable role even in a scientific anthropology. Although some anthropologists do employ experimental methodologies, the status of anthropology as a science depends upon speaking in terms that are testable by someone, if not by the ethnographer. We do not, for example, explain possession mediumship by reference to supernatural entities, but rather by recourse to social and economic variables. I.M. Lewis's work on this problem[77] is no less scientific because he did not himself conduct experiments. That step has been taken by other fieldworkers.[78]

These considerations, we believe, allow us judiciously to use claims about the social sciences generally in arguments about anthropology specifically. We use this nonanthropological literature conservatively. For example, most of the problems faced by the anthropologist drafted into the role of the expert witness in litigation will be identical to those of the sociologist, so any research on the latter can be applied to the former. We believe our practice is rational and defensible. Ultimately, the reader must decide.

The third limitation of our argument parallels the second. There we justified our use of source materials from categories that are broader but encompassing of anthropology, such as "social science." Here we must defend the opposite strategy. While our discussion concerns "law" in some wider sense, most of our direct examples are drawn from only one aspect of the legal system, the judicial.

In explanation, we appeal only partially to sheer convenience: court materials (briefs, case decisions, and the like) are simply more readily available than are comparable materials from the legislative or administrative branches. We might also rely upon the considered opinion that "although science and technology have become immeasurably more important to modern affairs of state, our leaders' knowledge of these subjects has dwindled to near zero."[79] Whatever might be the limitations of judges when dealing with scientific problems, including the anthropological, "they are rocket scientists compared to Congress."[80]

This negative assessment is only slightly exaggerated given past attempts of legislative bodies to pronounce on scientific issues. A most notorious example occurred in 1897. The Indiana House, by a unanimous vote, passed Bill No. 246, the object of which was to redefine the value of pi (the ratio of the circumference of a circle to its diameter, 3.14 ...). Only the lucky passing of a mathematics professor during the debate prevented its passage by the senate as well.[81]

Mathematics is not the only venerable discipline to suffer indignities at the hands of legislatures. Popularly elected bodies have repeatedly felt compelled to statutorily injure the biological sciences by either forbidding the teaching of its predominant theoretical model (Darwinian evolution), or by requiring the teaching of religious alternatives currently marketed under the terms "scientific creationism" or "intelligent design." If mathematics and biology, two of the more firmly established intellectual disciplines, regularly suffer such egregious insults, one can only shudder at what a legislature would do to a field whose principles and theories are less clearly defined and socially respected. In summary, one can wish for a better forum than the legislature in which to dissect the relationship between science and the law. Fortunately we can look to the judiciary.

The hoped-for improvement does not lie with the kind of person we find in the courtroom as compared to the legislature. "All judges and most legislators," law professor David Faigman notes,

> come from the ranks of lawyers. These are people who typically ended up in law school because their prospects in science and math were dim. Fewer than 10 percent of all students attending law school have undergraduate degrees in fields that require substantial math and science training, such as the natural sciences, math and statistics, computer science and engineering. Not only do they not have training in the particular subject, they have a more profound disability: most lawyers have little or no appreciation for the scientific method and lack the ability to judge whether proffered research is good science, bad science, or science at all.[82]

Faigman is not timid when conveying his low regard for lawyers' scientific acumen: "The average lawyer is not merely ignorant of science, he or she has an affirmative aversion to it."[83] He documents his conclusion with astonishing anecdotes of our national lawmakers in action.[84]

The advantage judicial materials have over the legislative record does not, therefore, rely upon judges being better educated than legislators. Rather, unlike other aspects of the legal establishment, the courts must justify the reasoning behind their decisions. When a judge (and not a jury) is the finder of fact, for example, the *Federal Rules of Civil Procedure* requires her to "find the facts specially and state separately its conclusions of law thereon."[85] This means that judges "are required to explain the factual and legal reasoning on which their judgment is based. They must explain what they found to be the facts and what law they actually applied to those facts to arrive at their ultimate judgment."[86] They must, in other words, "describe each link in the chain of fact and law that leads them to their conclusions."[87] If Faigman's pessimism is merited, at least a judge cannot hide faulty reasoning, false beliefs, or educational gaps nearly so easily as a legislator who is under no similar obligation to justify his position.

The problem for scholars can be even worse. Even if a legislator could be counted on to defend a bill with intellectual rigor, we may never hear about it. While Congress leaves a quantity of reports, hearings, and transcribed floor debates, some states (such as Louisiana) have no significant legislative history at all. But we almost always know why a court believes it decided the way it did, and sometimes this rationale can be more enlightening than the specific outcome of the case. This fact allows us to see better which arguments the court chose to credit and which to ignore. This information can be an effective window on contemporaneous cultural influences.

Finally, courtrooms are better contexts to consider the intersection of law and science than are legislatures because judges operate under a mandate formalized in *Daubert v. Merrell Dow Pharmaceuticals*.[88] This U.S. Supreme Court decision (discussed at length in chapter 2) "instructed federal judges to serve as 'gatekeepers,' aggressively screening out ill-founded or speculative scientific theories" which clever plaintiffs' attorneys seek to introduce to confuse juries.[89] To comply with *Daubert*, judges must at least sensitize themselves to the complexities of scientific issues, and where necessary, either take the time to educate themselves on the relevant issues or appoint a special master to summarize and instruct the court. Few judges will be as diligent as Patrick Higginbotham. Faced with a class action employment discrimination suit raising complex issues of statistical analysis, he "and his two clerks spent a year to produce an [127 page] opinion, devoting a full month to just this case" in an effort to sort through the technical details.[90] While this degree of willingness to self-educate on new issues remains unusual, *Daubert* requires that judges become more sophisticated consumers of any information offered as evidence in their courts. So while we may wish our legislators knew more about what they show no hesitation to discuss, our judges must meet the higher standard of an intelligent generalist.

Our weighting of judicial over legislative materials is therefore both convenient and rational. Again, as above, the reader must decide whether this heavy reliance on one dimension of the law has skewed our arguments.

Notes

1. *See* WILLIAM ROBERTSON SMITH, THE RELIGION OF THE SEMITES (New York: Meridian Books, 1889).
2. Robert Alun Jones, *Robertson Smith and James Frazer on Religion, in* FUNCTIONALISM HISTORICIZED: ESSAYS ON BRITISH SOCIAL ANTHROPOLOGY 31, 41 (George W. Stocking, Jr., ed., 1984).
3. *Id.*
4. *See* Ransom v. Kitner, 31 Ill. App. 241 (1889).
5. Speaking to the specific problem of governing traditional New Guinea societies, Peter Lawrence observed this same interdependence: "the emerging situation is one in which both the lawyer and the social anthropologist have a direct interest and much to contribute. Yet neither can realize his full potential unless he is prepared to go into partnership with the other and accept at least a partial amalgamation between the two disciplines in this common field of interest." Peter Lawrence, *Law and Anthropology: The Need for Collaboration,* 1(1) MELANESIAN LAW JOURNAL 40, 41 (1970).
6. Because we do not survey the whole of the universe of possible relationships between anthropology and other fields, we do not go so far as to assert that its relationship with law is unique. While some other discipline conceivably also stands in balanced reciprocity to anthropology, it is not immediately apparent to us which that might be.
7. Michael Freeman, *Law and Science: Science and Law, in* SCIENCE IN COURT 1 (Michael Freeman & Helen Reece eds., 1998).
8. Edited volumes that offer an extensive overview of legal anthropology theory and practice include those by LAURA NADER, LAW IN CULTURE AND SOCIETY (1969) and by PETER SACK & JONATHAN ALECK, LAW AND ANTHROPOLOGY (1992).
9. SIR HENRY SUMNER MAINE, ANCIENT LAW: ITS CONNECTION WITH THE EARLY HISTORY OF SOCIETY AND ITS RELATION TO MODERN IDEAS (New York: Dorset Press, 1986) (1861).
10. KARL N. LLEWELLYN & E. ADAMSON HOEBEL, THE CHEYENNE WAY: CONFLICT AND CASE LAW IN PRIMITIVE JURISPRUDENCE (1941). This book marks an early appearance of the practice continued in the present volume, the collaboration of an anthropologist and an attorney. Llewellyn was a noted lawyer; Hoebel, an anthropologist.
11. BRONISLAW MALINOWSKI, CRIME AND CUSTOM IN SAVAGE SOCIETY (1926).
12. An "ethnography" is literally a "writing about a people." A typical ethnography will begin with a description of the physical environment of the society, and then an his-

torical overview of the people's movements and interactions with neighbors. There-after, the ethnography will describe each of the major social institutions: its religion, subsistence practices, kinship systems, and often even the legal apparatus. As a rule, ethnographies eschew explicit theoretical perspectives and hypothesis testing, but are in the main strictly descriptive (although within any description, implicit theoretical assumptions are unavoidably embedded). A thorough ethnography will, however, provide the raw data against which later hypotheses can be cross-cultur-ally tested.

13. *See* MARGARET MEAD, GROWING UP IN NEW GUINEA (1928).
14. *See* MARVIN HARRIS, CULTURAL MATERIALISM (1979); COWS, PIGS, WARS AND WITCHES (1974).
15. *See* EDWARD T. HALL, THE SILENT LANGUAGE (1959).
16. Noted works by Dell Hymes include his FOUNDATIONS IN SOCIOLINGUISTICS: AN ETHNO-GRAPHIC APPROACH (1974). William Labov authored LANGUAGE IN THE INNER CITY: STUD-IES IN THE BLACK ENGLISH VERNACULAR (1972) and PRINCIPLES OF LINGUISTIC CHANGE (1994).
17. JAMES PEOPLES & GARRICK BAILEY, HUMANITY: AN INTRODUCTION TO CULTURAL ANTHROPOL-OGY 5 (2d ed., 1991).
18. A similar image is described in George W. Stocking, Jr., *Functionalism Historicized*, *in* FUNCTIONALISM HISTORICIZED: ESSAYS ON BRITISH SOCIAL ANTHROPOLOGY, *supra* note 2, at 3, 4.
19. DAVID HUME, A TREATISE OF HUMAN NATURE xix (L.A. Selby-Bigge ed., Oxford: Claren-don Press, 1888) (1739-40).
20. Charles Lindholm, *Logical and Moral Dilemmas of Postmodernism*, 3 JOURNAL OF THE ROYAL ANTHROPOLOGICAL INSTITUTE 747, 758-759 (1997).
21. BENJAMIN N. CARDOZO, THE NATURE OF THE JUDICIAL PROCESS 21 (1921).
22. BLACK'S LAW DICTIONARY 207 (7th ed., 1999).
23. John M. Conley & William M. O'Barr, *Legal Anthropology Comes Home: A Brief His-tory of the Ethnographic Study of Law*, 27 LOYOLA OF LOS ANGELES LAW REVIEW 41, 44 note 19 (1993).
24. A critical analysis of legal education can be found in Duncan Kennedy, *Legal Edu-cation as Training for Hierarchy*, *in* THE POLITICS OF LAW 40 (David Kairys ed., 1982).
25. BLACK'S LAW DICTIONARY, *supra* note 22, at 889.
26. *See* Carl T. Bogus, *The Death of an Honorable Profession*, 71 INDIANA LAW JOURNAL 911 (1996) ("The legal system is not best understood by lawyers, but by social scien-tists"((citing George L. Priest). As an example of the unsatisfying attempts to define generic law, we can point to the assertion that "What is meant by 'law' here is the standard legal scholarship to be found in law reviews articles." Freeman, *Law and Science*, *supra* note 7, at 1.
27. E. ADAMSON HOEBEL, MAN IN THE PRIMITIVE WORLD (1949).
28. John T. Pardun, *Good Samaritan Laws: A Global Perspective*, 20 LOYOLA OF LOS ANGE-LES INTERNATIONAL AND COMPARATIVE LAW JOURNAL 591, 606 (1998). Good Samaritan laws require bystanders to come to the aid of another person in grave danger.
29. According to the National Gay and Lesbian Task Force, as of June 2001, five states (AR, KS, MO, OK, and TX) specifically criminalize only same-sex consensual sex-ual activity. Twelve other states (AL, FL, ID, LA, MA, MI, MN, MS, NC, SC, UT, VA) have sodomy laws that apply to certain acts regardless of the sex of the partners.
30. Joel Greenberg, *Here Come Israel's Passover Police!* NEW YORK TIMES, April 11, 2001, at A6.
31. *See, e.g.*, ANTHONY GELLNER, ANTHROPOLOGY AND POLITICS 50 (1995) ("A culture is a system of constraints, limiting the endless viable set of possibilities, within bounds which are themselves also very complex, and apply to a wide range of situations.").

32. Bronislaw Malinowski, *Introduction, in* H.I. HOGBIN, LAW AND ORDER IN POLYNESIA: A STUDY OF PRIMITIVE LEGAL INSTITUTIONS lxii (1934).

33. Adultery falls midway between social acts that are proscribed but not criminalized (like fornication), and those that are criminalized but primarily for symbolism (like sodomy). Unlike sodomy, adultery continues to be prohibited by statutory provisions in many states. Outside divorce actions, however, prosecutions for this crime are rare. *See* 2 AMERICAN JURISPRUDENCE 2D *Adultery and Fornication* § 1 (2000). One exception is the military, which prosecutes adultery on its own authority under 10 U.S.C. § 934 (2000); most states prosecute (when they prosecute at all) only when the aggrieved spouse complains.

34. Robert Redfield, *Primitive Law*, 33 UNIVERSITY OF CINCINNATI LAW REVIEW 1, 2 (1964). For further definitions of law by an anthropologist, *see also* LEOPOLD POPISIL, ANTHROPOLOGY OF LAW 81-82 (1971), in which Popisil avers that law may be examined through its four attributes: (1) authority, (2) intention of universal application, (3) obligato, and (4) sanction.

35. *See* MARTIN OTTENHEIMER, FORBIDDEN RELATIVES: THE AMERICAN MYTH OF COUSIN MARRIAGE (1996); Gregory C. Leavitt, *Disappearance of the Incest Taboo: A Cross-Cultural Test of General Evolutionary Hypotheses*, 91 AMERICAN ANTHROPOLOGIST 116 (1989).

36. This distinction between universal and idiosyncratic law bears some resemblance to the divide between natural and positive law discussed in chapter 3.

37. James A. Coriden concisely identifies four functions of law in any society: (1) law aids society in the achievement of its goals; (2) law affords stability to society by providing good order, reliable procedures, and predictable outcomes; (3) law protects personal rights, provides avenues of recourse, redresses grievances and resolves conflicts; and (4) law assists in the education of the community by reminding everyone of its values and standards. *See* JAMES A. CORIDEN, AN INTRODUCTION TO CANON LAW 5-6 (1991).

38. COLIN TURNBULL, THE FOREST PEOPLE 110 (1962).

39. JOHN LOCKE, THE SECOND TREATISE OF GOVERNMENT 5-6 (J.W. Gough ed., 3d ed., Oxford: Basil Blackwell, 1966) (1690).

40. LLEWELLYN & HOEBEL, *supra* note 10, at 239.

41. As one crude measure of the potential interaction between law and anthropology, the concept of "human nature," the object of anthropological inquiry, occurs in opinions of the U.S. Supreme Court at least 130 times.

42. MURRAY J. LEAF, MAN, MIND, AND SCIENCE: A HISTORY OF ANTHROPOLOGY 190 (1979).

43. Conley & O'Barr, *supra* note 23, at 42.

44. For a compact yet erudite explanation of how the modern legal traditions emerged from the classic and medieval precursors, *see* PETER STEIN, ROMAN LAW IN EUROPEAN HISTORY (1999).

45. FRANCIS LIEBER, MANUAL OF POLITICAL ETHICS, DESIGNED CHIEFLY FOR THE USE OF COLLEGES AND STUDENTS AT LAW (2d ed., Philadelphia: J.B. Lippincott, 1876).

46. *See* LAUREL OATES ET AL., THE LEGAL WRITING HANDBOOK 520, 538 (2d ed., 1998).

47. STEVEN M. STANLEY, THE NEW EVOLUTIONARY TIMETABLE 19 (1981).

48. *Id.* at 18.

49. KLAUS-PETER KOEPPING, ADOLF BASTIAN AND THE PSYCHIC UNITY OF MANKIND 9 (1983).

50. MAINE, *supra* note 9, at 141.

51. LEWIS H. MORGAN, ANCIENT SOCIETY (New York: Henry Holt & Co., 1877).

52. KOEPPING, *supra* note 49, at 7.

53. *Id.* at 31.

54. *See, e.g.,* BRADD SHORE, CULTURE IN MIND: COGNITION, CULTURE, AND THE PROBLEM OF MEANING (1996).

55. LEAF, *supra* note 42, at 83-84.

56. *Id.* at 107.

57. *Id*. at 112.
58. *Id*.
59. Max Weber, The Protestant Ethic and the Spirit of Capitalism (London: Unwin Paperbacks, 1985) (1904).
60. Claude Lévi-Strauss, The Elementary Structures of Kinship (Boston: Beacon Press, 1969) (1949).
61. Leaf, *supra* note 42, at 254.
62. *See* Claude Lévi-Strauss, The Raw and the Cooked (1969).
63. Edmund Leach, Claude Lévi-Strauss 2 (1970).
64. John M. Conley & William M. O'Barr, Just Words: Law, Language, and Power 101 (1998). *See also* the autobiographical account of his former classmate, Hilda Kuper. Hilda Kuper, *Function, History, Biography: Reflections on Fifty Years in the British Anthropological Tradition*, in Functionalism Historicized: Essays on British Social Anthropology, *supra* note 2, at 192.
65. *See* Max Gluckman, The Ideas in Barotse Jurisprudence (1972).
66. Max Gluckman, Order and Rebellion in Tribal Africa 112 (1963).
67. Lawrence Rosen, *The Anthropologist as Expert Witness*, 79 American Anthropologist 555, 558 (1977).
68. Conrad Phillip Kottak, Cultural Anthropology 299-300 (5th ed., 1991).
69. Rosen, *supra* note 67.
70. Conley & O'Barr, *supra* note 23, at 44.
71. We searched WESTLAW's MARQUIS database, which contains all of the *Who's Who* publications. The search term "Anthropolog!" drew 3,359 hits (persons). However, of these, only 161 also include the words "law" or "legal." Assuming all these hits are relevant, and that the sample of anthropologists with *Who's Who* entries is representative, then less than 5 percent of anthropologists have formal training in law.
72. For example, see William Vogeler, *He Got an "A" for Argument: Jurist Made the Grade in Law after Flunking Anthropology*, Los Angeles Daily Journal, March 11, 1993, at 1.
73. Many gaps in our current knowledge may not be practical limitations that we can fill in later. Some are irresolvable by virtue of the kinds of creatures that we are, and the ways in which the physical world is structured. Complete predictability may consequently be impossible for any field at all, including the physical sciences. *See* James M. Donovan, *Espying the Limits of Human Knowledge*, 38(3) Anthropology Newsletter 16 (March 1997).
74. We should not be distracted by the admission that some conclusions in physics are probabilistic; a good deal more of them are deterministic. In contrast, *no* social science conclusion is deterministic.
75. Anthropologists incorporating postmodern philosophies, for example, deny that anthropology was, is now, or ever should be a science. If their argument were successful, then our use of statements about the social sciences to support arguments about anthropology would be objectionable. We are not persuaded by the postmodern arguments. *See* Stanley R. Barrett, Anthropology: A Student's Guide to Theory and Method 31-32 (1996). We should also note that postmodernists deny the existence of a human nature, the elucidation of which we have described as the main task of anthropology. From our perspective, then, postmodernists necessarily deny the existence of a meaningful anthropology at all because it lacks a subject matter.The postmodern project seeks to cripple modern science and philosophy by rejecting such premises as the existence of an objective reality, the possibility of a single truth, and the necessary characterization of science as purely political in nature. The tenets of this philosophy are described in detail in several interesting books, particularly Paul R. Gross & Norman Levitt, Higher Superstition: The Academic Left and Its Quarrels with Science (1994). This problem as it affects anthro-

pology particularly is reviewed by LAWRENCE A. KUZNAR, RECLAIMING A SCIENTIFIC ANTHROPOLOGY (1997); JAMES LETT, SCIENCE, REASON AND ANTHROPOLOGY (1997); and MARVIN HARRIS, THEORIES OF CULTURE IN POSTMODERN TIMES (1999).

76. ROBERT PARK, VOODOO SCIENCE: THE ROAD FROM FOOLISHNESS TO FRAUD 39 (2000).

77. *See, e.g.*, I.M. LEWIS, ECSTATIC RELIGION (2d ed., 1989).

78. *See, e.g.*, James M. Donovan, *A Brazilian Challenge to Lewis's Explanation of Cult Mediumship*, 15(3) JOURNAL OF CONTEMPORARY RELIGION 361 (2000); Maria Lima Leão Teixeira, Transas de um Povo de Santo: Un Estudo sobre Identidades Sexuais (1986) (unpublished Master's thesis, Universidade Federal do Rio de Janeiro).

79. DAVID L. FAIGMAN, LEGAL ALCHEMY: THE USE AND MISUSE OF SCIENCE IN THE LAW 123 (1999).

80. *Id.* at x.

81. *See* PETR BECKMANN, A HISTORY OF _ (PI) 170-173 (1970).

82. FAIGMAN, *supra* note 79, at 53-54.

83. *Id.* at xi.

84. One senator, for example, resolutely declared that "All the science that is used to explain [the topic] will not change my mind to the cold hard facts." *Id.* at 163.

85. FEDERAL RULES OF CIVIL PROCEDURE 52a (2000). In contrast, legislatures have not been required by the U.S. Supreme Court to give their reasons for passing a law. *See* U.S. R.R. Retirement Bd. v. Fritz, 449 U.S. 166 (1980) ("[T]his Court has never insisted that a legislative body articulate its reasons for enacting a statute.").

86. STEPHEN C. YEAZELL, CIVIL PROCEDURE 712 (5th ed., 2000).

87. *Id.* at 666.

88. 509 U.S. 579 (1993).

89. PARK, *supra* note 76, at 164.

90. Judge Higginbotham's decision in *Vuyanich v. Republic National Bank*, 505 F. Supp. 224 (S.D. Texas 1980) is discussed in STEPHEN E. FIENBERG (ED.), THE EVOLVING ROLE OF STATISTICAL ASSESSMENTS AS EVIDENCE IN THE COURTS 19-26, 72 (1989).

Chapter One

PRACTICAL BENEFITS OF
ANTHROPOLOGY TO LAW

Legislators, judges, and lawyers should be especially avid consumers
of anthropological literature. At every turn, the legal profession invokes concepts that are the stock in trade of anthropology. Whenever
culture and custom are relevant factors—and in legal practice, they frequently are—the obvious source of information should be anthropology.[1] The outcome of at least one important U.S. Supreme Court case
hinged upon the substantial impact of well-considered anthropological
data. In *Wisconsin v. Yoder*[2]

> it was the testimony of John A. Hostetler, an anthropologist and expert
> witness who was himself raised in the Amish community, to which the
> Court frequently referred in its opinion. The Court found that the Amish
> religion and mode of life were inseparable and interdependent, and that
> the social repercussions of compulsory high school attendance for the
> Amish would necessarily infringe on the well-being of the community as
> a religious entity.[3]

The relevance of anthropology to law is considerable. Examples
include prosecutions for imported cultural practices such as female circumcision[4] and "marriage by capture,"[5] debates over alternative languages
in American school systems,[6] and arguments over ownership of culture
and its products.[7] More directly, laws such as the National Environmental
Policy Act mandate "the integrated use of the natural and social sciences"
so as to achieve the goal of preserving "important historic, cultural, and
natural aspects of our national heritage."[8] A strong command of anthropology would be necessary to fulfill the spirit of this and other legislative

---

Notes for this section begin on page 63.

acts, such as the 1990 NAGRPA (Native American Grave Protection and Repatriation Act). NAGRPA requires the return of objects of aboriginal origin found on federal lands to native communities. If no clear linear descendents exist, or if no such group currently owns the land where the objects are found, then the objects must go to that group with the "closest cultural affinity."[9] The determination of cultural affinities is clearly a task for the anthropologist. This clause became central to two cases that received much press: to whom did the unearthed remains of "Kennewick Man" belong,[10] and who owned the rediscovered brain of Ishi?[11]

This list of problematic intersections of law and anthropology, which includes examples from each of the four subfields of anthropology, demonstrates how many aspects of the legal project involve the topics meticulously studied by anthropologists. Whether the law, through its practitioners, judges, and academics, adequately avails itself of that expertise is a different question. More than one overview has concluded that the law is usually content to rely upon the "commonsense" perspective, with little concern for the accuracy of the layperson's view. For example, despite its seeming relevance, no decision by the U.S. Supreme Court articulating what is or is not a "religion" has cited even one social scientific reference.[12] Similarly, although many issues that the Supreme Court claims to consider when deciding abortion cases plainly fall within the expertise of social scientists, almost none of that literature has been cited in the final opinions.[13]

One context in which cultural data are overtly considered arises in criminal proceedings. In such cases, the defendant accused of a particular crime may offer evidence of culture as a basis for a claim that a mitigating circumstance exists,[14] and that therefore the law should be applied differently to his or her situation.[15] This "culture defense" is similar to those offered by psychologists and sociologists who argue that because a defendant lived in a tough neighborhood, experienced racial discrimination, or suffers from a mental abnormality, he or she should be excused from the crime altogether, or be assessed a lesser punishment.[16] While considering culture as a mitigating factor, thus far the courts have declined to go the next step in this analysis and ask whether a law itself unfairly embodies a cultural perspective or bias.

Law might be more receptive to the use of anthropological data were it more sensitive to its own status as a cultural institution, and to its dynamic exchanges with other such institutions. On the one hand, "Legal processes provide cultural narratives for imposing order and asserting the primacy of community";[17] on the other, cultural narratives provide the imagery and vocabulary from which law is formed.[18] The social sciences allow this process to be engaged purposefully and to best effect by offering insight into the community that law is to serve.

Peter Lawrence offers one practical example when he describes the necessity of anthropological insight for the effective Australian administration of its New Guinea colony.[19] Accordingly, without proper reference to, inquiry by, or utilization of the social sciences—especially anthropology—law becomes detached from society and instead focuses upon the static words of its own jurisprudential canon.[20]

One can still detect in many legal actions the influence of anthropological arguments even when they have not been explicitly consulted. But because the law lacks mechanisms, standards, and a tradition availing itself of these data in a routine and conscientious manner, the practical benefit of anthropology to law remains in many ways merely a potential benefit rather than an actual one. Consequently, this chapter offers two arguments. First, it examines in detail why the law should care what social scientists have to say. This contention is primarily philosophical in nature; we look into the fundamental relationship between anthropological fact and legal act.

Second, we apply this philosophical template to a specific intersection between anthropological fact and legal final act. The case study critiques the reasons offered by the courts for the criminalization of polygamy. The primary court decision upholding polygamy's criminalization argues that it merits prosecution because of its correlative and even causative implications for other undesirable social outcomes. The problem becomes, What should be done when these proffered associations are factual errors? What are the duties of the law to reflect accurately our current state of knowledge on social matters the law has itself identified as important?

The Philosophical Background: "Is" versus "Ought"

A word of encouragement should be given about the present section. It may appear to the reader to be strictly "philosophical," and even ponderously so. Its relevancy to our purposes might be doubted on that ground alone. But—and perhaps even to our own surprise—practically every significant discussion in this book will need to refer to this problem of the "naturalistic fallacy."

Recall our initial premises about both anthropology and law. As set forth in the introduction, we approach anthropology as a science devoted to the task of ascertaining facts about a real world. Although the relationships sought cannot be framed as determinative laws like those in physics, they remain independent of our desire whether they should exist or not. Anthropology ultimately addresses what "is." On the other hand, law is wholly a cultural creation, which arises and persists because, in important ways, we want it that way. Law is not thrust upon us the way gravity is, but is instead an artificial construct. Law, in other words, is about what "ought" to be. As a result of these two assumptions—that anthropology deals with facts and law with desires—the claims of anthropology are of a different character than those of law. If the proper relation of the one to the other is to be understood, we must first confront this fundamental difficulty.

We begin by articulating more carefully the ethical grounds of legal prescriptions. The legal enterprise concerns itself with both sides of the visionary coin. The judiciary, charged with the application of law, is devoted to hindsight. It asks what *happened* (empirical, past tense) in a particular case, either What are the facts? or What did the drafters mean? Legislators, who create the laws, contrarily look ahead and ponder what *should be* the case; theirs is an ideal inquiry designed to be a cause in future situations, and not merely a restatement or distillation of past ones. Thus in law the past and future, descriptive and prescriptive, mutually influence one another.

Our attention is drawn particularly to the fact that, in the end, both aspects of the legal project involve an "ought." Judicially we are told what we ought or ought not to have done to have avoided being haled into court. Legislatively, we have prescribed for us what we ought or ought not do in particular circumstances. I "ought" to pay my taxes; otherwise I shall suffer penalties. That we "ought" to help our neighbors is justification enough, some would argue, for us to pass further "Good Samaritan" laws[21]—the kind that received wide exposure in the famous last episode of the television program *Seinfeld*.[22]

A reasonably curious person will ask the source of all these legal "oughts." We insist that the answer to this question matters. Practically, it becomes easier to convince someone to comply with an "ought" if he or she knows why things, in fact, ought to be that way. This inquiry is the purview of the social psychologists and political scientists. But there are also theoretical and philosophical reasons why the inquiry is important.

The rationality of a reason why something ought to be the case can change with varying circumstances, either temporal or cultural. Although many people continue to invoke "the will of God," we cannot miss the fact that that justification no longer possesses the explanatory power it may once have enjoyed. If a good rationale is required to justify a new ought, then good rationales should be required to maintain old oughts. *The adequate rationale and the acceptability of an ought should be concurrent.* Too often the rationale is treated as an initial threshold requirement, necessary to accept a new ought but irrelevant to maintain it.[23] The outcome then reduces to a claim that something *ought to be* simply because it *has been*. Prior existence becomes the sole rationale for continued existence in perpetuity, perhaps in the belief that that earlier existence had better justification, even if we have now forgotten what that was. The law is replete with such claims elevated to the level of high principle, such as common law's *stare decisis* ("to stand by the things decided," i.e., don't overturn precedent).[24]

The lesson we need to learn is that frequently the justification of a contemporary ought is merely the reliance upon past invocations of that same ought. This kind of reasoning is certainly circular, and in any event, wholly unsatisfactory. As we go forward, we will want to keep the rationale for a particular ought in sight since oughts tend to become self-justifying in a way that should make one suspect the integrity of the reasoning pervasive in the legal system.

If it is unsatisfactory to justify an ought in terms of itself, what elements would make a rationale adequate? Most people expect the explanation for an ought to link up with something external to itself, something either empirical ("we ought to promote equal opportunity in employment because that will better distribute economic benefits throughout the population") or ideal ("we ought to promote equal opportunity in employment because that is a good thing, regardless of its impact on economic distribution"). Such explanatory chains can become fantastically long and nuanced. What is "better"? What is "good"? But the point for us is that the explanation for one thing should depend upon something other than itself, and it is these explanatory links that make our body of knowledge the unitary corpus that Edward O. Wilson advocates.[25]

So again we can ask, What is the (philosophically interesting, external) source of legal oughts? Why ought the *ought* to be what it is: an "ought"? Now that we have effectively blocked the usual recourse to self-justification, there are only two logical options: either the legal ought is grounded in something else, or it is not. We need not consider the latter situation. Although it is entirely possible for a new ought to be legislated solely upon the random whimsy of a sponsor, such arbitrary acts (if there are any) do not lend themselves to the critical analysis and insight we aim for here. Anarchy is always a possibility, but not a very interesting one.

The immediate advantage to the stipulation that an *ought* be grounded is the implicit concession that without that ground, the *ought* ought not be. Consequently, to ascertain whether any legal ought should be maintained, the first step is to identify its ground. We can identify at least four possible grounds for a legal ought.[26]

The Four Grounds for Legal "Oughts"

GENETIC "OUGHTS"

A legal ought may be *genetically* related to another ought. The link here can be logical. If I ought not murder, then neither should I help someone else commit a murder. The fuller achievement of the first ought motivates the discovery of the second. In practice, this ground is contained in the maxim that what the law forbids directly cannot be done indirectly (if the police cannot search you, neither can an agent acting on behalf of the police). This ground is also the one upon which we build the hierarchy of oughts (constitutional oughts have priority over statutory oughts, for example).

When grounded genetically, lower ranked oughts are simply means to achieve the higher oughts. To assert a ground of this kind allows us to reason backward to identify the primary ought that is not always made explicit. For example, criminal codes (and their application by the courts) may punish less severely the actual killing of someone by accident than they do the collusion to hire someone else to commit the murder or the verbal exhortation that someone should be killed.[27] This seems an odd state of affairs if the higher ought were simply that we ought not kill: actual killing would then always be worse than talking about or conspiring to kill. That the codes dictate differently shows that the higher ought does not forbid killing per se, but only intentional, deliberate killing, and that intention matters more heavily than the naked act. If society somehow came to believe that all acts are intentional, that there are no true accidents (a conclusion commonly attributed to Freud), then the exception for accidental killings would no longer support the higher ought. The dependence of the former upon a genetic link to the latter would lead us to expect that under this imaginary scenario the distinction between negligent and intentional homicide would disappear.

CATEGORICAL "OUGHTS"

The link between two legal oughts can be *categorical*. If I should not do X, then that proscription alone suffices to expect that I ought not do anything that is conceptually equivalent to X. Surely an "ought not" does not become permissible merely by relabeling it, when the referent or underlying idea remains the same. Contrarily, this judgment might be different if the relabeling does involve a reconceptualizing or re-identification of the focus.

For example, what is for some a "murder" can be for others a "mercy killing," with the difference not simply being a change in nouns. Inherent in the idea of "murder" is "against the victim's will," a qualifier absent from "mercy killing." While a "mercy killing" can be against the victim's will, it is also possible that the victim did give consent (as was argued in the Jack Kevorkian trials). But to consent to one's own murder is logically impossible because that consent makes the act not a murder, a contradiction missing in the idea of the victim consenting to a mercy killing.[28]

Discerning when a difference of terms reflects a difference in concept can be difficult. Indeed, it is a common rhetorical ploy to make distinctions without a difference. Some would preclude such sophistry by locating the marker of a categorical link between oughts, not in the underlying idea, but rather in the objective outcome. That is, the categorical link should depend upon behavioral equivalencies and the like. Murder would thereby be recognized solely as the killing of another human being, rendering the underlying intention irrelevant. But we have already shown that this approach has been rejected by modern criminal codes: murder is the killing of another human being, but with nonobvious elements such as "intent" (which distinguishes it from manslaughter) and lack of consent (which distinguishes it from some mercy killings). It is not apparent to the senses whether a particular killing qualifies as a "murder." Because this behavioral alternative fails to capture the established distinctions, we must return to our first model, whereby oughts are categorically linked when they share the same conceptual structure. Although a more difficult standard, it is not, like the other, patently false.

The attractiveness of any particular instance of this principle will depend on one's tendency to lump or to split. We would want to treat *X* and *Y* similarly if we consider them but two members of a single conceptual class, *A*. What sense is there in regulating our responsibilities to dogs, but not to cats, since we interact with them in nearly identical ways and both are members of the class of "domestic household pets"? Splitters, on the other hand, would argue that *A* is not the proper level of analysis, since it collects together tokens of dissimilar kinds. Although no one has been mauled to death by a cat, the same cannot be said about dogs. Cats and dogs are not members of a class "domestic household pets," but are rather each members of the separate classes "non-threatening domesticated animals" and "potentially threatening domesticated animals," and therefore should be differentially regulated.

Finally, the principle of categorical oughts provides a basis for the legal claim that likes (technically, "those similarly situated") should be treated alike. The practical difficulty would be to establish what is truly "like" in any particular context, a problem discussed by Aristotle in his *Nicomachean Ethics*.

Traditional "Oughts"

An anthropologist would not fail to emphasize what to her would be the most obvious ground of a legal ought: *tradition* or authority. We ought not work on the Sabbath because our elders have told us not to, and presumably they have done this because God revealed compliance with this rule to be his will. Traditional oughts form the bulk of "folk law."[29]

Unlike the previous two types, there need be no connection between traditional oughts other than the originating source. They do not, in other words, necessarily constitute a system. Consistency is not a requirement, although upon inspection, genetic or categorical links can often be identified in a set of mainly traditional oughts. This class of oughts can no more be the subject of philosophical treatment than the class of the wholly arbitrary.

EMPIRICAL "OUGHTS"

The genetic and the categorical links between oughts differ from the fourth type in that whereas the former can be forged wholly "in the head," the latter requires a relationship of some kind with the external world. The link here is not with a prior ought, but with an independent fact. The world imposes constraints, both physical and social. The articulated legal rule springs from, responds to, or is directed at some specifiable set of facts or state of affairs: "While judges and scholars have not typically identified facts as a source of *authority* for determining constitutional meaning, facts play, and historically have played, a pivotal role in exactly this capacity."[30] An *empirical* ought acquires its status because that ought produces results that we both expect and desire, either to maintain the status quo or to edge society progressively toward some envisioned end condition.

"Expect" is the critical criterion in that last sentence. This does not mean that the anticipated result must occur, but only that we have articulable reasons to anticipate that result instead of some other—and not just any articulable reasons, but ones that have the potential to be demonstrably wrong.[31]

We can possess knowledge only about real things because they are not under the control of our imaginations. Only the real world can surprise us (the use of surprise to distinguish imagination from perception was an important element of Husserl's phenomenology). While defining what is "real" can be contentiously partisan, we need only understand reality in the sense credited to novelist Philip K. Dick: "Reality is that which, when you stop believing in it, doesn't go away." This posture assumed legal significance in *Daubert v. Merrell Dow Pharmaceuticals*, wherein Justice Blackmun quotes philosopher of science Karl Popper to clarify how a judge is to ascertain whether a theory qualifies as scientific knowledge: "The criterion of the scientific status of a theory is its falsifiability, or refutability, or testability."[32]

This real world is presumed to be mostly predictable at the physical level, less so at the social level. Still, if we can identify, isolate, and manipulate the relevant factors, we can construct lives at least somewhat of our own design. Too often in postmodern discourse the conclusion that not everything is under our control justifies the assertion that nothing is. We dismiss this conclusion as being *ideo*logical, not logical. This goal of maximizing the control of our lives is the function of the empirical ought. So, for example, sociological studies and labor statistics might support an empirical ought that "All citizens, even the childless, ought to be taxed for public education" because we know that the benefits of a well-trained and educated work force and electorate redound to the benefit of all.

The temptation here is to succumb to the conflation of the empirical ought with the other grounds, especially the traditional. Could it not be said that we should pay education taxes simply because it is the "right" thing to do, regardless of whether it has any particular benefit?[33] And, indeed, many of our recognized empirical oughts probably began this way because we lacked the knowledge that would permit us to isolate the elements connecting the legal prescription to its real-world impact. One of the benefits of anthropological knowledge is the transformation of nonempirical oughts into empirical oughts. In contemporary Western culture, this change is not merely a transition, but a promotion. Classic works that have effected this transformation of traditional into empirical oughts include Mary Douglas's *Totem and Taboo*, wherein she finds a rational basis behind the abominations of Leviticus.[34] Marvin Harris and his theory of ecological materialism gave a firm empirical basis to the oughts governing the Hindu worship of cows and the refusal of Jews and Moslems to eat pork.[35]

Within the American legal tradition, an ought may be based legitimately on any of the four grounds we have identified, and examples of all kinds abound. Traditional oughts are favored by original interpretationists like U.S. Supreme Court Associate Justice Antonin Scalia who argues that the law, and especially constitutional law, can only embrace what the drafters of the language explicitly had in mind, and nothing further. If the nation's founders accepted school prayer, that fact alone suffices to conclude that such activities are constitutionally permissible, even if that practice can be conclusively demonstrated to contravene the scope of the Constitution's explicit language.

An alternative source of traditional oughts is religion, either specifically sectarian or generally civil:[36] we ought to relate to the rest of the world in particular ways that are a function of our privileged position of being among God's elect. This belief causes our politicians to disdain any form of government that does not mirror our own republican democracy, regardless of whether the alternative better serves its own people.[37]

Genetic oughts are overabundant in administrative law. To achieve some vague and general goal of the good, innumerable—and often insufferable—regulations are imposed. As amply demonstrated by Frank Anechiarico and James B. Jacobs in their book, *The Pursuit of Absolute Integrity: How Corruption Control Makes Government Ineffective*, the presumption that these regulations advance that goal is demonstrably false.[38] Categorical oughts are behind the long strings of apparent synonyms in legal language, making the typical legal document a dense and obtuse text, unreadable to the vast majority of citizens and even some lawyers.[39]

While we may each have preferences about which ground for an ought is the most appropriate for jurisprudence, that debate need not be reviewed here. Our limited focus shall be upon when law *itself* identifies which kind of ought it is propounding. Specifically, we are interested in those occasions when the legal rationale explicitly claims to establish an ought upon empirical grounds. If, for example, studies have found a correlation between some action and a desirable social outcome, then the antecedent condition may be encouraged through policy choices, or in some instances, mandated as a legal requirement. At this writing, the current example would be President George W. Bush's proposal, based upon a correlation between single mothers and poverty, to fund projects to encourage these women to marry. The gist is that if we know what the facts are, we can determine what we ought to do to maintain those facts or to change them in a controlled way. To the extent that law is concerned to ground its oughts empirically, its need for anthropology is self-evident. Anthropological facts can serve as legitimate bases for empirical legal oughts.

The Naturalistic Fallacy

Students of philosophy will recognize that the structure of the empirical ought brings us perilously close to committing the "naturalistic fallacy." The naturalistic fallacy is the unwarranted movement from an "is" to an "ought." The modern recognition of this problem is credited to David Hume.[40] In his *Treatise of Human Nature, Book Three: Of Morals*, Hume "argues that it is 'altogether inconceivable' that a proposition containing the modal term 'ought' can be *deduced* from other propositions that contain no such term. He argues, that is, that those who suppose they have rationally deduced obligations from merely factual premises have committed a logical blunder."[41] This germ of an idea matured in the work of G.E. Moore's *Principia Ethica* (1903). It was Moore who labeled this problem "the naturalistic fallacy," which he defined as the attempt to define moral goodness in terms of some natural property. For Moore, goodness is "a foundational and unanalyzable property," one "not capable of being explained in terms of anything more basic."[42] If Hume and Moore are right (and in the case of Hume, this conclusion certainly seems to be an inevitable result of his radical empiricism), then any "is" can be consistent with any ought since the "is" is the premise of no argument supporting (or contradicting) that ought.

Stop for a moment and think what this argument entails. *No* factual observation is relevant to *any* evaluative conclusion; *every* state of affairs is consistent with *every* moral belief. How often do we hear others (or perhaps even ourselves) suggest that "God is good because *X* happened," or even that we should not kick the neighbor's dog because it causes him pain? According to the naturalistic fallacy, this kind of reasoning is absolutely irrational, even silly, because it tries to extract ethical conclusions from factual premises.

This cautionary note might seem to be unnecessary were it not so commonly transgressed, not only by unreflective practice but even in thoughtful argument. In an otherwise excellent text, David Faigman asserts that "[w]hile what *is* might very well assist us to decide what *ought to be*, it never dictates what *must be*."[43] Faigman has it exactly backwards. What *is* can never tell us what *ought to be*, although it can often tell us what *must be*. The fact that the earth revolves means that the sun will rise tomorrow morning, but that fact does not mean the sun's rising ought to happen. The astronomical facts tell us what will happen, not what would be good to have happen.

For obvious reasons, we would like the naturalistic fallacy to go away; we would feel better about what the law tries to do if we could reasonably derive an ought from an is. And, indeed, some believe there is no such problem. E.O. Wilson holds that the opposing of the "is" and the "ought" is itself a fallacy. The usual framing of the problem opposes an empirical, factual "is" on the one side, and an ethereal, ideal "ought" on the other. But upon reflection, the reader will note that the ought becomes of interest to us only if we can attribute existence to it: the ought "is." And indeed, we easily use the verb "to be" in relationship to the ought, and one of the senses of "to be" is the existential. To say that something "is" is to say that it exists. The ideal becomes materialized, even if only as an idea, but more frequently as a standard or limit against which the material world "bumps" if it tries to go too far. So Wilson is not obviously wrong when he argues that if "*ought* is not *is*, what is?"[44] For Wilson, everything ultimately reduces to a material cause, which is the "is," leaving no room for an immaterial or ideal ought. Goodbye naturalistic fallacy.

Where Wilson would dissolve the problem, other scholars claim to solve it. Heretofore it has been assumed that the transition from empirical fact to moral judgment can be made only with the addition of a third, intermediate premise that is itself evaluative. John Searle tries to show that this need not be the case, offering as illustration the following series of statements:

> Jones uttered the words "I hereby promise to pay you, Smith, five dollars."
> Jones promised to pay Smith five dollars.
> Jones placed himself under (undertook) an obligation to pay Smith five dollars.
> Jones is under an obligation to pay Smith five dollars.
> Jones ought to pay Smith five dollars.[45]

Searle believes that "the relation between any statement and its successor, while not in every case one of 'entailment,' is nonetheless not merely a randomly contingent relation."[46] The intermediate statements connecting the purely empirical with the fully evaluative do not involve any evaluative statements, moral principles, or anything of the sort.[47] He recognizes that "to promise" is a problematic concept in this series. Perhaps this concept imports hidden evaluative and moral precepts into the ostensibly empirical series.

Searle parries this objection by resort to "institutional facts":

> It is often a matter of fact that one has certain obligations, commitments, rights and responsibilities, but it is a matter of institutional, not brute fact. It is one such institutionalized form of obligation, promising, which I invoked above to derive an "ought" from an "is." I started with a brute fact, that a man uttered certain words, and then invoked the institution in such a way as to generate institutional facts by which we arrived at the institutional fact that the man ought to pay another man five dollars. The whole proof rests on an appeal to the constitutive rule that to make a promise is to undertake an obligation.[48]

It is not clear that Searle has successfully answered the objection that "to promise" is to presume the ought one is trying to generate. But if he has, we can see the heightened necessity for anthropology to establish the requisite set of "institutional facts" that would allow us to do away with the naturalistic fallacy, thus clearing the stage for the rational construction of empirical legal oughts.

Without some such solution to the challenge of the naturalistic fallacy, we can here only note the philosophically obscure progression that transmutes anthropological fact into a legal rule. But for present purposes we can set this difficulty aside, and rely instead on the assurances law itself offers that it has reliably effected this alchemy.

Empirical Fact as Legal Justification

What the reader should take away from the preceding discussion is that some legal prescriptions explicitly justify themselves as having been demanded by the facts of the situation. Having identified cause and effect relationships, a specific set of facts prompts a particular legal response. To achieve social ends, certain intermediate conditions must be either promoted or discouraged. It is the business of science generally to determine what is or is not the case, and of the social sciences, including anthropology, to offer conclusions about what is real in the sociocultural context.

We have seen that there are many candidate grounds for legal oughts. When a pronouncement itself explicitly identities itself as being an "empirical ought," we will accept that claim on its face. Certainly, sometimes the purported empirical ground is a sham, intended to bestow illegitimate credibility upon a conclusion that is otherwise without any ground at all, or an illegitimate one.[49]

Why laws are passed makes a difference, at least within our constitutional framework. At the minimum, we are not permitted to enact laws whose sole or primary purpose is to advance sectarian causes.[50] What we cannot enact if our reason is to promote religion, we can enact if that same legislation promotes some secular goal primarily and only incidentally correlates with religious objectives.[51] The laws against murder here are an easy example: secular society has good reason to outlaw murder beyond the enforcement of the Ten Commandments. The trick is that religious motivations can be hidden behind the flimsiest of secular purposes, as was the case with the Defense of Marriage Act, an act creating for the first time a federal definition of "marriage," the sole purpose of which was to bring state power to enforce one religion's idea of the proper family unit.[52] When mere secular gestures are found to divert attention from the primary sectarian objectives, the law falls. The antievolution statutes at issue in cases from *Epperson v. Arkansas*[53] to *Edwards v. Aguillard*[54] all toppled before this principle.

What if the empirical ground is not a devious gloss, but a well-intentioned error? Should laws claiming to have an empirical ground be stricken when the alleged factual justification for that law fails? This empirical failure can come about for two reasons. First, either the legislature or court innocently misunderstood or unfairly represented the actual facts. These cases are distinguishable from the aforementioned antievolution cases. In *Epperson* and *Aguillard*, the issue was "sham" science; in the present scenario the issue is not deception but bias or misunderstanding. Cases involving complex statistical testimony are especially prone to this error.[55]

A second type of empirical failure occurs when a legal conclusion solidly reflected the current state of knowledge on that subject when the law was passed or decision rendered. Improvement of our knowledge in that area, however, has shifted that empirical ground from beneath that legal superstructure. If the law does not keep pace with our improved knowledge, it may become irrelevant; if it does attempt to incorporate changing data, this attempt cuts against another legal goal, to provide final and certain outcomes. Either way, an important aspect of our legal system seems certain to suffer, leaving it either irrelevant or unsettled.

We will examine one case where our improved knowledge has removed the empirical support for early legal positions. If the conclusion in that context is that the law should change with the factual foundation, the same result must certainly apply to situations where the science was invoked in bad faith. There are many, many possible topics from which to choose: race and ethnicity, impact of social welfare programs, and the relationship between criminal behavior and criminal penalties are but a few. Instead of these more modern debates, however, we will focus on one that is treated as largely settled: the criminalization of polygamy. For over one hundred years, polygamy has been illegal in the United States, and the first major decision supporting the constitutionality of this position, *Reynolds v. U.S.*, continues to be cited with approval by the Supreme Court. The principle of *stare decisis* makes this result particularly entrenched and difficult to question: polygamy is a crime. But why?

Case Study: The Criminalization of Polygamy

The early Mormons[56] were unquestionably the victims of unrelenting oppression from the federal government. By the end of the nineteenth century Mormons had seen their religious practices criminalized, their church threatened with federal confiscation, and the mere profession of their faith sufficient to bar members from voting polls and juries. Much (but not all) of the popular distaste for this religion was a reaction to its early advocacy of polygamy. It is not immediately obvious why polygamy provoked this vigorous opposition. The only standard of comparison we might have today would be the rancorous debate over abortion, but possibly even this pales by comparison. Because both sides of the abortion question are given voice, one can hope that the net effect on the attentive individual is a tempering of the debate's worst extremes. Literally no one outside Utah was defending polygamy. Every public declaration was an uncontradicted opposition, giving free rein to wild generalizations and baseless characterizations. Little has changed

today with respect to polygamy, which remains, in the public imagination, an inconceivable perversion. Any time arguments favoring
same-sex marriage become dangerously reasonable and persuasive,
opponents can be counted on to avoid this concession by asking how it
would not lead to that greatest of horrors, polygamy.[57]

Certainly the charge against polygamy cannot be that it is "unnatural." At least 83 percent of human societies permit polygamy:[58] "Strict
monogamy, defined in terms of sexual encounters, is probably more a
human ideal than it is a common biological reality."[59] Even Western civilization came to the idea of monogamy relatively late: "Up to the
eleventh century casual polygamy appears to have been general, with
easy divorce and much concubinage."[60] Bigamy in England was "both
easy and common" as late as 1570.[61]

That the majority of societies are polygamous is obscured by the fact
that most unions within even those societies are, for reasons both biological and economic, monogamous. Only about 5 to 10 percent of men
actually avail themselves of this option where it is offered.[62] The Mormon
average in the pioneer era may have been only as high as 20 percent.[63]

The economic factors limiting recourse to polygamy should be obvious. More resources are needed to support two or more wives and their
children than one wife and offspring. Resources being a limited good,
not all males will accrue sufficient material wealth to afford extra wives.
In the Koran, Muhammad revealed that a man may marry up to four
wives, subject to equitable treatment:

> marry such women
> as seem good to you, two, three, four,
> but if you fear you will not be equitable,
> then only one, or what your right hands own;
> so it is likelier you will not be partial.[64]

The biological limitations are more subtle:

> The ratio of male to female babies guarantees that polygamous matings must
> be the numerical exception, however favored or preferred they may be. Only
> monogamy and group marriage are compatible with the natural sex ratio and
> permit a majority of the population to follow the norm of marriage.[65]

Many features of human life are rare without being thereby disparag-
ingly termed "unnatural." The material accumulation of a Bill Gates, for
example, is rare, but not often criticized as unnatural. By no measure is
polygamy "unnatural"; quite the contrary.[66]

Few antipolygamists would disagree with the characterization of
monogamy as "the moral nexus" of our society:

To talk about monogamy is to talk about virtually everything that might matter. Honesty, murder, kindness, security, choice, revenge, desire, loyalty, lying, risk, duty, children, excitement, blame, love, promising, care, curiosity, jealousy, rights, guilt, ecstasy, morals, punishment, money, trust, envy, peace, loneliness, home, humiliation, respect, compromise, rules, continuity, secrecy, chance, understanding, betrayal, intimacy, consolation, freedom, appearances, suicide, and, of course, the family. Monogamy is not simply about these things, among others; but when we talk about monogamy we cannot help but talk about these things as well.[67]

If polygamy stands as the antithesis of monogamy (which the author of this list denies; for him the opposite of monogamy is not polygamy, but infidelity), then presumptively polygamy also opposes every good thing on the list, especially "the family." Without delving too deeply into the subconscious motivations of an entire cultural movement, we may expect that some such associational thinking underlies the strident opposition to Mormon polygamy. Such was the abhorrence of plural marriage that "even such a liberally minded American revolutionary as Thomas Jefferson wrote the Virginia law of 1779 that decreed castration for all men convicted of rape, sodomy, bestiality (sex with animals), or polygamy."[68]

The Congressional Reaction against Polygamy

Fully in step with its constituents, Congress enacted several laws that outlawed polygamy,[69] including the Morrill Act of 1862,[70] the Edmunds Act of 1882,[71] and the Edmunds-Tucker Act of 1887.[72] Such was the vigor with which this crime was prosecuted that "from 1882 to 1890 [there were] federal indictments, arrests, prosecutions, and imprisonments of more than 1,300 polygamist Mormons."[73]

The prosecution of George Reynolds under the Morrill Act afforded the opportunity for the United States Supreme Court to author one of the most influential decisions in the nation's history. As then codified, the relevant statute stated that

Every person having a husband or wife living, who marries another, whether married or single, in a Territory, or other place over which the United States have exclusive jurisdiction, is guilty of bigamy, and shall be punished by a fine of not more than $500, and by imprisonment for a term of not more than five years.[74]

Reynolds v. United States[75] ultimately found itself in the Supreme Court, which upheld Reynolds' conviction in 1878.[76] This case is hardly an obscure episode of constitutional law of only antiquarian interest. On the one hand, the precedent of *Reynolds* upholding the illegality of polygamy has been invoked as recently as 1990.[77] The principle enunciated by *Reynolds* to reach this outcome—particularly its rigid distinction between protected religious beliefs and unprotected religious acts—was cited with great approval by the U.S. Supreme Court in that same year.[78]

Our interest lies in the reasons given for the decision. How does the Court justify the criminalization of polygamy? In terms of the previous section, upon which of the four identified grounds for a legal "ought" did the Court choose to build its argument that a man ought not have more than one legal wife? Clearly the opinion penalizes the religious observances of Mormons, so one might have expected them to be entitled to a First Amendment free exercise exemption from an otherwise valid law.[79] On the other hand, the law commits the enforcement powers of the State to the marriage practices of particular Christian sects. Why is this not an unconstitutional establishment of religion?

For a law to pass constitutional muster, it is necessary but not sufficient that there be independent secular justifications beyond the sectarian preference it may advocate (recall the example about the Ten Commandments and its prohibition of murder). The Court must find that the law criminalizing polygamy has a legitimate and primarily secular reason behind it, leaving its support of Christian tradition as only a happy coincidence. The discovery of this secular reason avoids the transgression of the Establishment Clause. Similarly, the protections promised by the Free Exercise Clause are not absolute, and may be withheld if a strong, secular reason exists (we will not allow, for example, human sacrifice in the name of religious observance).

The problem can be resolved on both constitutional counts, then, if overarching secular reasons for the law can be identified. To identify this reason, the *Reynolds* Court was satisfied to note that Europe had long outlawed polygamy,[80] and that the various states have followed this tradition.[81] Had the Court stopped here, the legal "ought" forbidding polygamy would have rested on a traditional ground. But the Court continued on, seeking to demonstrate the pragmatic wisdom of this tradition. It seeks, one might say, to conduct a Marvin Harris sort of analysis, that is, to find the cultural logic behind an otherwise inscrutable practice:

> [A]ccording as monogamous or polygamous marriages are allowed, do we find the principles on which the government of the people, to a greater or less extent, rests. Professor Lieber says, polygamy leads to the patriarchal principle, and which, when applied to large communities, fetters the people in stationary despotism, while that principle cannot long exist in connection with monogamy.[82]

By this reasoning, the State finds a strong secular justification for the criminalization of polygamy in the sociological depiction of polygamy as a corrupter of the democratic spirit. In other words, the Court selected a presumptively empirical ground to rationalize this particular legal ought. The only authority cited to substantiate this claim is Francis Lieber (more on whom below). These, then, are "the evil consequences that [are] supposed to flow from plural marriages."[83]

A later Supreme Court case, *Davis v. Beason*, elaborated in more colorful language the then-common perception of this Mormon practice and gave further specificity to the empirical ground articulated by *Reynolds*:

> Bigamy and polygamy ... tend to destroy the purity of the marriage relation, to disturb the peace of families, to degrade woman and to debase man. Few crimes are more pernicious to the best interests of society and receive more general or more deserved punishment.... To call their advocacy a tenet of religion is to offend the common sense of mankind."[84]

We wish to consider the merit of these empirical claims. Specifically, does polygamy entail "despotism," and does it necessarily "degrade" women? If the answer is, Yes, then a reasonable secular justification to criminalize polygamy presumptively exists, and the laws touching on this issue are not unconstitutional. If the answer is, No, then the asserted secular reasons are revealed to be at best an error obscuring the essentially religious motivations behind the marriage laws. In this second result, the laws against polygamy must fall.

Anthropology can inform us about the reality of the institution of polygamy. If the empirical ground to criminalize polygamy fails, can the criminalization of this behavior persist? More pertinently, *should* it persist? Those are legal (policy) questions. The philosophical issues are: Should legal principle yield to anthropological fact, especially when that principle was initially justified in terms of those same facts? If the criminalization of polygamy is an empirical "ought," can it still stand when that foundation is removed? Is the validity of the empirical justification only a threshold condition, and not a concurrent one?

The Influence of Francis Lieber

Although it can be asked whether the Supreme Court had any good reasons to assert its negative assessment of polygamy, it cannot be denied that there were few data at that time to conclude differently. This case is not one where the Court ignored a body of information that contradicted its policy decision. We would do well, therefore, to at least review the purported empirical basis upon which that decision was originally made. Thus we turn to consider Francis Lieber.

Born in Berlin in 1800, Francis Lieber received a Ph.D. in 1820 after four months of study from the University of Jena.[85] After emigrating to the United States in 1827, Francis Lieber began a long history of illustrious intellectual accomplishments, including editorship of the *Ency-*

clopedia Americana.[86] In 1835, he obtained a professorship in history and political economy at what is now the University of South Carolina: "There he remained for more than twenty years, most of them spent trying to leave."[87] He ended his career at the Columbia Law School where he served from 1865 until his death in 1872.[88]

In his more sober works, particularly his influential *Manual of Political Ethics*,[89] Lieber begins with first principles and, fleshing out the implications of these principles, reaches other results he expects to be logically unassailable. Few thinkers today work on such a large intellectual canvas. For Lieber, "the family is the focus of patriotism. Public spirit, patriotism, devotion to our country, are nurtured by family ties."[90] However, the state is not merely the family writ large.

> That which renders the family so admirable, so holy, is love, and a continued forgetfulness of a separate individual interest. The fundamental idea of the state, on the other hand, is justice, the right which exists between man and man. That which renders the state so great and important is, that it maintains right, protects and is a continual guard over the individual right of every one; that it demands of no member an obligation on his side alone, but knows of mutual obligations only. There shall be no duty in the state for the performance of which the citizen does not receive an equivalent. *Family and state, then, do not only differ as to size, but they differ in their characteristics and essentials, whatever confusion to the contrary may in many parts of the world exist.*[91]

Although the patriotic sensibility is birthed within the family confines, it must be transmuted into something different if a civilized state is to arise. Lieber is explicit about the social deformities arising from the application of the family model directly to the task of state-building:

> If the principle of the family is applied to a state of any extent ... it cannot otherwise than lead to absolutism and tyranny. For we have seen that one of the characteristics of the family is the discarding of strict right and the adhering to mutual attachment, while the just authority of the parent is restricted only by this personal attachment and the natural relations of consanguinity. But this personal attachment cannot exist in an extensive state, but in a very limited degree in the smallest one, so that nothing remains but unlimited authority without the moral control existing in the parental relation.[92]

If the right kind of state is to develop, it is therefore important that it be built upon the right kind of family:

> The family cannot exist without marriage, nor can it develop its highest importance, it would seem, without monogamy. Civilization, in its highest state, requires it, as well as the natural organization and wants of man.[93]

We may well ask why polygamous families are more prone to effect this outcome than are monogamous ones. The first guess might be that because polygamous families tend to be larger than monogamous families, they more closely resemble protostates, and therefore could be more likely to incline their members to attempt to apply familial dynamics to the organization of nations. But then Lieber should also caution against large families of any kind, and such warnings are not to be found. Presumably, polygamy acquires its flaw from the submission of multiple adults to a single head. If two or ten, why not two thousand or ten million? Alternatively, the product of a monogamous family will always associate family dynamics to the parental dyad, and will have no model for its application to larger groups.

We now see the theoretical basis for the conclusion by the *Reynolds* Court: "Professor Lieber says, polygamy leads to the patriarchal principle, and which, when applied to large communities, fetters the people in stationary despotism, while that principle cannot long exist in connection with monogamy."[94]

The foregoing characterizes Lieber's "sober" analysis. We are fortunate in having his specific views on Mormon polygamy. Writing in a popular magazine, Lieber lambastes these "blasphemers" and their "revolting assertions and deeds."[95] Mormonism, he says, "from its very beginning, has been encrusted with vulgarity, jugglery, license and muddy materialism."[96] The monogamy rejected by the Mormons is

> a psychological condition of our jural consciousness, of our liberty, of our literature, of our aspirations, of our religious convictions, and of our domestic being and family relation, the foundation of all that is called polity. It is one of the pre-existing conditions of our existence as civilized white men....[97]

Consequently, the Mormon example, if allowed to spread unchecked, threatened the moral and cultural superiority patently enjoyed by "civilized white men."

Lieber's unrestrained attack on the Mormons gives a taste of what was being said everywhere at that time, including both chambers of Congress.[98] In that respect, he is typical. His formative influence upon the Court, which should not be underestimated, lies not only in his argument for a firm and unyielding response to this viper in the national bosom. In this same article we read the very principle that *Reynolds* would elevate to a constitutional standard:

> We enjoy religious liberty, and mean to perpetuate it for our children; but this liberty has never been understood to mean a license of doing anything, provided it be called religious. Religious liberty means that no one shall be

troubled about his faith—his inner man; but acts remain for ever subject to the law.[99]

Although from our contemporary perspective Lieber may come off as small-minded and even racist, in his own day his was a voice of reason and intellectual seriousness. His work allowed the Court to base its decision on conclusions that had been promulgated throughout the academy. In other words, the Court most likely believed what it was saying. At the time it was rendered, the rational basis for the decision was unassailable, and by the standard of inductive methodology prevalent at the time, it probably even qualified as empirical. The next section considers whether our knowledge about polygamy has improved. Do our wider knowledge and more sophisticated analyses support or refute *Reynolds*'s holding that polygamy necessarily leads to despotism and the degradation of women?

Correlatives of Polygamy

Does Polygamy Promote Despotism?

No small irony exists in the finding of the Supreme Court that polygamy should be criminalized because of its relationship to political despotism. In 1869, some years before the *Reynolds* decision, John Stuart Mill had lambasted the traditional (i.e., monogamous) marriage practice for exactly the same reason. In Mill's words, in its present form

> [t]he family is a school of despotism, in which the virtues of despotism, but also its vices, are largely nourished. Citizenship, in free countries, is partly a school of society in equality.... Any sentiment of freedom which can exist in a man whose nearest and dearest intimacies are with those of whom he is absolute master, is not the genuine or Christian love of freedom, but, what the love of freedom generally was in the ancients and in the middle ages—an intense feeling of the dignity and importance of his own personality; making him disdain a yoke for himself, of which he has no abhorrence whatever in the abstract, but which he is abundantly ready to impose on others for his own interest or glorification.[100]

In theory at least, despotism seems the inevitable result whichever marriage form society encourages. If the goal is truly to stamp out the seeds of political despotism, the courts will have to look elsewhere than whether marriages are polygamous or not.

The first step in the attack on any problem is to clarify the terms of the question. First, "despotism," defined as the rule of a "king with unlimited powers,"[101] is more technically restricted to cases displaying "the *exercised* right of heads of societies to murder their subjects arbitrarily and with impunity."[102] Both definitions share the requirement that despots are heads of societies, meaning that heads of families can be despots only by analogy. That forces upon us the conclusion that even *if* polygamy does lead to despotism, this relationship is true and undesirable only at the national level. That is to say, Clinton's victories in presidential elections should not entitle him to take any and all women he desires to wife. His political power as head of state should not translate into sexual access. But this finding would not immediately require that we conclude also that polygamy is undesirable at the familial level, that is, with respect to men who are not heads of state and who cannot therefore be literal despots.

For clarification, one might briefly consider socialism. Suppose we were all to agree that socialism is unqualifiedly undesirable at the level of national policy. This was the unabashed epithet hurled at Clinton's proposed health insurance plan early in his administration, and by all appearances it was a highly effective one. This concession still would not change the fact that we expect socialistic policies to be operative within the family unit. Whenever one spouse is the sole wage earner, it is assumed that the other spouse shares in the benefits of that wage. Should divorce occur, each spouse may lay legitimate claim to material goods that were technically earned only through the labor of the other. As a general principle, what is good within the family may not be good for the nation, and contrarily, what is bad for the nation may not necessarily be bad for the family. Recall that this was precisely the point Lieber made when he argued that the emotional and authoritarian dynamics ideal for the family are dysfunctional when applied to governing nations.

The fear of despotism is technically a concern of national policy. Even if it were granted, all that would mean is that our national leaders should not be permitted unrestricted access to mates (e.g., harem-building) by virtue of their political power. This result does *not* entail that all other, ordinary men should be restricted to only one wife. Even if the claim asserted by *Reynolds* were true, therefore, additional arguments would be required before that would justify criminalizing polygamy in private contexts.

Second, we must notice that only polygamy is criminalized, but not polygyny in all its manifestations. Although often treated as synonyms,[103] there is an important distinction that is obvious from the Greek roots. *Gamos* (____s) means *only* "a wedding, marriage";[104] on the other hand, *gyne* (____) can mean "wife," but its more common meaning is simply "woman."[105] For example, other words sharing this root ("gynecology," "misogynist") refer to women generally and not to wives specifically. In this derivation polygamy refers only to the number of one's legally recognized wives; polygyny indicates multitudinous female sexual partners, wives or not.[106] "Hence monogamy does not imply fidelity."[107]

Even if Western civilization has been almost uniformly officially monogamist, it has also been unremittingly polygynist. The well-structured roles of concubine, mistress, intern, and prostitute, for instance, demonstrate society's history of tolerance, and even expectation, that males will seek sexual diversity apart from the marital relationship. The major difference is that the polygamist marries these other women and accepts responsibility for any offspring, rather than merely using them for sexual pleasure and ignoring the reproductive consequences. Mormons "asserted that the Gentile objection was not to a man's having more than one woman, but to his calling more than one woman his wife."[108] It is not immediately clear that the polygamist is thereby more morally reprehensible than the more prevalent monogamous polygynist, much less why one rather than the other should be the subject of legal sanction.[109]

Two observations follow from this distinction between polygamy and polygyny. First, arguments against polygyny should not be conflated with those against polygamy. Were the motivation to engage in polygamy merely an impulse of sexual promiscuity, as is often and loudly alleged, the polygamist has opted for the less effective strategy.

Whereas a polygamist is necessarily also a polygynist, a polygynist is not necessarily, and indeed is only rarely, a polygamist. The many ethnographic descriptions of harems within despotic societies illustrate that they are more polygynist than polygamist.[110] Although the ruler did exert exclusive proprietary rights over his women, only a very few of them attained the status of legal wife who could produce a legitimate heir.[111] So while polygamy was practiced, as a proportion of the women procured for sexual purposes, full marriage was a rare attainment. The crux of the despotism/polygamy argument is therefore actually an indictment against polygyny, of which polygamy was only a minor feature.[112] To the extent that laws—especially laws infringing on fundamental rights such as marriage and religion—should be tailored as narrowly as possible to achieve their stated ends, it would be possible to avoid despotism by criminalizing irresponsible polygyny generally, while permitting that small portion which entailed full legal marriage and commitment to the woman.

This comment segues into the second observation. Does it not contravene a sense of fair play, if not the principle of due process, to criminalize *only* one particular (religiously inspired) form of polygyny? If polygyny is socially detrimental, should not all of its varieties be precluded?[113] Why *only* the religious polygamous manifestation? The law should be closely scrutinized to ascertain that it is not unjustly underinclusive in its reach and subsequent implementation. Even if the *Reynolds* correlation between despotism and polygamy were valid, good grounds still exist to question the legitimacy of the antipolygamy laws.[114] The shortfall between the laws and their stated purpose may be so vast as to contravene our understanding of the constitutional guarantee of equal protection.[115]

But in fact, if the *Reynolds* claim is ill-conceived for these technical reasons, it is also simply untrue. The reasoning of *Reynolds* depends upon a universal characterization of polygamy as necessarily associated with other cultural features; it demonstrates the reasonableness of its posture by pointing to the undesirable correlates of this marriage form as they appear in other parts of the world. A recent cross-cultural analysis has, however, ponderously demonstrated that polygamy is not a monolithic institution. The correlatives of polygamy in one part of the world do not readily transfer to another. Peter Bretschneider exhaustively tested every candidate correlate of polygamy (including the economic, a popular explanatory variable), and reached this conclusion:

> The current findings strongly suggest, that [polygamy] is a multidimensional phenomenon and that arguments pointing out singular explanatory categories, such as purely socio-cultural, economic, demographic, or environmental circumstances only insufficiently explain this kind of marriage. I found, for example, the existence of bridewealth payments, high dependencies on fishing, or plow agriculture, war for plunder and captives, and homogenous, high quality environments to be most strongly related to [polygamy]. Other predictors, such as diverging devolution, fraternal interest groups, gathering, internal warfare, marriage of female captives, and pathogen stress, are of somewhat minor relevance. The impacts of extensive agriculture, pastoralism, hunting, female contribution to agriculture or overall subsistence, crop type, offensive external warfare, population size, certain climate conditions, food stress, and variables indicating the impact of Western contact upon traditional subsistence systems are found to be weakly correlated.... The length of a post partem sex taboo, the societal appreciation of children, the level of societal complexity, differences in marriage age, male mortality due to warfare, and high female contributions to gathering, finally, turn out to be completely unrelated to the occurrence of [polygamy].[116]

Most important for our purposes, Bretschneider goes on to say that

> predictors relevant to a worldwide context do not replicate cross-regionally, and vice versa. Divergences from the worldwide pattern are most obvious in the Eastern Eurasian/Insular Pacific world area and in the Americas. This strongly suggests that general, i.e., worldwide explanations of [polygamy] are of limited value only.[117]

If Bretschneider is correct, Mormon polygamy must be evaluated on its own terms. The undesirable implications of polygamy elsewhere are at best merely suggestive, and the burden should be on the government to prove a particular harmful manifestation inherent in Mormon polygamy. *Reynolds*'s appeal to other cultural traditions is therefore irrelevant, even misleading.

Among Bretschneider's specific conclusions is that "the form of political organization as such, cannot contribute very much to our understanding of [polygamous] marriage practices."[118] This concern was the one that most preoccupied the *Reynolds* Court. We are fortunate to have another study on precisely this issue.

At first blush, Laura Betzig's *Despotism and Differential Reproduction* (1986) would seem to support the claim that polygamy and despotism are related, just as Lieber argued. After reviewing over one hundred ethnographically described societies covering the full span of geography and human recorded history, she concludes that despotism does highly correlate with polygamy/polygyny. But *Reynolds* stipulates that polygamy should *cause* or at least stimulate despotism. Otherwise, nothing would be gained in the fight against despotism by criminalizing polygamy. But Betzig assigns the causal links in exactly the opposite direction: despotic rulers will use their power to accumulate women (polygyny) and perhaps wives (polygamy). In other words, despotism causes polygamy; polygamy does not cause despotism.

The full theory begins with the Darwinian assumption that men and women "have evolved to seek out positions of strength as a *means* to reproduction. Power, prestige, and privileged access to resources should be sought, not as ends in themselves, but as prerequisites to procreation."[119] Thus, whenever "conflicts of interest among individuals are not overridden by common interest, or by an overpowering force, [the individual interests] will be manifested."[120] Wherever possible, conflicts of individual interest are *always* resolved in favor of the more powerful contestant. Degree of bias in conflict resolution is directly proportional to the amount of polygyny practiced by the winners.[121] Sociopolitical power yields access to women, and supreme power (despotism) yields unlimited access (harems). Hence, polygamy stands at the *end* of this chain, and not, as Lieber presumed, its beginning.

So the secular reason asserted by *Reynolds*—that because polygamy stimulates despotism it may be criminalized—is false.[122] Even if scholars did not know this in 1878, we know it now, meaning that this Court's justification for criminalizing polygamy today lacks an adequate nonreligious foundation. Unless a new secular basis is found, the holding of *Reynolds* should be overturned.

Does Polygamy Degrade Women?

If the *Reynolds* rationale fails, perhaps the one expressed by *Beason* will suffice: does polygamy (as opposed to polygyny) degrade women? It is on this basis that at least one author argues that the United States and England "would be justified in prohibiting polygamy within their jurisdiction," and thus fulfill the spirit of the United Nations Convention on the Elimination of All Forms of Discrimination against Women.[123]

As in the previous section, it is prudent to begin with a clarification of terms. While everyone may share an intuitive sense of what it might mean to "degrade" someone, what is critically unspecified is who should be the judge. Modern feminism has frequently adopted the stance that there are universal standards of what is "right," standards to which westerners are specially privy. Any transgression of these standards is "wrong," regardless of the context. If the actors in that episode disagree, their ignorance is merely another token of their oppression or degradation.

This perspective has gained popular attention recently over the furor surrounding female circumcision.[124] Western culture has adopted the stance that this practice is wrong and inhuman in some fundamental sense, and that it is right to interfere in its performance, whether that be in the United States or abroad. That the women involved may not view the matter in this negative light is not deemed relevant. "The way that outraged 'western' women championed the cause has since been accused of revealing 'latent racism,' 'intellectual neo-colonialism,' and 'anti-Arab and anti-Islamic fervor,' and efforts to 'eradicate FGM [female genital mutilation]' have been seen as an imperialistic intervention from meddling Westerners of privilege."[125] The opinion above comes from the affected women, not the men. Despite protestations to the contrary from the women involved, *we* (westerners) know that female circumcision is wrong, and that alone is presumably sufficient.[126]

So, who judges if a women is "degraded"? Arguably, the judgment of the woman herself should be determinative. If *she* feels that she is degraded, she is presumptively degraded. If she believes herself *not* to be degraded, she is not degraded. She should not require instruction by outsiders to become dissatisfied with her life,[127] nor should she condescendingly be diagnosed as suffering from "false consciousness." This standard will be applied herein to ascertain whether polygamy degrades women.

We have good reason to doubt that Mormon women viewed themselves as degraded, especially as compared to their female contemporaries. Unlike most women of that era, they could vote—a privilege they lost only with the same federal legislation that outlawed their marriages.[128] One observer, fully prepared to be appalled by the "hopeless, dissatisfied, worn expression" on the faces of Mormon women,[129] came away convinced that these were sound, ordinary women. Although this observer never approved of polygamy, she became so taken with the independence and refinement of the Mormon women that she even stated, "I was willing to eat salt with them"[130]—an enormous public concession.

Specific instances can probably be cited on both sides of this question. But since the question pertains to the institution and not to any individual experience therein, the answer should be sought at that same level of generality. What are the overall trends? From this perspective, it again seems unlikely that Mormon women, as a group, viewed their lot as inferior to that of monogamously married women. On the contrary, to the modern ear, their condition sounds like a precocious foray into contemporary feminism:

> Many wives in pioneer plural families were self-sufficient and resourceful; ran businesses; were teachers, physicians, and writers; and were quite "liberated" in a contemporary sense. They had to be strong and independent for several reasons: wives in plural families were often geographically dispersed, they lived in a frontier subsistence economy, the men were occupied with church responsibilities and travel, and the fear of prosecution kept many husbands on the run.[131]

Although the female *role* was such that we would term it "inferior" to the male role within Mormon communities, it is extremely relevant that this inferior status was *not* justified by appeal to a mythology popular in much of Western culture (which has historically accepted as given the "hysterical" and irrational nature of women) that females were themselves inferior beings.[132] For Mormons, women were under male supervision because this was deemed the natural order, not because women were thought to be incapable of independent living. Males were themselves subordinated to their hierarchical superiors, and all were inferior to God. The important point is that among Mormons, the social hierarchy did not mirror a biological hierarchy.

Related to this question of women as self-sufficient entities is the locus of the decision to enter into a polygamous marriage. In rough terms, it may follow either the "female choice" model or the "male coercion" model. Much of the popular imagery of the late nineteenth century implied a male coercion model, wherein a lurid fictional literature depicted young, impressionable girls whose seductions into polygamous unions constituted "a socially-sanctioned, Victorian form of pornography."[133] It was incomprehensible that any woman of normal intelligence and moral development would willingly endure the degradations of polygamy.[134] Consequently, either the women were themselves ignorant and foolish, or they were tricked and deceived into submission.

What evidence rebuts this popular conception? Was polygamy an arrangement chosen by women as being in their own best interests? Proponents of polygamy as female choice can marshal several arguments. First, the women claimed that the very moral principles invoked to condemn polygamy actually made it the virtuous choice. According to this argument, the moral problem was not the degradation of women but the depravity of men:

> If most men were depraved and most women pure and lacking in passion [as was the common belief in this Victorian ethos], it followed that there were not enough good men to marry all the good women and thus allow them to fulfill their proper sphere [the home, again a Victorian virtue].[135]

Mormon critics had reversed the problem: it was monogamy that degraded women, since if forced women to marry beneath them morally or "to remain single and not fulfill their proper sphere as wives and mothers."[136]

A second reason a woman might consciously choose polygamy is that, in practice, it emphasized the relationships she may herself most value, that between mother and child, and that between women. Even Mormon polygamists conceded that plural marriage "inherently assaulted the ideology of romantic love"[137] (hardly a damning criticism in any event, since romantic love did not emerge as a "respectable motive for marriage" until late in the eighteenth century[138]). The "ties of sisterhood among plural wives" may have evolved as a "compensatory emotion function of this loss of romantic love."[139] Any woman who by nature preferred these relationships would be drawn toward polygamy.[140] Although some of these women would today have been labeled "lesbian,"[141] the point here is the preference for homo*social* relationships between the Mormon women, and only rarely homo*sexual* ones.

At least one feminist historian regarded polygamy as "an implied sealing of wives to wives."[142]

> Her conclusion derives from the well-known facts that "these women 'courted' other wives, placed their husband's hand on the new wife's, and were present at the sealing ceremonies." She concludes that this "qualifies as a same-sex covenant of eternal companionship between women who were, in effect, sealed to other women in polygamy."[143]

Although it is probably too much to conclude that wives "courting" future co-wives was the norm, a cautious conclusion would be that the participation by or at least consultation with wives regarding the addition of a new wife was far from uncommon.[144] Conversely, "it is recorded that some plural wives chose a family through affection for a previous wife."[145] By this reading, women willingly entered into polygamy, or at least remained in it, largely from the satisfying relationships they enjoyed with their co-wives.

An even more telling rebuttal to claims that women are somehow forced into polygamous marriages is the fact that they could freely initiate divorce proceedings, perhaps even more freely than could men.[146] In one study of a modern polygamous congregation, only three or four divorces had been granted in the previous year, all initiated by the wives.[147] Brigham Young, the successor to Joseph Smith, held that "a woman should 'stay with her husband as long as she could bear with him, but if life became too burdensome, then leave and get a divorce."[148] In the Mormon community, divorce was neither difficult nor stigmatizing.[149]

Women possessed freedom, then, to both enter and exit polygamous marriages as they saw fit. This ability supports the argument that on the whole women participated in this institution from their own choice, not from male coercion. So contented were the majority of the Mormon women that an "Industrial Home" in Utah whose purpose was "to provide employment … for the dependent women who renounce polygamy," failed "due to the scarcity of disillusioned and cast-off polygamous wives and children."[150]

Finally, we can also approach the problem of female choice in the terms introduced for the analysis of the argument on despotism, that is, male versus female reproductive strategies. In the female choice model, women will choose as husbands those "men with the most resources, even if this means mating with a man who is already married."[151] The male coercion model assumes that there is no benefit to females and that they would not choose polygamy if given a choice.[152] We shall assume women can only be degraded within the male coercion model. Although they may not actually be degraded in the male coercion model, they certainly are not degraded if polygamy is their own choice.

In general, "human polygyny research usually, but not invariably, finds that polygynous women have lower total fertility than monogamous women."[153] This fact would tend to support the male coercion model at the expense of female choice, and thereby lend indirect credibility to a broad claim that polygamy is degrading to some women.[154]

But even if most of the world's polygamy were instituted under male coercion, this does not necessarily mean that *Mormon* polygamy followed this pattern. Recall the conclusion from Bretschneider's cross-cultural review: few generalizations can be made about polygamy worldwide; each manifestation must be evaluated on its own terms. The specific data for Mormon marriages are equivocal. While one report merely observes that Mormons are, as a group, unusually fertile when compared to Utah and the nation,[155] two other studies—both using data covering the nineteenth century—seem to replicate the usually observed inverse relationship between fertility and polygamous marriage forms. In the first, eighty-one women had a *lifetime* reproductive outcome of 701 children, "demonstrating a fertility which ranks them very high among populations for whom such data has [*sic*] been studied."[156] Unfortunately, these data make no distinction between monogamous or polygamous marriages. For the kinship snapshot diagrams of 1874 alone,[157] however, a slight advantage accrues to monogamy: thirteen polygamous marriages, involving thirty-two women, had produced 76 offspring by 1874, for an average of 2.38 children per wife; by contrast, sixty monogamous unions generated 164 offspring, for an average of 2.73 children per wife.

A second study supports this aggregate analysis.[158] However, its authors suggest that such lumped studies are inappropriate because they mask internal trends. In this study of nineteenth-century Mormons, first wives in polygamous marriages produced *more* children as compared not only to their later co-wives but also as compared to monogamous unions.[159] In other words, reproductively speaking, the most prolific woman was the first wife in a future polygamous marriage. If we extend our focus to include subsequent generations, however, the picture changes. Although later wives had fewer children, they each averaged as many grandchildren as monogamous women, which means they achieved identical long-term reproductive outcomes with less personal investment.[160]

Mormon polygamous marriage, in the long run, turns out to be a more efficient reproductive strategy from the woman's view than is monogamy. The efficiency of these unions has often been highlighted:

> The nuclear family is a capital-intensive and inefficient enterprise with enormous excess capacity in almost all its facilities. A sizable shift toward cooperative and expanded family arrangement could markedly increase the efficiency of resource utilization. Such a shift would also require radical economic reorientation, and it would not be at all surprising to find the producers of consumer goods, especially appliances, aligned on the side of the traditional family against social change.[161]

The contemporary furor over the possibility of gay marriage has led many people and state agents to voice the belief that the primary function of marriage is to birth and raise children. If these advocates are to be taken at their word, then they must favor polygamy over monogamy since it achieves this function more efficiently than does monogamy.

From the perspective of reproductive strategy, the most conservative statement is that polygamy was not the clear example of male coercion among Mormons that it seems to be among many other studied groups. Coupled with the expressed views of the women themselves, there seems little ground to assert a claim that polygamy, at least as practiced by Mormons, constitutes a degradation to women.[162] We should again emphasize that we are speaking of polygamy as an institution. The conclusions at that level will not apply to all marriages. Some women are unquestionably ill-served by their participation in plural marriages,[163] just as some are the worse off for their involvement with monogamous attachments. Still, the preponderance of the data forces the conclusion that *Reynolds* and *Beason* are wrong. Polygamy is not an unreasonable choice for women, and may, in fact, have advantages over monogamous arrangements.[164] One ethnographer has concluded that women in contemporary polygamous marriages "are empowered more fully" than their mainstream (nonpolygamous) Mormon counterparts.[165]

This generalized outcome matches the Supreme Court's own level of analysis, which is to say, it speaks in the abstract about the generic woman. The standards of today's legal doctrine demand something more specific. Neither *Reynolds* nor *Beason* moves from the general to the particular evils supposed to have been committed by the respective defendants. Where was the despot? Where the degraded woman? No fingers were pointed at actual victims of polygamy, *even in those cases*. No wife of George Reynolds was complaining to the federal agents about her miserable life, nor did the courts illustrate their point with stories of Reynolds's despotic, or even merely unseemly, behavior.

> At the least, government plainly has the burden of producing nonspeculative evidence that the harm it fears will actually come about.... Even in the prison and military contexts, where there is a judicial "tradition of giving due deference to the experience and expertise" of administrators, ... "mere speculation, exaggerated fears, and trumped-up or post-hoc rationalizations for thoughtless policies will not suffice...."[166]

Although this statement was made in the specific context of the now-stricken Religious Freedom Restoration Act, the principle holds generally. If a woman had brought charges, for instance, claiming to have been victimized by polygamy, the charge would be specific and appropriate. The institution should not be attacked on its general, theoretical, or possible evils if none are *actually* in evidence.[167] Since any and every act or social arrangement can be or might be detrimental to some persons, legal action should be reserved for those instances that are actually injurious to specific individuals. There are no persuasive data that such injuries existed or are to be expected from Mormon polygamy, either then or now.

Conclusion

Reynolds based its secular justification for the criminalization of polygamy on empirical grounds that we know today to be false. By today's standards, *Reynolds* and *Beason* were wrongly decided.[168] Presumably the Supreme Court thought its information about Mormon polygamy was accurate and the need urgent. The Justices could point to learned treatises by Francis Lieber to provide a factual basis for their decisions. But today we know better. Due to the extensive investigations of social science now available, no student of Mormon polygamy could support the factual conclusions expressed by the *Reynolds* and *Beason* Courts.

This scholarly conclusion mirrors the pragmatic approach that modern society adopts in regard to a polygamy that it no longer sees as threatening to the very fabric of democracy.[169] "[O]fficials have stated publicly that they will not initiate charges against [polygamists] because no significant harm to the community is being perpetrated."[170] Likewise, although a recent case found that an Arizona constitutional prohibition against polygamy is valid and that it can be used to revoke a peace officer's certification,[171] that state's Law Enforcement Officer Advisory Council ruled that such decertification "should be dismissed because 'there has never been … any determination that polygamy is a practice inconsistent with the peace and safety of the state.'"[172]

This discussion reveals two important points. First, the Supreme Court was not acting unreasonably when it voiced its policy decision to criminalize polygamy. If at that time there were any data at all on this point, they all pointed in the direction the Court chose. Second, the true empirical bases are such that they would today produce the opposite result. What, if anything, should be done when judicial precedent deviates from anthropological facts? Although our case study has focused on polygamy, this more general difficulty is not restricted to that context alone. Every time the law articulates its understanding of social facts, the same potential conflict arises.[173]

One judge has expressed the conclusion from his own experience that "[j]ust as a raconteur will seldom let the facts interfere with a good story, judges seem to have seldom allowed sociology to interfere with a good theory."[174] Another practitioner makes the same point more deeply: "Lawsuits are not scientific inquiries—they are highly individualized, and therefore non-repeatable, experiments best resolved by analogical reasoning. *More data do not necessarily improve the analogies.*"[175]

Supreme Court Justice Benjamin Cardozo once observed that "[s]tare decisis is at least the everyday working rule of our law."[176] In that vein, the Supreme Court has concluded that "[j]udicial precedents are presumptively correct,"[177] and indeed, that bad law left standing long enough becomes good law.[178] This rule holds for lower courts as well. The federal Fifth Circuit, for example, considers itself a "strict *stare decisis* court" wherein "one panel ... cannot disregard, much less overrule, the decision of a prior panel."[179] By this principle, the fictions of *Reynolds* and its progeny, having endured for over a century, are not to be undone by something so nettlesome as a contrary fact.[180] Polygamy here will remain criminalized. "[I]t is questionable whether the Court would reconsider, much less reverse, *Reynolds* despite the decision's significant weaknesses."[181]

This refusal to reconsider *Reynolds* is especially ironic given that the Court looked to the authority of Francis Lieber to buttress its holding. But Lieber also gave other advice of a more purely jurisprudential nature. He warned against an "idolatry of precedents" as would let *Reynolds* stand once its basis has been removed:

> If the subject which they relate to has changed, or if we are convinced after patient inquiry, which includes a thorough knowledge of the subject-matter, that we ought in justice to deviate from former decisions, we act wrongly in perpetuating that which is unjust or injurious; for whatever may be said, *reason is and must remain above law and precedent....* There is such a thing as idolatry of precedents, and an idolatry it is, which, at times, has slaughtered Justice at her own altars.[182]

The more sensible approach, and the one we certainly support, is to amend laws or overturn decisions whose self-proclaimed empirical bases are shown to be inadequate or even false. Precedents of this kind do exist. Two decisions by the Vermont Supreme Court held that the original rationales that justified a law may become outdated and thereby fail "to establish a reasonable relation to the public purpose in the light of contemporary circumstances."[183] The U.S. Supreme Court has, on occasion, expressed similar views, giving the impression that the Court espouses two contradictory positions as to the determinative effect of *stare decisis*. When considering whether *Roe v. Wade* should be overturned, for example, the Court established as one criterion "whether *Roe*'s premises of fact have so far changed in the ensuing two decades as to render its central holding somehow irrelevant or unjustifiable in dealing with the issue it addressed."[184]

It is also not unheard of for a factual reevaluation to be preemptively applied to decisions from the U.S. Supreme Court:

> There is some precedent for a lower court engaging in the anticipatory overruling of a higher court decision where that decision is predicated on an empirical circumstance that has changed over time. Courts and commentators have offered principled reasons for refusing to follow higher

court precedent. The higher court, of course, can then review the lower court decision, including the new empirical information upon which its rule of law rests. As we have stated, the higher court would not be bound by the lower court's evaluation of the research, and therefore would be free to reinstate its original rule of law.[185]

It would be naive to believe that only reason dictates which course a court chooses. Other factors are surely involved, not the least of which is the raw power of public opinion or politics.

Much clamor is heard these days about the benefits or evils of an "activist" U.S. Supreme Court, which (mis)reads the Constitution to find new unenumerated rights. Taken for granted by many in these debates is that the Court by virtue of the Constitution has this power, which we only wish them to use wisely. But in actuality, very little constitutional justification exists for the extensive judicial review employed by the Supreme Court. Rather, it assigned itself these responsibilities in the landmark *Marbury* case.[186] This means that the Supreme Court (and thereby all the inferior courts) exercises its expansive powers largely by public permission, which could (in theory at least) be withdrawn. This does not happen because the Court enjoys the benefits of high prestige: "The Court has no power over the purse or the sword; its power instead resides merely in the persuasive force of its judgment."[187] The best interests of the Court require that it do nothing that needlessly diminishes its prestige in the eyes of the American citizenry. The "loss of faith in the legitimacy of the Court's decisions would jeopardize the Court's ability to function effectively."[188] The tenuousness of the Court's legitimacy became especially apparent in the wake of the 2000 presidential election and the Supreme Court's involvement in determining its outcome. The "public's confidence in the Court itself … is a public treasure. It has been built slowly over many years…. It is a vitally necessary ingredient of any successful effort to protect basic liberty and indeed, the rule of law itself."[189]

One of the surest means to reduce the Court to the object of scorn and derision is for it to habitually base judicial decisions on alleged facts that are patently false.[190] Only slightly less debilitating is a chronic refusal to adjust a decision that, while made in good faith, assumed facts that we now know to be invalid. An error is no more tolerable for being an old error. And although we are speaking specifically of the high court, the same conclusion holds for all aspects of the law generally. A legislature that seeks to establish a new value for pi (for example) is not a body that will long enjoy the deference and respect of the citizenry.

The Court is not required to identify an empirical basis for its decisions. Even in *Reynolds* and *Beason* the empirical claims were included among other kinds of "oughts" we discussed above. Combined with purely constitutional principles, these other "oughts" might have suf-

ficed to support the Court's conclusion to preserve the statutory criminalization of polygamy. But since the Enlightenment, empirical facts
(a.k.a. "scientific knowledge") have had a credibility-imbuing aura that
appeals to the critical thinker.[191] No argument suffers for being supported by the sciences.[192] The Court is under no obligation to use empirical facts, but having chosen to do so, it must use them wisely. Anytime
a legal position is allowed to drift too far from the empirical facts that
purportedly generated it, that legal position becomes increasingly irrational.[193] Any Court that continues to endorse irrational positions does
so at the cost of its prestige. A loss of prestige will, in time, result in a
diminution of the powers of the judiciary: "persistent misapplication of
empirical data undermines the Court's legitimacy. Rulings that rest on
faulty premises have little or no persuasiveness, for they lack rationality and judgment—the source of judicial power."[194]

Anthropology has an important contribution to make to prevent
any diminishment of the Court in the eyes of the public. As a social science, anthropology can make certain that the legal machinery at least
begins with good information. If the Court properly utilizes the available anthropological evidence, it can reduce the likelihood that it will
make a decision that will later prove to be inconsistent with sociocultural reality. Also, anthropology can help to correct any such errors
when they do appear, preventing the Court from defending outmoded
positions with antiquated premises.

The practical benefit of anthropology to law, then, is that it can
keep law credible in the first place by providing it with valid data on relevant issues. Further, it can provide ongoing review of empirical justifications already asserted. This practice would not only keep the law
rationally compatible with our current state of knowledge about the real
world, but it would also help to preserve the high esteem and prestige
enjoyed by the Court.

Notes

1. *See* Agustin Fuentes, *The Importance of Teaching Introductory Courses in Anthropology*, THE CHRONICLE OF HIGHER EDUCATION, June 15, 2001, at B16 ("Anthropology
   has much to offer the public. The issues of human behavior, race, and gender are
   central facets of U.S. society today, and anthropologists have participated in the
   debates about those issues for the last century and a half.").
2. 406 U.S. 205 (1972).
3. ROSEMARY J. ERICKSON & RITA J. SIMON, THE USE OF SOCIAL SCIENCE DATA IN SUPREME
   COURT DECISIONS 21 (1998). The anthropologist as expert witness, and John A.
   Hostetler particularly, will be considered in greater detail in chapter 2.

4. *See* Carol M. Ostrom, *Hospital Debates Issue of Circumcising Muslim Girls*, TIMES-PICAYUNE (New Orleans), September 29, 1996, at A14; Barbara Crossette, *Mutilation Seen as Risk for the Girls of Immigrants*, NEW YORK TIMES, March 23, 1998, at A3; Barbara Crossette, *Testing the Limits of Tolerance as Cultures Mix: Does Freedom Mean Accepting Rituals That Repel the West?* NEW YORK TIMES, March 6, 1999, at B9. Female circumcision will be further discussed below.

5. *See* Deirdre Evans-Pritchard & Alison Dundes Renteln, *The Interpretation and Distortion of Culture: A Hmong "Marriage by Capture" Case in Fresno, California*, 4(1) SOUTHERN CALIFORNIA INTERDISCIPLINARY LAW JOURNAL 1 (1994).

6. *See* William Labov, *Objectivity and Commitment in Linguistic Science: The Case of the Black English Trial in Ann Arbor*, 11 LANGUAGE IN SOCIETY 165 (1982).

7. *See* Michael F. Brown, *Can Culture be Copyrighted?* 39(2) CURRENT ANTHROPOLOGY 193 (1998); Mary Riley & Katy Moran (eds.), *Culture as Commodity: Intellectual Property Rights*, 24(4) CULTURAL SURVIVAL QUARTERLY 1-57 (2001).

8. THOMAS F. KING, CULTURAL RESOURCE LAWS & PRACTICE: AN INTRODUCTORY GUIDE 36 (1998).

9. H. MARCUS PRICE, DISPUTING THE DEAD: U.S. LAW ON ABORIGINAL REMAINS AND GRAVE GOODS 32 (1991).

10. *See* ROGER DOWNEY, RIDDLE OF THE BONES: POLITICS, SCIENCE, RACE, AND THE STORY OF KENNEWICK MAN (2000). The legal case of Kennewick Man continues at this writing. [UPDATE]

11. *See* Bruce Bower, *Ishi's Long Road Home: A California Indian's Preserved Brain Accentuates His Tragic, Mysterious Life*, 157 SCIENCE NEWS 24 (January 8, 2000). The life of Ishi was recounted in the film *Last of His Tribe* (HBO, 1992).

12. *See* James M. Donovan, *God Is As God Does: Law, Anthropology, and the Definition of "Religion,"* 6(1) SETON HALL CONSTITUTIONAL LAW JOURNAL 23 (1995). The legal definition of "religion" will be a topic for chapter 3.

13. *See* ERICKSON AND SIMON, *supra* note 3, at 42:

> In short, the majority opinion [in *Roe v. Wade*] relied on medical, legal, philosophical, and religious literature, yet it makes no citations to the social science literature. Blackmun addresses social science issues, when he says that maternity may force a distressful life or future; psychological harm may be imminent; mental health may be taxed by child care; there can be the distress of an "unwanted child"; a woman may be psychologically and otherwise unable to handle pregnancy or motherhood; and there is the stigma of unwed motherhood. But Blackmun does not make any reference to the social science literature on any of those subjects.

All told, only four of the twenty-two abortion cases on which the Supreme Court ruled between 1972 and 1992 refer to social science literature in the majority or concurring opinions. *Id.* at 87. This literature is less likely to be cited by those Justices aiming to overturn *Roe. Id.* at 88. One implication of this contrast might be that the abortion debate is, in its essence, a struggle between worldviews. Those who favor science will tend to favor the right to choose an abortion; those who give higher priority to theological reasoning will deny that right. The fate of *Roe*, then, can depend directly upon society's attitude toward science in general at the moment the Court decision is to be rendered.

14. *See, e.g.*, State v. Finlaysen, 956 P.2d 283 (Utah App. 1998) (Defendant in a rape case argued that his defense was prejudiced when the lower court denied admissibility of expert testimony regarding "saving face" in Japanese culture when the defendant sought to attack rape victim's credibility); Bui v. State, 717 So.2d 6 (Ala. App. 1997) (Defendant's expert witness testified that defendant, having discovered that his wife was cheating on him, murdered his wife and children to save face in accordance with Vietnamese culture).

15. *See generally* Leti Volpp, *Blaming Culture for Bad Behavior*, 12 YALE JOURNAL OF LAW & THE HUMANITIES 89 (2000).
16. The "culture defense" will be discussed in chapter 2.
17. Paul Schiff Berman, *An Anthropological Approach to Modern Forfeiture Law: The Symbolic Function of Legal Actions against Objects*, 11 YALE JOURNAL OF LAW & THE HUMANITIES 1, 19 (1999).
18. *See* ANTHONY G. AMSTERDAM & JEROME BRUNER, MINDING THE LAW (2000).
19. *See* Peter Lawrence, *Law and Anthropology: The Need for Collaboration*, 1(1) MELANESIAN LAW JOURNAL 40 (1970).
20. Lawyers will recognize this contrast as that between the "jurisprudence of concepts" and the "jurisprudence of interests."
21. "Good Samaritan" statutes require "a person to come to the aid of another who is exposed to grave physical harm, if there is no danger of risk of injury to the rescuer." John T. Pardun, *Good Samaritan Laws: A Global Perspective*, 20 LOYOLA OF LOS ANGELES INTERNATIONAL AND COMPARATIVE LAW JOURNAL 591 (1998). "Generally, common law jurisdictions disfavor a general duty to assist [with some notable exceptions, such as where a special relationship exists between the victim and the rescuer, or if the rescuer has either caused the danger to the victim, or has attempted rescue and thereby dissuaded others from doing likewise], whereas civil law jurisdictions prefer such a duty." *Id.* at 592.
22. Good Samaritan laws "became the catalyst for the final episode of the popular television show *Seinfeld*. In that episode, the main characters, Jerry, Elaine, Kramer, and George were taking a walk in a small New Hampshire town when, just a few feet from them, a stranger was robbed at gunpoint. The victim cried for help, but rather than doing anything to help him, the four characters continued their conversation, part of the time commenting and joking about the crime they were witnessing. A moment later, a police officer walked up and announced that they were under arrest. 'But, why?' Elaine asked, 'We didn't do anything.' To which the officer answered, 'That's just it, you didn't do anything.'" Kathleen M. Ridolfi, *Law, Ethics, and the Good Samaritan: Should There Be a Duty to Rescue?* 40 SANTA CLARA LAW REVIEW 957, 968-969 (2000).
23. A legal example of such a threshold is the requirement of good faith in a claim for acquisitive prescription. *See* Louisiana Civil Code articles 3475, 3480, and 3482 (2000). "Good faith" refers to one's reasonable belief that he is the owner of the thing he possesses. If one has possession of the thing for ten years in good faith (and some other elements), then he comes to own the thing in fact whether or not he was the actual owner at the commencement of the possession. The element of good faith need only apply at the commencement of the adverse possession. Should the possessor later realize that he is not the owner of the thing, that later bad faith is irrelevant. Good faith and possession are *not* co-occurring conditions for acquisitive prescription, but only initial conditions. The opposite standard holds in Roman Catholic Canon law: "No prescription is valid unless it is based on good faith, *not only in its beginning, but throughout the whole time required for the prescription....*" Canon 198 (1983) (emphasis added).
24. Civil law jurisdictions such as Louisiana, by contrast, do not recognize *stare decisis*. *See* Joseph M. Simon, *Donations Omnium Bonarum—Article 1497: Who May Object to Such Donations*, 6 LOUISIANA LAW REVIEW 98 (1944) ("Louisiana does not recognize stare decisis.").
25. *See* EDWARD O. WILSON, CONSILIENCE: THE UNITY OF KNOWLEDGE (1998).
26. Supreme Court Justice Benjamin Cardozo offers a parallel analysis. He identifies four methods for extracting legal principles: the method of *philosophy*, which follows a logical progression, the method of *evolution*, which follows "the line of historical development," the method of *tradition*, which follows "the line of the

customs of the community," and the method of *sociology*, which follows "the lines of justice, morals and social welfare, the *mores* of the day." *See* BENJAMIN N. CARDOZO, THE NATURE OF THE JUDICIAL PROCESS 30-31(1921).

27. For example, in Louisiana the penalty for negligent homicide is imprisonment for 0-5 years. Criminal conspiracy to commit a crime punishable by death or life imprisonment (like first-degree murder) shall be punished by imprisonment for 0-30. Inciting a felony such as first-degree murder is punishable with prison for 0-2 years.

28. This conclusion comports with Aristotle's assertion in the *Nicomachean Ethics* that a person cannot be the voluntary victim of an injustice.

29. *See* ALISON DUNDES RENTELN & ALAN DUNDES (EDS.), FOLK LAW: ESSAYS IN THE THEORY AND PRACTICE OF *LEX NON SCRIPTA* (1994).

30. DAVID L. FAIGMAN, LEGAL ALCHEMY: THE USE AND MISUSE OF SCIENCE IN LAW 96 (1999).

31. This, admittedly, is a softer sense of "know" than is usually found in philosophical discourse. There, one "knows" only those things that *are* true and that one also *knows* to be true, and implicitly why they are true. To adhere to true claims without this knowledge of why they are true is not to have knowledge, but right opinion. "Belief" is something else altogether, being a function of one's willingness to act on a proposition that one thinks might be true, but for reasons unknown to the believer.

32. Daubert v. Merrell Dow Pharmaceuticals, 509 U.S. 579, 593 (1993), citing KARL POPPER, CONJECTURES AND REFUTATIONS: THE GROWTH OF SCIENTIFIC KNOWLEDGE 37 (1965). Karl Popper was adamant in his conviction that there was a "truth" with a capital "T," unlike many other philosophers of science like Thomas Kuhn, best known for his THE STRUCTURE OF SCIENTIFIC REVOLUTIONS (1970). Where Popper envisioned progress toward an ever more complete grasp of the "Truth" of the real world, Kuhn saw merely change from one incommensurable paradigm to another. Popper's view is out of fashion among the contemporary postmodern intelligentsia, so his selection by Blackmun is particularly significant.

33. This, incidentally, is a typically Kantian position: one does the right thing without consideration of whether it is particularly good or beneficial.

34. *See* MARY DOUGLAS, PURITY AND DANGER: AN ANALYSIS OF THE CONCEPTS OF POLLUTION AND TABOO (London: Ark, 1984) (1966).

35. *See* MARVIN HARRIS, COWS, PIGS, WARS AND WITCHES (1974).

36. Civic or civil religion is "that religious dimension ... through which it interprets its historical experience in the light of transcendent reality." ROBERT N. BELLAH, THE BROKEN COVENANT: AMERICAN CIVIL RELIGION IN TIME OF TRIAL 3 (2d ed., 1992). American civil religion contains elements that are broadly "Christian," but these are usually so distilled and generic as to bear little relationship to the theology of any particular sect. This fact helps ostensibly religious elements, such as the motto "In God We Trust," to survive Establishment Clause challenges.

37. So pervasive is this political parochialism that republican democracy has been included as one of the enumerated "human rights." *See* UN Universal Declaration of Human Rights Article 21.

38. *See* FRANK ANECHIARICO & JAMES B. JACOBS, THE PURSUIT OF ABSOLUTE INTEGRITY: HOW CORRUPTION CONTROL MAKES GOVERNMENT INEFFECTIVE (1996).

39. The punch behind this tongue-in-cheek illustration comes from its underlying truth:

> Professor Charlton said to Cecilia, one of his law students, "Now, if you were to give someone an orange, what would you say to him?"
> The student replied, "Here. I'm giving you this orange."
> "No! No! No! Think like a lawyer, Cecilia!" shouted Professor Charlton. "Okay. I'd say, 'I hereby give and convey to you all and singular, my estate and interests, rights, title, claim and advantages of and in, said orange, together with all its rind, juice, pulp, and pits, and all rights and advantages with full power to bite, cut, freeze, and otherwise eat, the same, or give the same away

with and without the rind, skin, juice, pulp, or pits, anything herein before or hereinafter or in any other deed, or deeds, instruments of whatever nature or kind whatsoever to the contrary in anywise notwithstanding....'"

SID BEHRMAN, THE LAWYER JOKE BOOK 20 (1991).

40. Some believe this attribution is erroneous, that the famous paragraph which seemingly makes this point is making quite another. Oliver Curry, in a useful posting to the Evolutionary Psychology internet discussion list, argues this point, and cites, among others, L. Arnhart (DARWINIAN NATURAL RIGHT (1998)) and N. Capaldi (*Hume's Rejection of "Ought" as a Moral Category*, 63 JOURNAL OF PHILOSOPHY 126 (1966)) as defending this alternative interpretation.

41. David Fate Norton, *Hume, Human Nature, and the Foundations of Morality*, *in* THE CAMBRIDGE COMPANION TO HUME 169 (David Fate Norton ed., 1993). The discussion in Hume occurs in section 1 of book 3, p. 469.

42. *Naturalistic Fallacy*, THE INTERNET ENCYCLOPEDIA OF PHILOSOPHY, *at* www.utm.edu/research/iep/n/nfallacy.htm (last visited January 6, 2003).

43. FAIGMAN, *supra* note 30, at 14.

44. Edward O. Wilson, *The Biological Basis of Morality*, 281(4) ATLANTIC MONTHLY 53 (1998).

45. John R. Searle, *How to Derive "Ought" from "Is,"* 73(1) PHILOSOPHICAL REVIEW 43 (1964).

46. One can think here of the distinction George Lakoff draws so effectively between variables that *motivate* a particular outcome, as opposed to those that *determine* it. *See* GEORGE LAKOFF, WOMEN, FIRE, AND DANGEROUS THINGS: WHAT CATEGORIES REVEAL ABOUT THE MIND 65 (1987).

47. Searle, *supra* note 45, at 44. A similar argument can be found in JUDITH JARVIS THOMSON, THE REALM OF RIGHTS (1990).

48. *Id.* at 56.

49. Some suggest that this intellectual veneer is the primary utility of the social sciences to the law. Even when an appearance is given that the facts have motivated the legal outcome, in actuality, the basis may lie altogether elsewhere. *See* John Minor Wisdom, *Random Remarks on the Role of Social Sciences in the Judicial Decision-Making Process in School Desegregation Cases*, 39(1) LAW AND CONTEMPORARY PROBLEMS 134, 142 (1975).

50. Sadly, this limitation does not extend to decisions of the judiciary. The decision in *Bowers v. Hardwick*, 478 U.S. 186 (1986), was unabashedly intended to maintain the fundamentalist Christian status quo. Modern "[r]esearch [on homosexuality] was ignored in favor of history and morality." ERICKSON & SIMON, *supra* note 3, at 10.

51. *See* Harris v. McRae, 448 U.S. 297, 319 (1980) ("[I]t does not follow that a statute violates the Establishment Clause because it 'happens to coincide or harmonize with the tenets of some or all religions.'").

52. *See* James M. Donovan, *DOMA: An Unconstitutional Establishment of Fundamentalist Christianity*, 4(2) MICHIGAN JOURNAL OF GENDER & LAW 335 (1997).

53. 393 U.S. 97 (1968).

54. 482 U.S. 578 (1987).

55. *See* STEPHEN E. FIENBERG (ED.), THE EVOLVING ROLE OF STATISTICAL ASSESSMENTS AS EVIDENCE IN THE COURTS (1989).

56. The Church of Jesus Christ of Latter-day Saints has recently announced that "it no longer wants to be referred to as 'the Mormon Church.'" Jeffery L. Sheler, *Don't Call it "Mormon,"* 130(11) U.S. NEWS & WORLD REPORT, March 19, 2001, at 51. It is still acceptable to use "Mormon" in proper names, and church members may continue to be called Mormons "although many prefer the title 'Latter-day Saints.'" *Id.* We have attempted to adhere to this preferred usage.

57. For only one example, *see* syndicated columnist Jeff Jacoby, *Just Another Nontraditional Family*, BOSTON GLOBE, May 17, 2001, at A13: "No one who supports same-sex marriage can logically oppose the legalization of polygamy." Other examples appear in the sundry selections within Andrew Sullivan's edited volume, SAME-SEX MARRIAGE: PRO AND CON (1997). For a more detailed discussion of the alleged relationship between polygamy and same-sex marriage, *see* James M. Donovan, *Rock-Salting the Slippery Slope: Why Same-Sex Marriage Is Not a Commitment to Polygamous Marriage*, 29 NORTHERN KENTUCKY LAW REVIEW 521 (2002).

58. *See* DAVID M. BUSS, THE EVOLUTION OF DESIRE 178 (1994).

59. TIMOTHY H. GOLDSMITH, THE BIOLOGICAL ROOTS OF HUMAN NATURE 56 (1991). Peggy Vaughan describes monogamy as an achievement, not an assumption. *See* PEGGY VAUGHAN, THE MONOGAMY MYTH 171 (1989).

60. LAWRENCE STONE, THE FAMILY, SEX AND MARRIAGE IN ENGLAND 1500-1800, at 29 (1979).

61. *Id.* at 35.

62. *See* HELEN E. FISHER, ANATOMY OF LOVE: THE NATURAL HISTORY OF MONOGAMY, ADULTERY, AND DIVORCE 69 (1992).

63. *See* IRWIN ALTMAN & JOSEPH GINAT, POLYGAMOUS FAMILIES IN CONTEMPORARY SOCIETY 39 (1996).

64. Sura 4.:3, quoted by KAREN ARMSTRONG, MUHAMMAD: A BIOGRAPHY OF THE PROPHET 190 (1992).

65. LARRY L. & JOAN M. CONSTANTINE, GROUP MARRIAGE 14 (1973). Kwasi Wiredu makes much the same point. He says that "little imagination" is required to think of circumstances that would make polygamy more favorable than monogamy. His own example is a heavily skewed sex ratio. *See* KWASI WIREDU, CULTURAL UNIVERSALS AND PARTICULARS: AN AFRICAN PERSPECTIVE 70 (1996). Also, the aforementioned verse of the Koran was concerned about the fact that during Muhammad's time, there was a surplus of unmarried women. Karen Armstrong writes that "[t]here was probably a shortage of men in Arabia, which left a surplus of unmarried women who were often badly exploited. The Qu'ran is most concerned about this problem and resorted to polygamy as a way of dealing with it." ARMSTRONG, *supra* note 64, at 190.

66. According to Plato, "the common possession of women" would be the greatest good, if indeed it is possible." But for many reasons, he doubted that this would be possible. PLATO, REPUBLIC 132 (G.M.A. Grube trans., Indianapolis: Hackett, 1992).One interesting observation relates our extended life spans with our new lifestyles. "A lifelong monogamous marriage when the life expectancy was forty or fifty is very different from a lifelong monogamous marriage when the life expectancy has increased so dramatically [to seventy or eighty]." VAUGHAN, *supra* note 59, at 193. *See also* FISHER, *supra* note 62, at 304. If valid, this would account for the perception that what was "natural" is now crumbling. But instead of accounting for this change in terms of moral degeneration, the alternative reading would be that marriages are lasting as long as ever they did; it is we who are outliving the marriages. For this reason, Stone suggests that "modern divorce is little more than a functional substitute for death." STONE, *supra* note 60, at 46.

67. ADAM PHILLIPS, MONOGAMY i-ii (1996).

68. D. MICHAEL QUINN, SAME-SEX DYNAMICS AMONG NINETEENTH-CENTURY AMERICANS: A MORMON EXAMPLE 35 (1996).

69. An able review of the congressional debates surrounding the passage of the antipolygamy laws can be found in Robert G. Dyer, *The Evolution of Social and Judicial Attitudes towards Polygamy*, 5(1-3) UTAH BAR JOURNAL 35 (1977).

70. Morrill Act, ch. 126, 12 Stat. 501 (July 1, 1862).

71. Edmunds Act, ch. 47, 22 Stat. 30 (March 22, 1882) (amended 1887, repealed 1909).

72. Edmunds-Tucker Act, ch. 397, 24 Stat. 635 (March 3, 1887).

73. QUINN, *supra* note 68, at 282-283.

74. Sect. 5352, Revised Statutes.
75. Reynolds v. United States, 98 U.S. 145 (1878).
76. Later, in 1885, despite this conviction, George Reynolds took a third wife. This fact prompted Ray Davis to relay the following limerick:

> There was a young fellow of Lyme
> Who lived with three wives at a time.When asked, "Why the *third*?"
> He said, "One's absurd,
> And bigamy, sir, is a crime."

Ray Jay Davis, *Plural Marriage and Religious Freedom: The Impact of* Reynolds v. United States, 15 ARIZONA LAW REVIEW 287, 291 note 25 (1973).
77. Barlow v. Blackburn, 798 P.2d 1360 (Ariz. App. 1990) (Arizona constitutional prohibition against polygamy is valid). This court concluded that even if Barlow practiced polygamy as part of a sincere religious belief, his certification as a peace officer was revocable because the state had "an overriding interest in assuring that law enforcement officers ... evidence respect for the very laws and constitution that peace officers had sworn to uphold." *Id*. at 1366. An amusing sidebar to this case is that if read literally, the court and the defendants were less exercised about Barlow's practice of polygamy than they were about "his *open* practice of polygamy." *Id*. at 1361 (emphasis added). Compare this with the Louisiana ban of open concubinage, not concubinage per se. *See* Ralph Slovenko, *The De Facto Decriminalization of Bigamy*, 17 JOURNAL OF FAMILY LAW 297, 301 (1978-79).
78. *See* Employment Division, Dept. of Human Resources of Oregon v. Smith, 494 U.S. 872 (1990).*Reynolds* can be cited for either of two points: the general constitutional principle articulated that while the First Amendment guarantees absolute freedom of belief, actions—whether religiously motivated or not—fall within the purview of governmental regulation notwithstanding the guarantees of free exercise; or the application of this principle to turn aside claims to a constitutional privilege to practice religiously motivated plural marriage. Most modern citations to *Reynolds* are in fact related to the first issue, the general constitutional principle.For that reason it makes sense that *Smith* (authored by Justice Scalia) should cite *Reynolds*, since both cases achieve the same end, specifically in *Smith*, albeit only incidentally in *Reynolds*. That is, both cases effectively repeal the Free Exercise Clause of the Constitution by saying that no religious actions have any constitutionally required protections. Since speech and belief are already protected by the Free Speech Clause, this removes any substantive meaning of the Free Exercise Clause. *Cf*. Edwin B. Firmage, *Religion & the Law: The Mormon Experience in the Nineteenth Century*, 12 CARDOZO LAW REVIEW 765, 772-774 (1991).Cases like *Barlow v. Blackburn*, 798 P.2d at 1360, and *Potter v. Murray City*, 760 F.2d 1065 (10th Cir. 1985), however, are modern invocations of *Reynolds*'s second issue, the specific criminalization of polygamy. In practice, however, these two points are difficult to separate: to carve out an exception for religious polygamy would require a reformulation of the rule in *Reynolds*; overturning the rule would force a reconsideration of its application to the criminalization of polygamy. For our purposes, therefore, it is not critical to note the specific context that provokes the citation to *Reynolds*.
79. Jesse Choper suggests that the criterion for Free Exercise exemptions should be the presence of extratemporal consequences for failure to perform the demanded act (or, alternatively, compulsion to perform the forbidden act). JESSE CHOPER, SECURING RELIGIOUS LIBERTY 74-80 (1995). Polygamy within Mormonism meets this standard: "the failing or refusing to practise polygamy by such male members of said church, when circumstances would admit, would be punished, and that the penalty for such failure and refusal would be damnation in the life to come." *Reynolds*, 98 U.S. at 161. Ira C. Lupu agrees that, contrary to *Reynolds*, "[t]he prohibition on polygamous marriage at issue in *Reynolds* ... would present a clear case of free exercise

burden." Ira C. Lupu, *Where Rights Begin: The Problem of Burdens on the Free Exercise of Religion*, 102(5) HARVARD LAW REVIEW 933, 973 (1989).

80.   *See Reynolds*, 98 U.S. at 164 ("Polygamy has always been odious among the northern and western nations of Europe, and, until the establishment of the Mormon Church, was almost exclusively a feature of the life of Asiatic and of African people. At common law, the second marriage was always void (2 Kent, Com. 79), and from the earliest history of England polygamy has been treated as an offence against society."). We may assume a strong correlation between the criminality of polygamy in western Europe and its disallowal by the Catholic Church. According to Philip L. Kilbride, polygamy was not definitively forbidden until the Council of Trent in 1563. Apparently part of the rationale for this action was as a rebuke to Martin Luther, who would "prefer bigamy rather than divorce." *See* PHILIP L. KILBRIDE, PLURAL MARRIAGE FOR OUR TIMES: A REINVENTED OPTION? 63 (1994).

81.   *Reynolds*, 98 U.S. at 165 ("[T]here has never been a time in any State of the Union when polygamy has not been an offence against society, cognizable by the civil courts and punishable with more or less severity."). Citations to the various state code sections that outlaw plural marriages are succinctly listed by Slovenko, *supra* note 77, at 307-308.

82.   *Reynolds*, 98 U.S. at 165-166.

83.   *Id.* at 168.

84.   133 U.S. 333, 341-342 (1890). This case has also been cited with approval by Justice Scalia in his dissent to *Romer v. Evans*, 116 S.Ct. 1620, 1635-1636 (1996). Justice Scalia's point is that if polygamy can be outlawed—indeed, if *advocating* polygamy can be outlawed—then surely actions against gays and lesbians such as Colorado's Amendment 2 must be constitutional. Although his argument is specious, Scalia unwittingly does make one good point: the fate of gay marriage is almost certainly tied to the legal treatment of polygamy. The first cannot be achieved without a radical reconsideration (but not necessarily acceptance) of the other.
      The extreme right will take such a statement as a sign that the goal of gay marriage is to destroy American society. But rather, all that is asserted here is that if polygamy is going to continue to be criminalized, better grounds for legal sanction will have to be found than the shoddy rationales offered thus far.

85.   *See* Michael Herz, *Rediscovering Francis Lieber: An Afterword and Introduction*, 16(6) CARDOZO LAW REVIEW 2107, 2100 (1995).

86.   *Id.* at 2110.

87.   *Id.* at 2111.

88.   *See id.* at 2113.

89.   1 FRANCIS LIEBER, MANUAL OF POLITICAL ETHICS DESIGNED CHIEFLY FOR THE USE OF COLLEGES AND STUDENTS AT LAW (2d ed., Philadelphia: J.B. Lippincott, 1876) [hereinafter *MANUAL*]. Our analysis focuses on the *MANUAL* as the primary source for Lieber's analysis of polygamy and its nefarious influence on democratic sentiment. Because *Reynolds* provides no citations, it is uncertain what the Court had in front of it. Another author has suggested Lieber's ON CIVIL LIBERTY AND SELF-GOVERNMENT as an alternative source. *See* James L. Clayton, *The Supreme Court, Polygamy and the Enforcement of Morals in Nineteenth Century America: An Analysis of* Reynolds v. United States, 12 DIALOGUE: A JOURNAL OF MORMON THOUGHT 46, 51 (1979), *reprinted in* CONSCIENCE AND BELIEF: THE SUPREME COURT AND RELIGION 58, 63 (Kermit L. Hall ed., 2000). The *MANUAL* came first (1838-39), as compared to the 1853 publication of ON CIVIL LIBERTY. Although the ideas may be more clearly articulated in the latter, they are fully present in the first.

90.   LIEBER, MANUAL, *supra* note 89, at 142.

91.   *Id.* at 145-146 (emphasis added).

92.   *Id.* at 146 note 1.

93. *Id.* at 139.
94. *Reynolds*, 98 U.S. at 165-166.
95. Francis Lieber, *The Mormons: Shall Utah Be Admitted into the Union?* 5(27) PUT-NAM'S MONTHLY 225, 226 (1855) [hereinafter *The Mormons*]. Lieber's answer to the title question: No.
96. *Id.* at 233.
97. *Id.* at 234.
98. For example, this from the House of Representatives:

> Amid the jealousies of a plurality of wives the respect of parental authority is lost, the gentleness of fireside instruction and hearthstone memories is destroyed. Crime of the most revolting character ensues; infanticide follows as a matter of course as soon as the husband finds he is getting more children than he can support.... Point me to a nation where polygamy is practiced, and I will point you to heathens and barbarians. It seriously affects the prosperity of States, it retards civilization, it uproots Christianity.... [E]ffeminacy and weakness, lack of intellectual strength, bodily energy, national decay, is its sad, unfailing result....

CONGRESSIONAL GLOBE, 33rd Cong., 1st Sess. 1100-1101 (1854). For another outburst contemporary to the Morrill Act, *see also* CONGRESSIONAL GLOBE, 36th Cong., 1st Sess. 1514 (1860).

99. Lieber, *The Mormons*, *supra* note 95, at 232.
100. JOHN STUART MILL, THE SUBJECTION OF WOMEN 44-45 (Cambridge, MA: MIT Press, 1970) (1869).
101. WEBSTER'S NEW WORLD DICTIONARY 374 (3rd College ed., 1988).
102. LAURA L. BETZIG, DESPOTISM AND DIFFERENTIAL REPRODUCTION: A DARWINIAN VIEW OF HISTORY 2 (1986) (emphasis added); *see also* JOHN LOCKE, THE SECOND TREATISE OF GOVERNMENT 87 (J.W. Gough ed., 3d ed., Oxford: Basil Blackwell, 1966) (1690). Chapter 6 of Locke's book describes his own views on the relationship of family structure to political power, which contrasts with those of both Mill and Lieber. Whereas Locke believed that the family was an autonomous set of power relationships, Mill, Lieber, and Hobbes argued that the state was, in many ways, the family writ large, and for this reason it was important to have the right kind of families. *See* THOMAS HOBBES, LEVIATHAN 129 (Oxford: Clarendon Press, 1909) (1651).
103. Whereas most writers will select one or the other, Jeremy M. Miller, *A Critique of the Reynolds Decision*, 11 WESTERN STATE UNIVERSITY LAW REVIEW 165 (1984), is unusual in that he uses both interchangeably; G. Keith Nedrow also stipulates the terms to be synonyms. *See* G. Keith Nedrow, *Polygamy and the Right to Marry: New Life for an Old Lifestyle*, 11(3) MEMPHIS STATE UNIVERSITY LAW REVIEW 303, note 1 (1981).
104. GREEK-ENGLISH LEXICON (abridged from Liddell and Scott's GREEK-ENGLISH LEXICON) 138 (1974). Diacritical markings from the Greek are omitted.
105. *Id.* at 147. *Gyne* would mean "wife" in the same colloquial way that pointing to a female and saying "She's my woman" can be taken to mean that she is your wife. In this case, it is the attached possessive pronoun that connotes spousal ties, and not the word alone.
106. A different and more common relationship between these terms is given by Bretschneider. He construes both words according to multiple marriages. However, he takes "polygamy" to be a superordinate category comprised of two subordinates, "polygyny" and "polyandry." *See* PETER BRETSCHNEIDER, POLYGYNY: A CROSS-CULTURAL STUDY 50 (1995). Although the definitions we offer are the more technically correct, we recognize that they are not the most conventional, and therefore they require some justification.Our approach better captures what we deem the pertinent contrast, which is not between multiple wives and multiple husbands, but whether a man has multiple legal wives or access to multiple females for purely sexual pur-

poses, with no legal entailments. The status of polyandry might seem to fall by the wayside in our analysis. Rather than show why this is not necessarily the case, our response to that criticism is to highlight one obstacle that serves to separate anthropology from law (others are considered in chapter 2).The issue of polyandry is a rare occurrence even in anthropology. *See* FISHER, *supra* note 62, at 69 ("only 0.5 percent of all societies permit a woman to take several husbands simultaneously."). Polygamy, on the other hand, is practiced by most of the world's cultures. Moreover, polyandry has never been an issue for American law. No national movement has emerged that requires a woman to take multiple husbands in the way that Mormonism arose to advance polygamy.To treat polyandry as a marriage form collateral with polygamy—a status it holds only logically, but neither ethnographically nor legally—is to exaggerate the former at the expense of obscuring important elements of the latter. That approach might be appropriate for some other purposes, especially those striving for intellectual understanding of a phenomenon. But law's goal is not to "make sense" of social data, but to resolve disputes. The question of polygamy is one example where these two interests diverge. An analytic approach that seeks understanding will not be one that necessarily provides utility.Law, in other words, does not require all-encompassing theoretical systems, only insight on the immediate issues it must decide. The law must deal with the practical problem of polygamy, not polyandry. We actually believe that our redefinition will ultimately enhance understanding; we confess, however, that it was designed to improve utility. To the extent that anthropology insists on conceptual systems that focus on issues of little or no relevance to law, those systems can be expected to be overlooked by the law.Our minority approach to the terms, then, has the virtue of framing the variables so that they are most likely to render a result useful to law.

107. FISHER, *supra* note 62, at 63.
108. Orma Linford, *The Mormons and the Law: The Polygamy Cases* (pt. 1), 9 UTAH LAW REVIEW 308, 311 (1964) [hereinafter *Mormons and Law* (pt. 1)].
109. A Mormon cleaning lady is on record as replying to men sent to Utah to enforce the antipolygamy laws that they also "lived in polygamy but they won't own up to it and marry the women." Joan Smyth Iversen, *A Debate on the American Home: The Antipolygamy Controversy, 1880-1890,* 1(4) JOURNAL OF THE HISTORY OF SEXUALITY 585, 596 (1991) [hereinafter *Debate on the American Home*].

> The Mormons unsuccessfully contended that monogamy could not be proved to be morally superior to polygamy, noting that infidelity, divorce, prostitution, and the like were common in monogamous populations, while such behavior was almost non-existent among the Mormons.

Slovenko, *supra* note 77, at 298. Stephen Macedo, *Homosexuality and the Conservative Mind,* 84 GEORGETOWN LAW JOURNAL 261, 288 note 105 (1995) would seem to agree.

It has been suggested that the proliferation of pornography and the detrimental side-effects therefrom are the result of suppressing innate polygynous tendencies into ill-fitting monogamous relationships. Joseph Shepher & Judith Reisman, *Pornography: A Sociobiological Attempt at Understanding,* 6 ETHOLOGY AND SOCIOBIOLOGY 103 (1985).

110. BETZIG, *supra* note 102.
111. In most contexts, offspring inherit the status of their mother. Thus, without the sanction of marriage, offspring between a noble and a socially inferior woman were relegated to the mother's lot, rather than expecting to share in the father's. BETZIG, *supra* note 102, at 71-73, reviews this issue, suggesting that one of the reasons the Romans freed so many of their slaves is because they were actually freeing their own illegitimate sons who had inherited their mother's slave status.
112. The relevant parallel, as highlighted by Macedo, *supra* note 109, at 264, is the "frequency with which conservatives translate their opposition to promiscuity and lib-

erationism into blanket condemnations of homosexual conduct [which] is as puzzling as it is illegitimate."

113. This observation was not foreign to the contemporary debate about the Mormons. At least one Congressman refused to vote for the Edmunds Bill "because it did not go so far as to outlaw adultery, fornication, lewdness, and related moral offenses." Linford, *Mormons and Law* (pt. 1), *supra* note 108, at 321.

Technically, there are indeed laws against many forms of polygyny, and of sexual conduct in general. The following paragraph pithily summarizes the law on this issue:

> You can't do it with your mother, father, son, daughter, and maybe even with some cousins. You can't do it with animals, and certainly not with dead humans. If you're a man, you're not supposed to do it with a man, or if you're a woman, with a woman, although in some states you can do it in private. You aren't supposed to do it at all in public. You aren't supposed to do it with more than one other person at the same time. And you aren't supposed to look at other people doing it, at least not through someone's window. You can't expose what you do it with. The law tells us what parts we can use and can't use. You can't do it with force, perhaps, even to your spouse. You can't whip, chain, or hurt someone in doing it even if they want it. You can't do it for pay. With or without pay, you can't do it until you're a certain age. If you're married, you can't do it with someone not your spouse, and if you aren't married, you'd better not do it with someone who is married. Even if both of you aren't married, you still can't do it in most places.

Stephen L. Wasby, *The Impotency of Sex Policy: It's Not All in the Family (Or: A Non-Voyeuristic Look at a Coupling of Sex and Policy)*, 9(1) POLICY STUDIES JOURNAL 117 (1980).

In practice, though, these laws are unevenly and only sporadically invoked. A recent case in Gastonia, North Carolina, wherein a judge sought to indict a young couple under a 191-year-old state law against fornication, was newsworthy because of its rarity. *See Viewpoint*, U.S. NEWS & WORLD REPORT, October 14, 1996, at 19. So while many polygynist activities are formally outlawed, they are hardly ever enforced. How many people are currently in jail for having committed adultery? Probably not very many. Slovenko, *supra* note 77, at 304, says such prosecutions are "as uncommon as meat on a drugstore sandwich." One recent exception: the primary culprits in the U.S. Army sexual harassment scandal were each charged with a variety of crimes, such as rape, forcible sodomy, conduct unbecoming an officer, and including adultery. Sonja Barisic, *Captain, 2 Sergeants Charged in Recruit Rapes*, TIMES-PICAYUNE (New Orleans), November. 8, 1996, at A7. But even this exception proves the point, in that it is the special case of military law. The point to be stressed here is that from the universe of outlawed polygynist practices, only polygamy seems to have been selected for special and vigorous enforcement.

114. An additional failing not discussed is the fact that the antipolygamy laws criminalized not simply polygamy, but also "the *form* or *appearance* of such marriages." Linford, *Mormons and Law* (pt. 1), *supra* note 108, at 355. This meant that a former polygamist could comply with the new laws not only by cohabitating and having sexual relations with only one of his wives, but also by abandoning all the others. The logic of the dominating non-Mormon Christians was that if a man is nice to a woman, he must be sleeping with her; they recognized no other reasons to associate with females. Therefore, were he seen to be attending to the material needs of his former wives and children, that created the criminal "appearance" of polygamy.

It seems ironic that outraged Christian America preferred him to abandon his polygamous families, leaving them destitute and unprotected, rather than to allow him to provide for their basic human needs. It must have been a higher order of logic which decreed that the "helpless victims of polygamy" would be better served by taking away in fines money needed for their food, clothing, and shelter and imprisoning their only provider.

Orma Linford, *The Mormons and the Law: The Polygamy Cases* (pt. 2), 9 UTAH LAW REVIEW 543, 586 (1965). Indeed, "It would seem that the only way that a polygamist could dispose of a plural wife to the satisfaction of the courts was to either publicly drive her and her children into the streets with a whip or to bring about her demise." Linford, *Mormons and Law* (pt. 1), *supra* note 108, at 370.

115. An example of a fatally underinclusive law is discussed in *Edwards v. Aguillard*, 482 U.S. 578 (1987).

116. BRETSCHNEIDER, *supra* note 106, at 183.

117. *Id.* at 184.

118. *Id.* at 119.

119. BETZIG, *supra* note 102, at 2. The state of the art of evolutionary psychology in general is contentious but improving constantly from its initial assertion into the modern scientific discourse by Edward O. Wilson in the 1970s. The "Bible" for the discipline of evolutionary psychology is generally conceded to be JEROME H. BARKOW, LEDA COSMIDES, & JOHN TOOBY, THE ADAPTED MIND (1992). An early effort to apply this perspective to law was made by JOHN H. BECKSTROM, SOCIOBIOLOGY AND THE LAW (1985).

120. BETZIG, *supra* note 102, at 9.

121. *See id.* at 88.

122. The expressed fear was that polygamy would lead to despotism. Avoid polygamy, it was thought, and you can avoid despotism. On the other hand, Plato believed that the surest way to encourage despotism would be to outlaw homosexuality. Symposium, *in* PLATO: ON HOMOSEXUALITY: LYSIS, PHAEDRUS, AND SYMPOSIUM 114 (Buffalo, NY: Prometheus Books, 1991).

123. CAROLYN HAMILTON, FAMILY, LAW AND RELIGION 72-73 (1995).

124. *See* Tina Kelley, *Doctor Fights Ban on Circumcising Girls*, SEATTLE TIMES, June 6, 1996, at B3; Neil MacFarquhar, *Egyptians Defy Ban on Ritual; Genital Mutilation of Females Unabated*, DALLAS MORNING NEWS, August 9, 1996, at 45A; Celia W. Dugger, *U.S. Outlaws Practice of Girls' Genital Cutting*, TIMES-PICAYUNE (New Orleans), October 12, 1996, at A14.

125. Bettina Shell-Duncan & Ylva Hernlund, *Female "Circumcision" in Africa: Dimensions of the Practice and Debates, in* FEMALE "CIRCUMCISION" IN AFRICA 1, 24-25 (Bettina Shell-Duncan & Ylva Hernlund eds., 2000).

126. It can be difficult to know just where to draw the line when cultures collide. A visiting Korean man was prosecuted for beating his wife. She refused to cooperate with the prosecution, and he argued that in his culture, he was justified in beating her. *See* John Ellement, *Korean Says Assault on Wife was OK*, TIMES-PICAYUNE (New Orleans), December 31, 1996, at A6. Iraqi men face child abuse and rape charges because the father, in keeping with their native custom, gave his 13- and 14-year-old daughters in marriage to adults. *See* Don Terry, *Immigrants' Traditions Clash with U.S. Customs and Laws*, FRESNO BEE, December 2, 1996, at D11.   If you believe in democracy, which presupposes that citizens are free and able to make their own decisions about their own lives, and are free and able to act on those decisions, it is extremely difficult to assert that crimes were committed in either case *if* the Korean woman and the Iraqi teenagers have no complaints about their situations. The "cultural defense" is considered in greater detail in chapter 2.

127. "[O]ne of the principal aims [of the nineteenth-century woman's organization, the National Woman Suffrage Association, was] 'to make those women discontented who are now content.'" Iversen, *Debate on the American Home*, *supra* note 109, at 597.

128. *See id.* at 591. The two issues were not unconnected. Discussion on the Senate floor expressed dismay that it was the vote of women which "sustained" polygamy in Utah. *See* 13 CONG. REC. 230 (1881). The speaker intended "to introduce a bill to

repeal woman suffrage in the Territory of Utah, knowing and believing that that will be the most effectual remedy for the extirpation of polygamy in that unfortunate Territory." *Id.*

> Congress took away the vote on the theory that the women in Utah cast their ballots as they were directed to do, which served to maintain the polygamist-dominated hierarchy in the Territory. 14 CONG. REC. 3057 (1883) (remarks of Senator Edmunds). This was a complete reversal of thinking on the subject; earlier, it had been suggested that if Congress gave the suffrage to the women of Utah, they would cast off the chains of polygamy. CONG. GLOBE, 41st Cong., 1st Sess. 72 (1869).

Linford, *Mormons and Law* (pt. 1), *supra* note 108, at 324 note 80. The Mormon women failed to respond as expected of women presumably being debased and abused. The reasonable conclusion would be that they were not, in fact, debased and abused.

129. CLAUDIA L. BUSHMAN, MORMON DOMESTIC LIFE IN THE 1870s: PANDEMONIUM OR ARCADIA? 6 (1999). This lecture examines the diaries of Elizabeth Kane, who passed extensive visits among the Mormons, for whom she expected to feel contempt and pity.The failure of Mormon women to feel degraded by their entry into polygamous marriages is at least partially explained by the small details of how these conflicting obligations were managed and balanced. Kane gives one insightful observation along these lines: She was "always surprised when the Mormons said 'my wife' and not 'one of my wives.' Snow brought in his wives individually rather than as a group, indicating that the relationship was between the husband and each wife, rather than the family." *Id.* at 21-22. These small details, in aggregate, can be powerful social modifiers.

130. *Id.* at 30.

131. ALTMAN & GINAT, *supra* note 63, at 311. See also Iversen, *Debate on the American Home, supra* note 109, at 597. These descriptions can be compared with this testimony from a lawyer who was one of nine wives: plural marriage "enables women, who live in a society full of obstacles, to fully meet their career, mothering and marriage obligations. Polygamy provides a whole solution. I believe American women would have invented it if it didn't already exist." Elizabeth Joseph, *With Polygamy, Lawyer-Moms* Can *Have It All*, 104(106) Los ANGELES DAILY JOURNAL 6 (May 28, 1991); *see also The Lawyer in the Family*, 5 NATIONAL LAW JOURNAL 43 (October 18, 1982).

132. *See* Seymour Parker, Janet Smith, & Joseph Ginat, *Father Absence and Cross-Sex Identity: The Puberty Rites Controversy Revisited*, 1 AMERICAN ETHNOLOGIST 687, 694 (1973).

133. KILBRIDE, *supra* note 80, at 70, quoting Lawrence Foster.

134. "Assuming that no conscientious females would accept polygamy, the text [of Marie Ward's fabricated story 'Female Life among the Mormons'] accused Mormon males of using hypnotic techniques to force females to accept a presumably unnatural wedded life." RALPH W. HOOD ET AL., THE PSYCHOLOGY OF RELIGION 321 (1996).

135. Julia Dunfey, *"Living the Principle" of Plural Marriage: Mormon Women, Utopia, and Female Sexuality in the Nineteenth Century*, 10(3) FEMINIST STUDIES 523, 529 (1984).

136. *Id.* at 530.

137. Joan Smyth Iversen, *Feminist Implications of Mormon Polygyny*, 10(3) FEMINIST STUDIES 505, 515 (1984) [hereinafter *Feminist Implications*]; *see also* ALTMAN & GINAT, *supra* note 63, at 344-346.

138. STONE, *supra* note 60, at 190.

139. Iversen, *Feminist Implications, supra* note 137, at 516.

140. *See* ALTMAN & GINAT, *supra* note 63, at 440.

141. *See* QUINN, *supra* note 68, at 243.

142. *Id.* at 260 note 89, discussing the views of Maxine Hanks.
143. *Id.*
144. *See* Altman & Ginat, *supra* note 63, at 97.
145. Iversen, *Feminist Implications, supra* note 137, at 517.
146. *See* Kilbride, *supra* note 80, at 80.
147. *See* Altman & Ginat, *supra* note 63, at 470.
148. *Id.*
149. *See id.*
150. Linford, *Mormons and Law* (pt. 1), *supra* note 108, at 328 note 93.
151. James S. Chisholm & Victoria K. Burbank, *Monogamy and Polygyny in Southeast Arnhem Land: Male Coercion and Female Choice,* 12 Ethology and Sociobiology 291, 292 (1991).
152. *See id.* at 293.
153. *Id.* at 298 (Australian Aborigines); *see also* Michel Garenne & Etienne van de Walle, *Polygyny and Fertility among the Sereer of Senegal,* 43 Population Studies 267 (1989); Warren M. Hern, *Polygyny and Fertility among the Shipibo of the Peruvian Amazon,* 46(1) Population Studies 53 (1992); and Kashem Shaikh, K.M.A. Aziz, & A.I. Chowdhury, *Differentials of Fertility between Polygynous and Monogamous Marriages in Rural Bangladesh,* 19 Journal of Biosocial Science 49 (1987). E x c e p - tions to this trend are reported by Nan E. Johnson & A.M. Elm, *Polygamy and Fertility in Somalia,* 21 Journal of Biosocial Science 127 (1989); Osei-Mensah Abo- rampah, *Plural Marriage and Fertility Differentials: A Study of the Yoruba of West- ern Nigeria,* 46(1) Human Organization 29 (1987); and Monique Borgerhoff Mulder, *Marital Status and Reproductive Performance in Kipsigis Women: Re-evaluating the Polygyny-Fertility Hypothesis,* 43 Population Studies 285 (1989).
154. For this forum, it is expedient to make the assumption that marriage form directly causes individual reproductive outcomes. Monique Mulder, *supra* note 153, at 303- 304, clarifies under what circumstances this assumption is valid:

> To argue that the low fertility of polygynously married women is a *consequence* of their marital status, a number of alternative explanations must be ruled out. First, there must be no evidence of a selective process whereby women of low reproductive potential, particularly those who are infertile, are more likely to find themselves in polygynous marriages. Secondly, secular changes, specifi- cally those that co-vary with marital status, must be carefully excluded as the causes of reproductive differences between monogamously and polygynously married women.

Possible examples of such "secular changes" include age of husband and lack of spousal co-residency. These factors would lower reproduction in any context, but are typical of polygamy rather than monogamy. *See* Garenne & van de Walle, *supra* note 153, at 282-283.

Having ruled out these alternative explanations, processes by which polygamy can lower reproduction include: (1) relative poverty, especially when wives are ranked in terms of seniority or favoritism; (2) higher incidence of venereal disease; and (3) "little advantage, in terms of economies of scale, to be derived from co-oper- ative relations among co-wives." *See* Mulder at 303-304.

155. *See* Judith C. Spicer & Susan O. Gustavus, *Mormon Fertility through Half a Century: Another Test of the Americanization Hypothesis,* 21(1) Social Biology 70 (1974). Spicer and Gustavus suggest that Mormon fertility may be related to the religion's belief in the "pre-existence of spirits," to whom Mormons owe the temporal "responsibility of offering these spirits the best possible hope for progress toward perfectibility and exaltation" by birth into a "'good' Mormon family." *Id.* at 71. Kil- bride, *supra* note 80, at 69, observes that in 1988 Utah's birthrate of twenty-one per thousand was higher than that of China.

156. Dean L. May, *People on the Mormon Frontier: Kanab's Families of 1874*, 1(2) JOURNAL OF FAMILY HISTORY 169, 182 (1976).
157. *See id.* at 190-192.
158. *See* L.L. Bean & G.P. Mineau, *The Polygyny-Fertility Hypothesis: A Re-evaluation*, 40 POPULATION STUDIES 67 (1986).
159. *See id.* at 72. The difference can be traced in part to the fact that first wives, as compared to only wives, (1) marry earlier; (2) are still producing children later in life; (3) have a smaller age gap between themselves and their husband; and (4) have shorter birth intervals. All of these differences are small in absolute terms, but in combination render the first wife more prolific reproductively over a lifetime.
160. *See* Steven C. Josephson, *Status, Reproductive Success, and Marrying Polygynously*, 14 ETHOLOGY AND SOCIOBIOLOGY 391 (1993).
161. CONSTANTINE, *supra* note 65, at 131.
162. A related claim to the degradation of women is the effect on children of being raised in a polygamous home.

> Another important antipolygamy contention was that there were deleterious effects on progeny of plural homes. A popular notion of genetics held that moral depravity led to inherited physical degeneracy. Angie Newman reported to Congress [in 1886] that there was "a physical deterioration" observable in the children of polygamy as well as mental inferiority. "They do not begin to measure up to the standard of American children of the same age."

Iversen, *Debate on the American Home, supra* note 109, at 593-594. Another opinion expressed in 1882 was that "children developed observably 'depraved tastes' and lost the innocence of childhood from being raised in polygamous homes." *Id.* at 594. The *Reynolds* decision contains similar language. Part of the case involved the trial judge's charge to the jury, which included this statement:

> I think it is not improper, in the discharge of your duties in this case, that you should consider what are to be the consequences to the innocent victims of this delusion. As this contest goes on, they multiply, and there are pure-minded women and there are innocent children,—innocent in a sense even beyond the degree of the innocence of childhood itself. These are to be the sufferers; and as jurors fail to do their duty, and as these cases come up in the Territory of Utah, just so do these victims multiply and spread themselves over the land.

98 U.S. 145, 167-168 (1878). As with the examination of the question of female degradation, some evidence can be found for either side of the question of the effect upon children of being raised in a polygamous family. One study conducted among Nigerians found that "male adolescents from monogamous families had better adjustment scores than those from polygynous families." Adenekan O. Oyefeso & Ademola R. Adegoke, *Psychological Adjustment of Yoruba Adolescents as Influenced by Family Type: A Research Note*, 33(4) JOURNAL OF CHILD PSYCHOLOGY & PSYCHIATRY 785, 787 (1992). On the other hand, family type had no impact upon the relationship between corporal punishment and academic achievement. *See* Varghese I. Cherian, *Corporal Punishment and Academic Achievement of Xhosa Children from Polygynous and Monogamous Families*, 134(3) JOURNAL OF SOCIAL PSYCHOLOGY 387 (1994). When considering many studies in concert, KILBRIDE, *supra* note 80, at 20, concludes that "nonconventional family arrangements per se do not have undesirable effects on the children."

As regards Mormons specifically, one study compared negative courtship experiences of Mormon and non-Mormon college students. It found the two groups to be indistinguishable, *except* in the case of non-Mormon women, who "report [more] unpleasant, aggressive, and abusive experiences in both past and current relationships," and who also "report having inflicted [more] negative behaviors on their partners." Mary Riege Laner, *Unpleasant, Aggressive, and Abusive Activities in Courtship: A Comparison of Mormon and NonMormon College Students*, 6

DEVIANT BEHAVIOUR 145, 156 (1985). For women, at least, a Mormon upbringing seems to lead to more placid and pleasant intersexual relationships. This finding is merely suggestive about the formative influence of Mormonism generally, since it involves children who presumably were not raised in polygamous households. More on point was a study by Parker et al., *supra* note 132, which tested the hypothesis that father absence leads to hypermasculinity, delinquency, and gender role confusion. Examining a community of Mormon fundamentalists who still practice polygamy, Parker et al. found no such deficiencies among boys raised in polygamous households as compared to those of the same community raised in monogamous households.

As with female degradation, then, the argument about negative effects upon children may be less valid for Mormonism specifically than for polygamy generally.

163. *See* Steve Kloehn, *Polygamists' Ex-Wives Speak Up*, TIMES-PICAYUNE (New Orleans), July 5, 1998, at A26.

164. Engels agreed with much of Lieber's claims about the benefits of monogamy for laying the groundwork for civilization. But one area where they disagreed was the effect of monogamy upon women. For Engels, it is monogamy, not polygamy, which degraded and oppressed women. He believed that the nuclear monogamous family arose as an economic unit, and that as the economy transformed from capitalism to socialism, monogamy would be either significantly altered or completely done away with. *See* FREDERICK ENGELS, THE ORIGIN OF THE FAMILY, PRIVATE PROPERTY AND THE STATE (New York: International Publishers, 1972) (1884).

165. KILBRIDE, *supra* note 80, at 77.

166. Thomas C. Berg, *What Hath Congress Wrought? An Interpretive Guide to the Religious Freedom Restoration Act*, 39(1) VILLANOVA LAW REVIEW 1, 34 (1994).

167. As observed by Wasby, *supra* note 113, at 118, "most violations of sex policy, with the important exceptions of rape and sexual abuse of children, are 'victimless' (or at least 'complaintless') crimes."

Within the arena of constitutional law, a person is not allowed to lodge a complaint unless he or she has "suffered a personal, *concrete* injury that would be remediable by judicial process." Carl Esbeck, *A Restatement of the Supreme Court's Law of Religious Freedom: Coherence, Conflict, or Chaos?* 70(3) NOTRE DAME LAW REVIEW 581, 587 note 19 (1995) (emphasis added). "Courts are to refrain from 'abstract questions' which amount to 'generalized grievances' shared by many others." *Id.* at 615 note 130. "[A]s to the kinds of questions which [are] the staple of judicial business, it [is] not for courts to pass upon them as abstract, intellectual problems but only if a concrete, living contest between adversaries called for the arbitrament of law." Coleman v. Miller, 307 U.S. 433, 460 (1939) (opinion of Frankfurter, J.).

The requirement of concrete injury is a commendable bar to frivolous complaints. The principle should work in reverse, as well. If I must be injured before I can gain standing to complain about the government, someone else should be injured before they *or* the government can complain about me. If my behavior harms no one, why should the state squander its resources to impede me?

Victimless crimes by definition have no legitimate purpose, *if* you agree that law should be restricted to the protection of personal rights. Laws that go beyond this limit to seek to protect not society, but individuals themselves from the consequences of their actions, are suspect. Mandatory helmet laws would be a good example here. A very persuasive argument can be made that at least some victimless actions cannot rationally be restricted unless one is willing to require that "the rights of some individuals to pursue happiness will have to be violated so that others can gain something that they are not entitled to." Robert W. McGee, *If Dwarf Tossing is Outlawed, Only Outlaws Will Toss Dwarfs: Is Dwarf Tossing a Victimless Crime?* 1993 AMERICAN JOURNAL OF JURISPRUDENCE 335, 354.

As regards sexuality, it is not a cognizable harm to others if they get overwrought thinking about what I might be doing in my bedroom. With no victim, there can be no crime. McGee argues that my right to use my body as I wish is an absolute that cannot be mitigated because it conflicts with no *rights* of others. That is, people do not have a right not to be offended, or a right to have their viewpoints accepted by everyone. Where no rights conflict, there exists no justification to interfere with that which is clearly a right, that is, the right to control my body for myself. Kent Greenawalt, *Legal Enforcement of Morality*, 85(3) JOURNAL OF CRIMINAL LAW & CRIMINOLOGY 710 (1995), disagrees, finding "public offense" a legitimate rationale to restrict victimless conduct, although even here the standard may not be so low as many Christian moralizers would assume.

Thomas Aquinas argued that *nothing* is *malum in se*, that is, evil in and of itself. *See* W. Norman Pittenger, *The Morality of Homosexual Acts, in* HOMOSEXUALITY AND ETHICS 139, 141 (Edward Batchelor ed., 1980). If that is true, then actions like sodomy are necessarily *malum prohibitum*, or something that is wrong *only* because it is socially prohibited, and not because it transgresses some higher natural order. *See* Richard L. Gray, *Eliminating the (Absurd) Distinction between* Malum in Se *and* Malum Prohibitum *Crimes*, 73 WASHINGTON UNIVERSITY LAW QUARTERLY 1369, 1374 (1995). "Crime against nature," then, is an oxymoron.

168. For a recent legal argument that the antipolygamy holding of *Reynolds* should be voided, *see* Keith E. Sealing, *Polygamists out of the Closet: Statutory and State Constitutional Prohibitions against Polygamy are Unconstitutional under the Free Exercise Clause*, 17(3) GEORGIA STATE UNIVERSITY LAW REVIEW 691 (2001).

169. *See, e.g.*, Florence Williams, *Polygamy Thriving Subculture; Government Looks Away*, TIMES-PICAYUNE (New Orleans), December 21, 1997, at A27. A lot of good cultural information can be gleaned from the obituaries. A death notice in the New Orleans paper included the information that "Survivors include two companions...." [Obituary for] *Dean Cloud*, TIMES-PICAYUNE (New Orleans), January 4, 2000, at B3. A repeat notice the next day deleted this information, listing only one companion. The initial announcement may have been a mistake. What is intriguing is that the newspaper, under the belief that the information was accurate, would publish the claim that he was a polygynist.

170. ALTMAN & GINAT, *supra* note 63, at 52. Mike Leavitt, governor of Utah, has declined to actively prosecute polygamists. Diego Ribadeneira, *New Debate Flares over Jefferson's View of Church and State*, BOSTON GLOBE, August 1, 1998, at B2. That position seemingly changed in May 2001 when Tom Green was found guilty of four counts of bigamy in a Provo, Utah, court. Julie Cart, *Verdict Rips Veil from Bigamy Practice*, TIMES-PICAYUNE (New Orleans), May 20, 2001, at A3. This case will probably remain unique for several reasons. First, Tom Green practically begged to be prosecuted by appearing repeatedly on national television shows discussing his polygamous marriages. Second, Utah may have felt the necessity to symbolically clean up its image before it hosted the 2002 Winter Olympics. It is unlikely, therefore, that the Green conviction heralds a renewed and systematic suppression of polygamy.

171. Barlow v. Blackburn, 798 P.2d 1360 (Ariz. App. 1990).

172. ALTMAN & GINAT, *supra* note 63, at 52.

173. As only one other example, we might consider the Supreme Court's rulings in *Lochner v. New York*, 198 U.S. 45 (1905), and *Muller v. State of Oregon*, 208 U.S. 412 (1908). In *Lochner* the Court invalidated a statute forbidding bakeries from contracting with its employees to work more than sixty hours a week. The theory is that such a statute would interfere with the right to contract, and that our laissez-faire economic system disdained such interference. A similar law was upheld in *Muller*, however, because that law targeted women. The Court believed that while

men were capable of being free agents in our economic system, women, because of the "inherent difference between the sexes" required more paternalistic protections. The state of knowledge about sex differences would not today sustain such a distinction.

174. J. Braxton Craven, *The Impact of Social Science Evidence on the Judge: A Personal Comment*, 39(1) LAW AND CONTEMPORARY PROBLEMS 150, 156 (1975).

175. Charles E. Hamilton, *Lawyers' Professionalism: Great (and Historical) Expectations*, in IN OUR OWN WORDS: REFLECTIONS ON PROFESSIONALISM IN THE LAW 25, 36-37 (Roger A. Stetter ed., 1998) (emphasis added).

176. CARDOZO, *supra* note 26, at 20.

177. U.S. Bancorp Mortgage Co. v. Bonner Mall, 513 U.S. 18, 26 (1994).

178. *See* STEPHEN C. YEAZELL, CIVIL PROCEDURE 235 (5th ed., 2000):

> In Ankenbrandt v. Richards, 504 U.S. 689 (1992), the Court reaffirmed a nineteenth century decision holding that suits for divorce, alimony, or child custody fell outside the scope of diversity jurisdiction, even if the spouses were citizens of different states when suit was brought. *Ankenbrandt* went on to hold that some "domestic" cases could invoke diversity; for example, one former spouse could sue the other in tort for child abuse. It is fair to say that neither *Ankenbrandt* nor its nineteenth century predecessor, Barber v. Barber, 62 U.S. 582 (1858), are masterpieces of judicial persuasion. *Ankenbrandt* essentially says that *Barber* was wrong when decided but that its holding has become settled practice without congressional response, so that the passage of time has made bad law into good law.

179. Ford v. Cimarron Insurance Co., 230 F.3d 828, 832 (5th Cir. 2000).

180. "At least within the academy, conventional wisdom now maintains that a purported demonstration of error is not enough to justify overruling a past decision." Caleb Nelson, *Stare Decisis and Demonstrably Erroneous Precedents*, 87(1) VIRGINIA LAW REVIEW 1, 2 (2001).

181. Keith Jaasma, *The Religious Freedom Restoration Act: Responding to* Smith; *Reconsidering* Reynolds, 16 WHITTIER LAW REVIEW 211, 213 (1995). The author concludes that "under the standard set forth in *Lukumi*, the anti-polygamy law that was examined in *Reynolds* would be considered neither neutral nor of general applicability," and would thus fall before the First Amendment, much as George Reynolds first argued it should a century ago. *Id.* at 257.

> One federal court—writing before *Lukumi*—had explicitly rejected the argument that later cases have functionally overturned *Reynolds*. *See* Potter v. Murray City, 760 F.2d 1065 (10th Cir. 1985). Despite this pessimism, at least one Supreme Court Justice has predicted that "the state prohibition of bigamy will eventually be ruled constitutionally infirm." MARK STRASSER, LEGALLY WED 65 (1997) (referring to William O. Douglas's dissent to *Wisconsin v. Yoder*).

182. FRANCIS LIEBER, LEGAL AND POLITICAL HERMENEUTICS (1860), *reprinted as* 16 CARDOZO LAW REVIEW 1879, 2036 (1995) (emphases added).

183. Baker v. Vermont, 744 A.2d 864, 873 (2000). The two cases cited are *Choquette v. Perrault*, 569 A.2d 455 (1989), and *MacCallum v. Seymour*, 686 A.2d 935 (1996).

184. Planned Parenthood of Southeastern Pennsylvania v. Casey, 505 U.S. 833, 855 (1992).

185. John Monahan & Laurens Walker, *Social Authority: Obtaining, Evaluating, and Establishing Social Science in Law*, 134(3) UNIVERSITY OF PENNSYLVANIA LAW REVIEW 477, 516 note 130 (1986).

186. *See* WILLIAM E. NELSON, *MARBURY V. MADISON*: THE ORIGINS AND LEGACY OF JUDICIAL REVIEW (2000).

187. FAIGMAN, *supra* note 30, at 121. Faigman is paraphrasing Alexander Hamilton's Federalist Paper No. 78.

188. Nelson, *supra* note 180, at 69.

189. Bush v. Gore, 531 U.S. 98, 157 (2000) (Breyer, J., dissenting). The Supreme Court often expressed concern that it do nothing to injure its prestige in the eyes of the public. *See* Planned Parenthood of Southeastern Pennsylvania v. Casey, 505 U.S. 833, 865 (1992) ("The Court's power lies, rather, in its legitimacy, a product of substance and perception that shows itself in the people's acceptance of that Judiciary as fit to determine what the Nation's law means and to declare what it demands".).

190. With perhaps more optimism than realism, the occasional writer will opine that the legitimacy of legislatures and their pronouncements is also a function of the factual rationale for their works:

> To achieve legislation with a rational basis, legislators must be guided by an adequate theory of marriage, tested against historical and cross-cultural data. If no such theory exists, marital regulations will appear to be no more than senseless government interventions into personal liberties and will have no social force.

MARTIN OTTENHEIMER, FORBIDDEN RELATIVES: THE AMERICAN MYTH OF COUSIN MARRIAGE 16 (1996).

191. Some observers, for example, have worried that "jurors often ascribe a 'mystic infallibility' to scientific evidence." FIENBERG, *supra* note 55, at 292. Research has shown this concern to be unwarranted. *Id.* at 297.

192. The appeal for legitimization by the sciences occurs in the most unlikely contexts. The Catholic Church, when propounding its unfriendly conclusions about homosexual persons as being objectively disordered tending toward intrinsic evil, states first that the moral perspective to follow is one "which finds support in the more secure findings of the natural sciences." Congregation for the Doctrine of the Faith, *Letter to the Bishops of the Catholic Church on the Pastoral Care of Homosexual Persons*, October 1, 1986. This evaluation, incidentally, is false, not least because the sciences do not deal in the categories of "good" and "evil."

193. *See* Hans Kelson, *General Theory of Law and State* (1945), *reprinted in* JURISPRUDENCE: TEXTS AND READINGS ON THE PHILOSOPHY OF LAW 675, 684 (George C. Christie & Patrick H. Martin eds., 2d ed., 1995) ("a normative order loses its validity when reality no longer corresponds to it, at least to a certain degree. The validity of a legal order is thus dependent upon its agreement with reality, upon its 'efficacy.'").

194. FAIGMAN, *supra* note 30, at 116. Fienberg notes two instances when the Supreme Court based legal decisions on a faulty grasp of the underlying social science: the constitutionality of juries of fewer than twelve persons, and parental rights. FIENBERG, *supra* note 55, at 299.

Chapter Two

PRACTICAL BENEFITS OF LAW TO ANTHROPOLOGY

Chapter 1 identified as the practical benefit of anthropology to law the resources for laying an empirical ground for relevant legal findings. The thesis of balanced reciprocity expects that anthropology, too, will receive practical benefits from its relationship with law. To identify one such benefit, we look first at what we believe are some of the outstanding needs of anthropology. Finding that anthropology suffers from an ambiguous identity and low public esteem, we will suggest that law could use its high prestige in our society to elevate anthropology into more prominent public view.

The Identity and Stature of Anthropology

Anthropology is a fractured discipline, and perhaps that is to be expected. The introduction in this book characterized anthropology as the confluence of all the separate intellectual endeavors, converging in one mental space to answer a single question, What does it mean to be human? Despite this ultimate amalgamation, each field has its own customary rules and foundational premises that can conflict with another's. The intermixing of disciplines essential for anthropology, although necessary for a complete answer to its central question, should not be expected to be effortless.

But the centrifugal tendencies within academic anthropology are more primal than interdisciplinary conflicts. Contemporary anthropology has endured an intradisciplinary identity crisis as it struggles to answer

Notes for this section begin on page 114.

the question, Is the practice of anthropology a science or a humanitarian art? That we have staked out our own position in this debate does not blind us to the discipline's larger failure to reach a resolution. This fight is no mere quibble over terms or style: where one stands determines the appropriate standard of argumentation and method of proof. In terms introduced in the previous chapter, the scientific anthropologists adhere to some descendent of a Popperian philosophy of science, with the twin goals of testability and generalization. Humanistic anthropologists, on the other hand, look for inspiration to Thomas Kuhn for whom there is no truth toward which we approach with greater knowledge, but only one incommensurate social convention replacing another. Whereas the scientific anthropologist would aspire to generate quantifiable data applied to falsifiable theories, the humanistic anthropologist would prefer empathetic ethnographies intended to convey worldview and cultural perspective. In other words, the analytic contrast would be the objective/etic versus the subjective/emic.[1] Every anthropologist probably has his or her preferred method.

These distinctive approaches crystallize around their leading proponents. The ranks of scientific anthropologists would include William Durham[2] and Roy A. Rappaport.[3] These workers are not afraid, when appropriate, to measure, weigh, statistically analyze, and formally argue. Humanistic anthropologists are led by Clifford Geertz[4] and Claude Lévi-Strauss.[5] These ethnographers deal more with the intangibles of cultural life such as ritual symbolism and meanings, generally features that cannot be usefully quantified without destroying the phenomena of interest; their preferred methodological approach is largely qualitative.

We can set aside the issue of whether these two ways of doing anthropology are *necessarily* antagonistic. Although in the introduction we denied that science and humanism are intrinsically adversarial, in current practice they can barely abide one another. This conflict was formerly held in check by the earlier discussed "four field approach" to anthropology. Every subfield with its specific methodologies was taught to every student, subverting institutional favoritism and rendering each professional at least minimally conversant in all the major methods. For a while, all anthropologists were speaking the same language even when they chose to tell different stories. The real success of this method at defusing professional conflict was perhaps always questionable. But its ultimate failure burst through the veil of courteous misattention when, in 1998, the anthropology department at Stanford University split into two independent units along just this conceptual fault line. The anthropology department dissolved, and in its place arose the Department of Cultural and Social Anthropology and the Department of Anthropological Sciences.[6] After so many years of putting on a public united front, our dirty little family secret has become neither little nor secret.[7] Without this fundamental self-confidence about what we do, we have failed also to take several other developmental steps, and thereby impeded our connection with society at large.

Anthropologists have not been very successful at marketing their intellectual products to the wider society, either within the academy or to the general public. Consequently, one reviewer for the *New York Times* does not hesitate to begin a column with the declaration that "[A]nthropology has never had a particularly good reason for existing."[8] Some of this inability to effectively sell ourselves may lie with our insecurities about what we have to sell. Excepting only some few, sporadic examples (a list of which would include Ruth Benedict's *The Chrysanthemum and the Sword*[9]), anthropological study does not produce the useful commodities for consumption expected from chemistry, physics, and the other hard sciences. We are not the inventors of the better mousetrap having the doors of investors slammed in our faces; we are more akin to Socrates, speaking to any who will listen, with the only sure goal being to disturb their complacency about what they thought they already knew. Cultural introspection can be no more pleasant than personal introspection.

Another possible explanation for our failure to find a popular audience lies not in what we are selling but in the personalities of the salespeople. A convincing argument can be made that anthropologists do what they do so well—that is, enter into and adapt to foreign, alien, and from some perspectives even bizarre environments—because they are misfits in their own cultures:

> Most anthropologists describe themselves as "outsiders"—individuals who have gone through life believing that they never really belonged. In high school they were nerds, beatniks, hippies and skanks, never Student Council presidents, Varsity football players or A-squad cheerleaders. In college they discovered that their status as misfits prepared them admirably for an involvement with those "others" in the world whom modern society had similarly excluded: tribal peoples, Third World postcolonials, exotic fringe or "subculture" groups within national societies. They became cultural anthropologists, a community of outsiders.[10]

The football quarterback and prom queen rarely go on to become anthropologists. It is the awkward, overlooked "geek" who spent her adolescence observing those around her. Unable to relate, she came instead to learn what these "others" were doing, insight that might otherwise have been clouded by too-close involvement.[11] Nascent anthropologists are less likely to experience crippling culture shock in the field because they depend relatively less upon their own culture to reinforce their personal identities. To the extent that culture has given them an identity at all—a social role to play—it is often one they are eager to shed.[12]

This disconnect between the anthropologist and his own culture, which serves him well in the work itself, handicaps him when it comes to the social networking back home to get that work noticed and appreciated. Anthropologists may know all about schmoozing, but are themselves not very good schmoozers.

For all the reasons we have discussed, and perhaps more, anthropologists are rarely consulted on many of the pressing social issues and burning eternal questions that absorb society's attentions, even though they are the obvious resource. That neglect is disappointing enough, but easily swallowed with the consoling belief that we are not consulted due to our low profile: *These outsiders do not know we have the very data they need to answer their most pressing questions. If they only knew!* But this depressing oversight from ignorance becomes infuriating humiliation when anthropologists fail to be included even in discussions about the one thing everyone knows anthropologists study, if they know anything about anthropology at all: culture.[13] We gave the word to the general public, and it remains the simplest answer (albeit not necessarily the most accurate) to questions about what we study. Yet when the concept gained currency via policy debates about "multiculturalism" and the like, anthropologists were conspicuously uninvolved.[14]

Part of the blame unquestionably belongs on our own shoulders as anthropologists. We are simply too obtuse, too mired in detail for our own good.

> When CNN covers an important event or news item concerning anything but bones or Neanderthals, anthropologists seem to be the last experts consulted for a deeper understanding—even when it is a topic we are supposed to know something about, such as culture. As a professor once said when asked why CNN never consults anthropologists to comment on news events, "Would you want to listen to what most anthropologists have to say?"[15]

This author does not exaggerate his characterization of an anthropologist's attempt to explain something as simple as what it is she does:

> When asked, we give some kind of academic, socially awkward response. To Wit: "Well, I am comparing modes of social discourse among consumers, ages 15 to 25, who live in western Pawtucket county and attend community college, on their views of goods advertised on TV between the hours of 2:00 and 6:00 a.m. in an effort to develop a model of enculturation that allows for...."[16]

This satirical characterization stings because it is accurate. Here is an actual description of fellowship-winning research: it "investigates the relationships among the globalized discourse of human rights, state legal and normative orders, the local production of cultural identities and gender norms and forms of resistance in the indigenous communities of Chiapas."[17] While the work we do can be important and fascinating, we habitually cloak it within obscuring verbiage, daring the unwashed to penetrate into our secret knowledge.[18] Indeed, this obscurantist style could well lead the uninitiated to conclude that "behind these walls of jargon and clever phrasing, ethnographers really have no findings to report at all."[19] Perhaps we should hire lobbyists and public relations consultants, and take out advertisements, to better communicate to society what we have to offer, since we seem to be so inept in doing so for ourselves.[20]

This uncovering of anthropology's many insecurities underscores the pressing practical need that law can best fulfill. In the previous chapter it was briefly mentioned that the law has been imbued with a social dignity and authority that it does well to husband carefully. There we pointed out that anthropology can assist in the law's effort to preserve that dignity and authority by grounding it in social reality. Law can, in exchange, confer on anthropology a measure of the same. If, on appropriate occasions, the law defers to and acknowledges the relevance and importance of anthropology, other sectors of society will begin to do likewise. The "reflected glory" of the law upon anthropology would provide the opportunity for anthropology's own achievements to be noticed—a positive esteem that might even translate into increased popular support for the funding of anthropological work.[21] This chapter examines the context in which such "appropriate occasions" might arise.

There are ample data supporting the assertion that, heretofore, few niches of the legal machine take anthropology seriously. As one rough measure of law's neglect of this discipline, the word "anthropology" appears in opinions of the United States Supreme Court only nineteen times, in any context. The references to "economics," in contrast, number in the thousands, and "psychology" gets over five hundred mentions. Even "sociology" gets noticed by the Court eighty-five times. All of the federal circuit courts of appeal have used the word only 169 times, again in any context whatsoever. Even if every use of the word were substantive (which it is not), this meager result indicates either that the courts are ignoring anthropology altogether, or that they are open to using anthropology's findings but without giving it due credit. In either case, the law (or at least the judiciary) is demonstrably niggardly in its recognition of anthropology.

Some readers are perhaps surprised to learn that we consider the legal profession so abundantly awash in social prestige that it can afford to share some of it with anthropology. Aren't these the same lawyers who are the butt of endless jokes?[22] (Here's a classic: How can you tell if it's a skunk or a lawyer that's been run over on the road? There are skid marks around the skunk.[23]) Few scenes in the movie *Jurassic Park* got bigger cheers than when the dinosaur ate the lawyer in the loo. And the truly evil characters on the popular television shows *Buffy the Vampire Slayer* and *Angel* are not the demons and vampires, but the lawyers at Wolfram and Hart. Even the main characters of *The Practice* are, to put it politely, ethically challenged. Contemporary law practitioners seem to have regressed to the low opinion they suffered during our nation's founding: "The first lawyer who arrived in the Plymouth colony in 1624 or 1625 is said to have been jailed and then expelled from the colony for scandalous behavior. For a time, the *Bodies of Liberties* (1641) of the Massachusetts Bay Colony prohibited 'pleading for hire'; Virginia excluded lawyers from her Courts in 1645; Connecticut also prohibited them."[24] Forget about surplus prestige; the legal profession hardly seems to have enough to tend to its own image. Couldn't the opposite argument be better made? Anthropologists have a much lower profile in the public imagination, but when they do appear in popular culture they are almost always forces for good: Indiana Jones in the movies, and on television the sidekick on *The Sentinel* and the lead in *Mysterious Ways*. Perhaps law should be looking to anthropology for a character reference.

But this assessment confuses the ephemeral popular appraisal with the more fundamental privileges which law enjoys, and which anthropology does not. These privileges are indicative of the true regard in which law is held, even when it seems to be in general disrepute. These privileges derive from the status of law as a "profession." In common parlance the term "profession" is used rather loosely, almost as a synonym for "occupation."[25] But true professions share special qualities:

> Generally, professionals have a substantial amount of education and training, certification by others in the profession, a commitment to public service, high social prestige, and high income. Professionals provide a service that is vitally needed. They are generally self-regulatory, setting the standards, and controlling admission and discipline of those within the profession.[26]

Society concedes two important and related privileges to professions: self-regulation and monopoly. The privilege of self-regulation is addressed directly within the American Bar Association's (ABA) *Model Rules of Professional Conduct*:

> The legal profession is largely self-governing. Although other professions [such as medicine] also have been granted powers of self-government, the legal profession is unique in this respect because of the close relationship

between the profession and the processes of government and law enforcement. This connection is manifested in the fact that ultimate authority
over the legal profession is vested largely in the courts [rather than the
legislature].[27]

The *Rules* go on to explain why the lawyer's privilege of self-regulation
is especially important to preserve:

> To the extent that lawyers meet the obligations of their professional calling,
> the occasion for government regulation is obviated. Self-regulation also
> helps maintain the legal profession's independence from government dom-
> ination. An independent legal profession is an important force in preserv-
> ing government under law, for abuse of legal authority is more readily
> challenged by a profession whose members are not dependent on govern-
> ment for the right to practice.[28]

If it were within the power of the government to decide who may or
may not practice law, then all it would need to do to silence an unwel-
come gadfly is revoke her license. Withholding this ability from the
government preserves the freedom to challenge government actions
within the courts, an important element of the American political system. The self-regulation of lawyers is therefore essential in a way that
the self-regulation of even medicine is not.
    Closely tied to the power of self-regulation is the right of monopoly:

> The monopoly over the practice of law the bar enjoys is the result of a
> "bargain" between the state and the profession in which the bar provides
> competence and access to legal services to the public, but refrains from
> partisan politics, and avoids the excesses of the market. In exchange the
> state grants the bar the right to establish the rules by which it restricts its
> market (including entry into the profession and the disciplining of its mem-
> bers) and allows it to extract monopoly rents.[29]

The bar's right of monopoly is especially apparent when it empowers
persons of its own choosing to assume the role of attorney. Only persons with licenses can practice law, otherwise they commit a crime.
And only other lawyers determine who gets a license. To get a license,
one must take and pass a state bar exam; with few exceptions, only
those who have graduated from a law school accredited by the American Bar Association may sit for the exam.[30] By contrast, anyone at all
can practice anthropology, and no training is legally required to do so.
The American Anthropological Association does not certify departments of anthropology, nor limit its membership only to those persons
trained therein. Although the American Anthropological Association
has its own code of ethical conduct, no penalty follows from its violation other than, perhaps, shame before one's colleagues.

The lawyer provides a service that is "vitally needed," and is allowed to perform that service with little oversight by outsiders. That dispensation bespeaks an enormous amount of deference on the part of society. Irrespective of the low levels to which the popular reputation of lawyers may sink, at no point is the stature of the law itself ever seriously challenged. No shame attaches to the parent proudly proclaiming that her child is attending law school. It is this institutional capital to which we refer when we speak of the law's prestige, and this it has in abundance to share with anthropology.[31]

Obstacles to the Legal Use of Anthropological Data

The use of anthropological data by the law seems to be only common sense. So many of our public debates involve premises to which anthropology speaks directly (as we saw to be the case with polygamy). Surely one side or the other would want that kind of support for their legal argument. But despite the potential aid of anthropology to lawyers, in practical terms, the law has demonstrably underutilized this resource.[32]

For some in both fields, this neglect is a good thing. On the legal side, a judge from the Tenth Circuit argues that "social science evidence is not valuable," at least in constitutional matters.[33] "We would," he says, "pose a greater danger to our 200 year experience in constitutional democracy if we were to rest constitutional interpretation on social science data rather than on the bedrock of a coherent constitutional principle." He does not, unfortunately, tell us how he would handle problems such as those raised by *Reynolds*. Agreeing with him from the other side is sociologist Andrew Greeley: "the law would be very unwise to place undue emphasis in its arguments and decisions" on social science research, failing as it does to be "definitive."[34] A "good rule of thumb would be that when judges and lawyers find themselves listening to sociologists arguing with each other, it is time, perhaps past time, to declare a mistrial."[35] We need not be so pessimistic. But Greeley's cautionary note does suggest that the explanation for the failure of the law to apply anthropological facts goes beyond mere ignorance of their existence.

The Growth of Knowledge

Greeley faults the social sciences for their inability to offer "definitive" positions on issues of social and legal importance. This lack of definitiveness has at least two dimensions: anthropological knowledge is not static but instead increases (and one hopes, progresses), and anthropological knowledge is probabilistic, not determinative. This section addresses the first shortcoming, and begins with a worst-case scenario.

An early implicit interjection of social science data into legal thinking occurred in 1896[36] with *Plessy v. Ferguson*,[37] the case that justified the practice of racial segregation. Underlying that decision was the inappropriately named theory, "social Darwinism."[38]

> There is little doubt that sociological and psychological theories controlled the Court's decision, even though they were not formally presented or recognized. The Court ruled first that the statute was enacted in good faith, not as an annoyance; second, that racial segregation was a custom or tradition in the South; third, that law which followed custom was reasonable (while law that conflicted was unreasonable); and finally, that the law was incapable of restructuring racial instincts.[39]

Although it is popular nowadays to consider *Plessy* a ridiculously bigoted decision, we should be aware of how little it deviates from current constitutional law. The first point is the same argument used in *Employment Division, Department of Human Resources of Oregon v. Smith*,[40] the case that held that "where once states could interfere with religious observances for only the most pressing reasons, now ... states had free reign only so long as they did not directly target religions. Religions ... were due no special protections or exemptions from otherwise generally applicable laws."[41] In other words, a law passed in good faith and not as an "annoyance" can still be upheld regardless of its actual impact. The third holding of *Plessy* foreshadowed the reasoning in *Bowers v. Hardwick*,[42] the decision upholding the constitutionality of sodomy laws largely due to their reasonableness as based in long-standing social custom.

The holdings about good faith and reasonableness are points of law. The other two concerning customary practice and racial instincts are conclusions premised by social facts. The first, that segregation was a Southern tradition, no one would contest. But the last point in *Plessy*, "that the law was incapable of restructuring racial instincts," is the nub of the claim that the Supreme Court "implicit[ly used] social science in endorsing the separate-but-equal doctrine."[43] In short,

> The majority of the justices were not inclined to see the statute as oppressive, because they believed that racial segregation simply implemented and confirmed the natural inequality of the two races and that laissez-faire policies, given social Darwinism, complemented natural processes that worked toward the improvement of the human species.[44]

If, the Court reasoned, it was the conclusion of the social sciences that "one race be inferior to the other socially, the Constitution of the

United States cannot put them upon the same plane."[45] Separation of the races was, therefore, in keeping with the best available social theory of the day, and was in the best interests of both. Any harm attributed to that separation "is not by reason of anything found in the act, but solely because the colored race chooses to put that construction upon it."[46]

The point is that the Court *was* using the best available social science in its day. And given that science, the opinion's conclusions followed reasonably, even though into error. And *that*, claim the opponents of the use of social science data by the law, is precisely the problem: the "courts are uneasy in the presence of the ultimate facts or conclusions of the social sciences because we have many times consumed large quantities of social science only to have to regurgitate it."[47] Conclusions of law are notoriously rigid, whereas conclusions of fact are comparatively fluid: "Attaching constitutional meaning to scientific opinion, even when scientists agree, condemns the Constitution to fluctuations in meaning as scientific knowledge changes." Better we put our legal faith solely in the former, and ignore the latter.

The *Plessy* scenario is not unique to judicial reasoning, as we saw in the *Reynolds* claims for polygamy, and as we shall see again. But in retrospect, we can visualize the kinds of safeguards that should be in place to minimize their occurrences. For example, it was not the acquisition of more information that later overturned Spencerian "social Darwinism"; it was a careful examination of the premises available all the while. Simply put, social Darwinism was an *analogy* from the argument in Darwin's *Origin of Species*; it was not an extension. Whether the analogy is valid is an independent question that could be legitimately posed. But advocates of social Darwinism traded on the popular and tight arguments of Darwin as somehow certifying their own theories. The Court could be faulted for having so heavily relied upon a theory which, however popular, had so little actual basis, even by the standards of its own day. If the invocation of social science is limited to those theories for which there are independent evidences, at least errors of the magnitude of *Plessy* can be avoided.

Many of these same problems arise in the first major case to explicitly invoke social science data, *Muller v. Oregon*.[48] At issue was the constitutionality of a state law forbidding women from working in a factory or laundry more than ten hours a day. The court had already, in the famous *Lochner* case, ruled that such laws were unconstitutional when directed toward men.[49] The only issue was whether the application of this law to women made the case distinguishable. The high court found that "the inherent differences between the two sexes, and in the different function in life which they perform,"[50] justified this kind of protective legislation for women, legislation that "is not necessary for men and could not [for men] be sustained."[51]

The Court referred to, and apparently relied heavily upon, a 113-page brief filed by future Supreme Court Justice Louis Brandeis. He collated over one hundred extralegal source materials documenting "that women could not tolerate the same working hours as men."[52] The brief was "immediately recognized as an innovation in American advocacy,"[53] and all future such briefs have been called "Brandeis briefs" in recognition of this achievement.

Yet, again, we see the best available science at the time used as the basis for a crucial decision leading the Court into a regrettable outcome.[54] Surely results such as these should temper any call to put serious reliance on social science data lest we be forced at some later time to "regurgitate" them. Such data can reinforce decisions made on the basis of other criteria, enhancing the rationality of those, but are social science data ever really so solid as to warrant deference when the facts conflict with legal precedents? In other words, while social science data can *support* or uphold the law, can they also—given their inherent limitations—be invoked to change or void a law? If not, then we have identified a serious obstacle to the use of such data by the law.

The Probabilistic Explanation

Patrick Driessen has helpfully enumerated twelve reasons why members of the bar resist the introduction of social science data into the courtroom.[55] Ten of these are unproblematic in the long term because (1) they are restricted to certain judicial actors or social science practitioners, and not to the respective systems as a whole; (2) even if systemic, the weaknesses are "remediable with reasonable effort";[56] or (3) even if systemic and irremediable, the weaknesses are not unique to the courtroom, but are present in both the administrative and political spheres where the incorporation of social science is comparatively uncontroversial. Only two objections resist this analysis. As Driessen frames them:

> Legal reasoning is nonprobabilistic and is associated with a large tolerance for low-accuracy results. In contrast, social science is inherently probabilistic, and the degree of accuracy is important in distinguishing "good" from "bad" social science results; and
>
> Judges make normative/prescriptive decisions, whereas science attempts to be value-free; a basic tension exists.

We have already addressed the second objection in some detail in the previous chapter; it is the "is-ought" problem of the naturalistic fallacy, and need not be repeated here in detail. The gist of that argument that needs to be recalled is that one cannot deduce values from facts. Much of law, and consequently, many legal debates, are only ostensibly about facts; under that surface, they are really about values (the abortion controversy is perhaps a good example). The social sciences, which deal only in facts, cannot be much help on questions of values, and it can be misleading to draft them inappropriately into those kinds of arguments.

The remaining objection claims that the need for definitive judgments and determinations in legal analyses raises issues of compatibility with the nature of social scientific knowledge at a level more fundamental than simply that the latter's conclusions might be revised at a later time. Judges and legislators tend—perhaps even need—to think in dichotomous "yes-no," "did he or didn't he" terms. But definitive answers, even complexly generated or tentative-to-be-revised ones, are rare exceptions in the social sciences. Far more typical is the probabilistic response. The conclusions of anthropology, perhaps even more than all the other social sciences, are more nuanced than those sought by the law. Instead of "Yes," we say, "Yes, but"; never just "No," but rather "No, except." Where law restricts its focus to the actual deeds of a specific individual, anthropology concludes with statements about tendencies of populations.

By "large tolerance for low accuracy," Driessen is talking about what happens when you collapse a 51 percent probability that *X* will not happen into a flat, "No, it doesn't happen." "Courts," it has been observed, "are made uneasy by uncertainty and often act as though uncertainty does not exist."[57] In an adversarial context such as the courtroom, any admitted lack of complete certainty leaves you vulnerable to attack. If all you can claim is an 80 percent probability, you may as well be claiming no possibility at all. Unless you can assert with absolute certainty that *X* causes *Y* in all cases, the door is opened to the jury to conclude that in at least *this* case, *X* did not cause *Y*. All that is needed in most criminal cases to free the defendant is a reasonable doubt. The prosecutor will not do the defense attorney's job for him by underscoring where the data are "soft." Consequently, probabilities are recast as determinators, resulting in the law's "large tolerance for low accuracy." David Faigman humorously terms this the "'syndromic lawyer syndrome,' a pathological acceptance of simplistic explanations for complex human behavior that supports otherwise desirable legal outcomes."[58]

Simply put, what law and anthropology each considers to be a "good answer" to a question are fundamentally at odds with one another. There exists a basic incompatibility between what anthropology has to say and what the legal actors expect to hear. The danger is that because law will inevitably seek to repackage anthropological findings into a form compatible with its needs, law will necessarily misrepresent those findings and make them appear to be more final, absolute, and certain than they really are. Perhaps the data underlying the *Plessy* and *Muller* decisions (and all similar cases) are not strictly social science data, but social science recast into the legal idiom, which result no competent social scientist would have asserted in the first place. In that case, it would be bootless to try to argue against those decisions by reference to new or better information.

Social Difference versus Legal Egalitarianism

We may note one final obstacle why the law, and social policy generally, finds the nuanced incorporation of social scientific findings so very problematic. Beyond the issues of stability and complexity, the social sciences and the legal milieu presume different ideologies.

The U.S. political system and its attendant legal apparatus are predicated upon an ideal of egalitarianism.[59] Certainly the shortfalls in the implementation of this ideal have been great and tragic. Some would argue, however, that with the passing of time there has also been a progression toward fuller realization of that ideal which, encapsulated into a single phrase, holds that "Everyone in America stands equal before the law."[60]

Were all people actually equal in any strict sense, the social sciences would have very little to study. The equality asserted by law implies homogeneity. Structure, an important focus of the social sciences, presumes differentiation. Equality consequently suggests antistructure. True equality renders the social sciences superfluous.

This conflict of ideologies is more apparent than real, largely because the strong claim of universal legal equality is a fiction.[61] Even perfect realization of the ideal would leave several groups on unequal footing in the eyes of the law.[62] For example, minors, convicted felons, and military personnel all possess less than the full complement of rights, powers, and privileges bestowed on other citizens. Minors cannot drink, drive, vote, or consent to sexual relations; felons cannot vote or own firearms; military personnel do not enjoy the full measure of the first amendment right to free speech. Specifically, they cannot criticize their commander in chief, nor can they discuss their sexual orientation. Further, not everyone is subject to the death penalty, even having committed the same crime. Minors and the mentally disabled have been exempted from this risk. This list of categories of persons treated differently by the law could be much extended, undermining any claim that in practice all are equal before our law. The more accurate assessment is that "[v]irtually no legislation applies universally and treats all persons equally."[63] One glaring example of inequality before the law has emerged from the horror of the terrorist attack on the World Trade Center on September 11, 2001. The federal Victims Compensation Fund will allocate its money not uniformly according to the equal worth of human life, but rather according to the economic stature of the victim: "So now we have the United States of America, our country, saying that some people are worth more than others. Not just worth more but, at least by implication, are actually better people."[64]

The strong claim that all persons are equal before the law is therefore demonstrably false. The mantra of equality before the law is rather espoused to assert the weaker claim that irrelevant personal traits will not be invoked unduly to bias the legal system. Unlike the strong claim of absolute equality, this invocation of universal relevant equality is not immediately falsified by structural contradictions. The ideal is not that people will not be treated differently, but that they will not be treated differently for reasons irrelevant to the legal context. Americans, at least, have been shown to accept unequal legal treatment or outcomes if those differences "are justified by differences in the problems being dealt with ... [or are] justified by differences in the nature of the task."[65] Where unjustified bias does arise, it is idiosyncratic to the actors but not intrinsic to the system. The problem in this model is to ascertain exactly which traits are legally irrelevant.

Some would argue that some traits are so likely to inflame the triers of fact, most often a jury, that they are never relevant. We believe, on the contrary, that no fact about a party will always be irrelevant no matter what the circumstances. A "constitutional requirement that likes be treated alike cannot itself distinguish constitutionally relevant differences from constitutionally irrelevant ones."[66]

Gregory Herek argues that sexual orientation should be one difference that is always legally irrelevant. "[L]esbians and gay men, as a group, do not differ significantly from heterosexuals in their psychological and social functioning," at least for legal purposes.[67] In support of his argument, Herek identifies eight "myths" about gays and lesbians, and then proceeds to show why these are untrue.[68] A more critical examination of his thesis, however, finds it flawed because (1) some of his myths are either in fact true, or his rebuttal is inconclusive; and (2) the eight myths are not exhaustive of all the possible dimensions of variability between gays and heterosexuals.[69] Even were the eight myths truly myths, he still could not conclude that *no* significant differences exist. Yet contrary to Herek's position, one can easily imagine hypothetical situations where the variable at issue in each of the myths is indeed pertinent to the just outcome of a specific case.

The objective here is not to point out the problems with the "equality" claim, be it strong or weak. We mean to demonstrate only that the ideologies of law and social science contradict one another at a very fundamental level. As one social commentator concludes, "when it comes to the rising passion for equality and human rights secured against all authority, whatever its source, one sees no particular role for social science. For there we come to a real clash of values, one which will have to be fought out."[70]

This fight has been waged from the beginning of social scientific inquiry. The intellectual histories of sociology and anthropology reveal rises and falls between the polar answers to the question, Are people fundamentally the same? Early fascination with the indigenes of the New World and Africa—indigenes who seemed exotic to westerners—initially fueled a negative response. Later, Boasian anthropology, the intellectual progenitor of most American anthropology departments, had as its central claim that cultural evolution and physical evolution were independent, and that no biological "race" was therefore inherently culturally superior to any other.[71] While cultural differences can be marked and very real, they did not signify correlative differences in the physical types of persons within those cultures. All persons are, at the generic biological level, the same, and, for Boas, this meant a tabula rasa. This conclusion, when read in reverse, says that what we take to be "natural" in ourselves is but the impress of our culture; we possess very little in the way of innate predispositions. The purported demonstration of this thesis was the immensely popular *Coming of Age in Samoa* by Boas's student, Margaret Mead.[72] Her argument, now contested,[73] was that the angst associated with adolescence in Western culture, angst which was therefore deemed a natural concomitant of this developmental phase, did not exist in the island paradise of Samoa.

Much (but not all) contemporary social science seeks to find a middle ground between these two extremes of total unrelatedness and complete uniformity between human groups. Significant differences do exist. While these differences should not be taken out of context and blown out of all proportion, neither should they be ignored. At the physical level, women do differ in significant ways from men, and African-Americans from whites. These differences are particularly relevant in health issues. No one now contests that previously underrepresented groups need to be more adequately enrolled in drug trials and longitudinal disease studies,[74] since results from an all-white-male sample cannot necessarily be applied to other populations.

At the social level, the roles each of us occupies are also not equal, almost by definition. "[D]ecent social functioning ... [has] always taken for granted inequalities and differences in rights. The type case is the family, where children of different ages, mothers, and fathers, have different roles, roles which cannot be easily reconciled with our societies'—all our societies'—thrust to perfect equality."[75]

The discomfort of the law with recognition of group differences pre-sumed by the social sciences reveals itself in many ways. It has

> led to different evidentiary requirements for the same methodology depending on how it is used. One of the most influential effects of social interests on the treatment of scientific evidence in the courts may be found in relation to the use of cognitive ability tests in education and employ-ment. It has long been known that there are reliable differences between groups with regard to such ability-test performance.
>
> The social unpopularity of any type of methodology that results in find-ings of group differences has led to extraordinary government guidelines that specify in detail the requirements that an employer must meet to use a test for employee selection.[76]

The contrast to be made is with the use of the same tests in *clinical* set-tings, which are not hedged in by similar restrictions. A test deemed unsuitable to make employment decisions may be routinely incorpo-rated into the diagnosis and treatment of mental difficulties.

Peter Westen argued that "equality" is an empty concept, adding no new content to any situation where it is applied.

> Equality is an empty vessel with no substantive moral content of its own. Without moral standards, equality remains meaningless, a formula that can have nothing to say about how we should act. With such standards, equality becomes superfluous, a formula that can do nothing but repeat what we already know.[77]

To discover the emptiness of the legal belief that all persons are equal before the law does not, however, require recourse to deep theory. The claim that the rich defendant gets the same trial as does the poor one is simply false, as even a Supreme Court Justice has noticed:

> It is an unfortunate but undeniable fact that a person of means, by select-ing a lawyer and paying him enough to ensure he prepares thoroughly, usually can obtain better representation than that available to an indigent defendant, who must rely on appointed counsel, who, in turn, has limited time and resources to devote to a given case.[78]

At one extreme you have the O.J. Simpson double-murder trial, where Simpson could afford to be successfully defended by many "name-brand" attorneys who worked vigorously on his behalf; at the other extreme, you have the case of Calvin Burdine, whose court-appointed lawyer slept through much of the trial ending in Burdine's conviction and a sentence of death.[79]

Race also makes a difference. African-Americans face the death penalty more often for the murder of whites than do whites who mur-der blacks, and are more likely to face the death penalty generally.[80] These racial differences arise even under the assumption that the laws themselves are neutral to social facts, an assumption which is itself dubious. For example, although they are basically the same drug, possession of five grams of cocaine processed for smoking (crack) is a felony with a five-year sentence, whereas possession of cocaine in powder form for inhaling is a misdemeanor.[81] This disparity of punishments falls hardest on urban blacks, with the result that blacks constitute nearly 60 percent of persons in jail for drug offenses even though some have estimated that if powder and crack were punished equally, more whites would be going to prison than blacks.[82]

As every trial lawyer knows, the legal system also demonstrably treats defendants differently depending upon their level of physical attractiveness. Due to the "halo effect," juries tend to believe that good-looking persons are "less likely to commit negative, harmful behaviors.[83] Subsequently, they may be less likely to be assigned guilt and punishment when accused of a crime."[84] This effect is subject to all kinds of interesting qualifications. For example, the tendency to treat better the physically attractive defendant reverses when the jury feels that he or she used that attractiveness as an instrument in the crime to lure the victim, as in an embezzlement or a swindle. For these kinds of crimes, good-looking defendants are punished *more* severely than their less attractive counterparts.[85]

Anthropology's attention to differences is not insuperably incompatible with law's professed inattention to those differences only because the latter's claim to treat all persons equally is more prescriptive than descriptive. It might even be questioned whether this fictitious equality is even an appropriate ideal. There is something denuding about the concept of the generic person that grates against the other of America's great ideals, the individual worth of each person specifically, in all his or her idiosyncratic glory. The trick will not be to ignore all differences, but to decide which are operable in any particular case, and to deal with them honestly. Such difference can justify the invocation of a special defense (as with "culture defense" discussed below), or it can elicit remedial action by the system to remove the effects of that difference, such as guaranteeing to poor defendants the same quality of defense as is available to rich ones.

In sum, any claim such as Herek's that an important trait is never of legal relevance seems unlikely in the extreme. The inertial tendency of the law is to gloss over these differences, whereas that of anthropology is to underscore them. This clash can cause some lawyers to be uncomfortable with the use of anthropological data in the courtroom because by their very nature these data challenge the status quo.

Where, then, do we stand? Due to its lack of prestige and influence within its own society, anthropology would benefit from a stronger

alliance with the legal disciplines. Achieving that alliance will be difficult because, as we have seen, obstacles exist that make problematic
the easy use of anthropological findings in legal debates. First, anthropological data, like those from all social sciences, can change, develop,
and even reverse itself over time, making it an uncertain basis for
enduring legal principal. Second, the good anthropological explanation
is undesirable for direct insertion into adversarial legal proceedings
because it is too complex and too heavily hedged, nuanced, and qualified to benefit an adversarial proceeding. Finally, the elaboration of
social differences assumed by anthropology can conflict with the basic
legal maxim of complete equality that forms the basis of Western legal
systems. Notwithstanding these difficulties, the next sections consider
how anthropological data can be utilized productively by the law, in
ways that are also maximally beneficial to anthropology.

Anthropologist as Expert Witness

Having isolated problematic undercurrents that complicate the incorporation of anthropological findings into legal processes, we can now
set them aside. What follows assumes that the use of anthropology and
the resulting elevation of its social visibility and prestige could be
accomplished if the legal gatekeepers simply wished it so. How would
that be done? Law can recognize anthropology in either of two modes:
first, it can respectfully attend to what *anthropologists* have to say by
according them the status of "expert witnesses" in relevant matters, or
second, it can delegate to *anthropology* the role of arbiter of important
cultural facts of legal interest.

The first method by which anthropological views can find their way
into the legal arena is by the testimony of expert witnesses. Without
question this happens already, although not often. Anthropologists who
find themselves in this role at all, are likely only to fill "two such assign-
ments during their career."[86] What would be different, and what would
raise anthropology in social esteem, would be for this testimony to actually influence the outcome of the debate, be it legislative or judicial—in
short, for law with all of its prestige to actually defer to the considered
opinion of the anthropologist.

The Best Case: Wisconsin v. Yoder

We have often claimed that command of social facts seems only a reasonable expectation of workers in the legal system. No facet of that
enterprise fails to speak in terms that would lead one to believe that
those social facts have been carefully considered and allowed to appro-

priately influence the decision-making process. But often that belief is false. Both *Roe v. Wade* and *Brown v. Board of Education*, for example, are court decisions that prominently considered the pertinent social facts, leading some to believe that those facts actually influenced the outcomes of those landmark cases. Others, however, are more skeptical.

David Faigman suggested that a reasonable test of whether social science research has been taken seriously by the courts is to ask, What would be the result if the facts had been different? By that standard, neither *Roe* nor *Brown*, despite appearances to the contrary, depended on the facts they discuss at great length. "In both *Brown* and *Roe*, science offered a seemingly objective source of authority to lend legitimacy to decisions reached on other grounds."[87]

One of the few instances when the U.S. Supreme Court took official notice of anthropology *and* acted on that information, illustrates the promising benefit of this mutual assistance. In *Wisconsin v. Yoder*[88] members of the Amish community appealed a conviction for violating Wisconsin's compulsory school-attendance laws. Although the Amish had no problem with sending their children to public schools through the eighth grade, thereafter they believed both that it was more important for the children to learn the agricultural skills necessary for the maintenance of the community farms, and that exposure to outside influences in the impressionable teen years would be detrimental to the their moral and religious training.

The majority opinion written by Chief Justice Burger refers at length to the expert testimony that the respondents offered to support their claims. Foremost among these experts was anthropologist John Hostetler. The decision's footnotes cite liberally to his many works on Amish society. Even more impressive is his specific mention within the text of the opinion, repeating without contradiction or qualification his testimony "that compulsory high school attendance could not only result in great psychological harm to Amish children, because of the conflicts it would produce, but would also, in his opinion, ultimately result in the destruction of the Old Order Amish church community as it exists in the United States today."[89] Most remarkable in all this is the apparent fact that Hostetler's research and findings were instrumental in the Court's finding in favor of the Amish exemption. A "close reading of the Supreme Court opinion clearly demonstrates that the anthropological testimony in this case may well have been indispensable to the Court's assertion that enforcement of the school attendance law would have had an unusually harsh effect on the entire community of Amish people."[90] Framing its holding in the terms Hostetler introduced into the discussion, the Court stated its conclusion as follows:

Aided by a history of three centuries as an identifiable religious sect and a long history as a successful and self-sufficient segment of American society, the Amish in this case have convincingly demonstrated the sincerity of their religious beliefs, the interrelationship of belief with their mode of life, the vital role that belief and daily conduct play in the continued survival of Old Order Amish communities and their religious organization, and the hazards presented by the State's enforcement of a statute generally valid as to others. Beyond this, they have carried the even more difficult burden of demonstrating the adequacy of their alternative mode of continuing informal vocational education in terms of precisely those overall interests that the State advances in support of its program of compulsory high school education.[91]

The centrality of Hostetler's anthropological perspective to the outcome of *Yoder* is even more obvious when this case is put in the context of the developing theory of the Constitution's Religion Clauses. Heretofore, in the mid 1960s, the Supreme Court had been inching away from an understanding of religion as having a specific content such as a belief about God, and toward one highlighting the unique psychological status for the individual of his or her "ultimate concern." In contrast, *Yoder* assigns pride of place to the Amish for having a long history and established organization. One implication must be that the Amish exemption granted by *Yoder* would not be available to other religious claimants who lacked these structural elements. From this view Hostetler did his job too well, causing the Court to retreat from its earlier progressive tendency to liberally construe the word "religion." But the fact that the Court would follow him even into this error, forgetting its own precedents on the topic, amply demonstrates the powerful influence Hostetler exerted in this case.

To our knowledge, no anthropologist has exerted a similar influence in any other Supreme Court case even though, as we have suggested, the facts of many cases would seemingly demand this kind of expert opinion being both offered and incorporated into the Court's reasoning. In the next section we consider the legal procedures that determine whether the evidence from an anthropology expert witness would be admissible.

Federal Rules of Evidence

Devotees of popular culture crime dramas such as *Law and Order* will think themselves familiar with the standard by which courts admit expert testimony: scientific testimony can be admitted only if the principle "from which the deduction is made [is] sufficiently established to gain general acceptance in the particular field in which it belongs."[92] This rule, dating from 1923, is known as the "*Frye* test."[93] So long as the facts of the testimony were generally accepted by the relevant discipline, it could be heard by the jury.

However, it was not always clear exactly *what* had to enjoy "general acceptance." Some of the language of *Frye* suggests that so long as the *method* or "principle" were accepted, that would be enough. But the language also treats a "discovery" along with the "principle," implying that the end-product of the method must also be generally accepted. By the first reading, so long as the method employed to purportedly create "cold fusion" were generally accepted within the physics community, a jury could hear expert testimony about cold fusion. By the second reading, since the end-product of the method is far from generally accepted, it could not.

Under the *Frye* test an anthropologist could offer relevant expert testimony with little difficulty. The traditional methodology of anthropology, participant-observation fieldwork, is generally—indeed, universally—accepted within the discipline. Should the test extend to the "discovery" generated by the method, that too would present no insurmountable obstacle. Rarely do anthropologists claim the same fieldsite at the same time. Should one later follow after another, any discrepancy between conclusions could reasonably be attributed to the differing time frames of the fieldwork: That was then, this is now. Or the different conclusions may be the result of having asked different questions of different samples. For many reasons one anthropologist is rarely in a position to contradict another directly since the field experience is inherently unreplicable, unlike an experiment in the physical sciences. Derek Freeman's refutation of Margaret Mead is an exception. Freeman did not reach a different conclusion merely by working the same site; he also interviewed the very same informants Mead had relied upon.[94] This is as close as one can come to replicating an anthropological field experience.

The "general acceptance" test would therefore appear to be very conducive to the introduction of anthropological testimony into a judicial proceeding. Unfortunately, the *Frye* test is no longer the prevailing standard in the federal and most state courts. In 1975, Congress enacted the *Federal Rules of Evidence*, which stipulate the basis for the admission of expert testimony. The impact of this change was not felt until much later, in 1993, when the Supreme Court penned the decision of *Daubert v. Merrell Dow Pharmaceuticals*.[95]

Daubert concerned a suit against the manufacturers of Bendectin, a drug prescribed to prevent nausea, but which was later suspected of causing birth defects in the children of mothers who took the drug.[96] The defendant drug company accurately pointed out that the generally accepted method to determine causal links between drug ingestion and its later effects is to conduct human epidemiological studies. No study using this method had found Bendectin to cause birth defects. The plaintiffs presented their own expert testimony based on alternative analytic methods. These witnesses concluded that Bendectin did cause these defects. Because these conclusions were not based on human epidemiological evidence, but instead on animal-cell studies, live-animal studies, and chemical-structure analyses, the plaintiff's expert testimony failed the *Frye* test, and was excluded.

The Supreme Court vacated the decisions from the lower courts, which had applied the *Frye* test, holding that it had been superseded by the *Rules*. These rules do not require "general acceptance" as a necessary precondition to the admissibility of scientific evidence, although it can be one consideration. Instead, the Court directed the "trial judge [to] ensure that any and all scientific testimony or evidence admitted is not only relevant, but reliable."[97] The exact words of the central provision, Rule 702, are these:

> If scientific, technical, or other specialized knowledge will assist the trier of fact to understand the evidence or to determine a fact in issue, a witness qualified as an expert by knowledge, skill, experience, training, or education, may testify thereto in the form of an opinion or otherwise.[98]

While *Daubert* restricts its concerns to "scientific testimony or evidence," this is only one of the kinds of specialized knowledge addressed by Rule 702.

Preliminary determinations of whether a witness qualifies as an "expert," or whether the evidence is admissible, are assigned by Rule 104 to the court. This shift in emphasis was staggering. Before, each discipline had itself possessed the power to decide what was or was not to be accepted as reliable, obliging the court to accept these determinations passively; after *Daubert*, this determination was to be made by the court.

A sizable literature addresses the many unresolved questions raised by *Daubert*. How is a generalist judge expected to determine whether each of the scientific opinions, ranging over a potentially wide assortment of academic specialties, is either relevant or—most important— reliable?[99] Anticipating the need for some guidance, the *Daubert* opinion identified four nonexhaustive questions to determine "whether a theory or technique is scientific knowledge that will assist the trier of fact":[100] (1) "can it be (and has it been) tested"; (2) has "the theory or technique been subjected to peer review and publication"; (3) has the known or potential rate of error attached to the particular scientific technique been considered; and (4) has the theory or technique found "general acceptance" [the *Frye* test]?[101]

We should immediately note that the *Rules* are meant to be liberally applied, in the spirit of allowing the trial judge wide—but not unrestricted—latitude in determining the admissibility of expert testimony. But a strict application of these factors to the specific case of anthropology does not retain the conducive environment of the *Frye* test. The *Daubert* factors are plainly tailored to the physical sciences. Features characteristic of disciplines such as physics and chemistry, however, are not necessarily appropriate standards for others.

Anthropological theories and techniques are not easily amenable to the "testing" preferred by the first factor. One of the necessary elements of a true scientific test is the ability to control the relevant variables. By varying first one and then another independent variable, and observing the effects of these variations upon the dependent variables, the scientist can credibly interpret his results in terms of one "causing" the other. A "quasi-experiment" is one in which the independent variable is not controlled by the experimenter. Instead, he depends upon naturally occurring variation. For example, the scientist may compare two groups (males and females) to see if they differ on some dependent variable (the ability to manipulate spatial relationships). The true experiment would take the same subjects and alter their sexes and test for that ability, seeing whether the change in sex made a difference. That obviously cannot be done. Many hypotheses about the human condition are limited in this way; it is either impossible to test them, or, even if possible, unethical.

Anthropology has invested great energies in doing what it can to approximate the method of the quasi-experiment. One could go to the enormous expense of actually coordinating joint ethnographic research projects among carefully selected, disparate cultural settings. For obvious reasons, this approach is so rare as to be virtually nonexistent. In its stead are studies using data from the *Human Relations Area File* (HRAF). The HRAF is a coded database of ethnographic information that one can sample randomly to test for various relationships among culture traits.[102] An early and important use of this method documented the relationship between childrearing practices and later adult personality traits.[103] It is therefore possible for anthropologists to test theories, at least quasi-experimentally. But this is not the standard practice of the discipline, nor, as discussed in the introduction, is it a requirement of all anthropology, even in its scientific guise.

Most anthropologists called to offer their expert opinion will do so based upon their own insights and experiences which, whatever their virtues may be, have not been tested in any rigorous way. With notable exceptions, anthropologists will therefore fail to satisfy the first *Daubert* factor.

Even where testing is either conceivable or accomplished, few methods used by an anthropologist will be such as would generate an "error rate." HRAF analyses can generate numbers that might look like an error rate, but what would they mean? The familiar analogy here would be to the proverbial 2.1 children the census tells us are in the average family. What is .1 of a child? Similarly, the kinds of variables examined by anthropologists are discrete, and not interval. They do not lend themselves to the incremental values usual in determining a quantitative margin of error or confidence intervals. On this—the third *Daubert* factor—anthropology again fails to conform to the model anticipated by the Supreme Court.[104]

What this mismatch may mean is hard to predict. Several writers have noticed a tendency toward unfavorable treatment of the social sciences by *Daubert*.[105] That conclusion may be premature. Since "*Daubert*, evidence [from the behavioral and social sciences] has been excluded in isolated cases that would have been admitted pre-*Daubert*, but overall *Daubert* has not resulted in changes in the admissibility of behavioral and social science evidence."[106] This conclusion offers less consolation than it might appear, since the same authors admit that "the application of *Daubert* to behavioral and social science evidence has been so infrequent that the courts have rarely articulated how to interpret these criteria, and thus they provide little guidance to predict outcome."[107]

Conceivably, a consensus could emerge that anthropology is not sufficiently a "science" by *Daubert* standards to assist the trier of fact, failing largely on its demand for reliability. By some arguments, the *Daubert* factors are so limited that they preclude introduction of even commonly accepted evidence such as fingerprint identification.[108] If true, the poor evaluation of anthropology by those factors is hardly stigmatizing. Still, a potential outcome could be that testimony from anthropologists will not often be heard by the jury. If the goal is to increase the social prestige of anthropology by elevating its visibility via the increased use of its practitioners as expert witnesses, then the move away from the *Frye* test has made this goal more elusive.

Anthropology as Social Authority

Although there exist real obstacles to the increased presence of anthropologists within the legal system in the role of "expert witnesses," this tactic to raise the social esteem of the discipline has the virtue of being one whose components are already in place. By contrast, this section considers a more speculative strategy.

The Monahan and Walker Model of Social Authority

John Monahan and Laurens Walker, in a genuinely original article, first review the distinction between "'adjudicative facts'—facts that pertain specifically to the case at bar [hereafter simply 'facts']—and 'legislative facts'—facts involved in deciding questions of law or policy [hereafter simply 'law']."[109] The established rule is that questions of fact are settled by a jury, whereas questions of law are answered by the judge.

The traditional expectation has been that to the extent that social science data are admissible at all, they will be facts introduced by expert testimony. Monahan and Walker argue contrarily that social science research should be treated by the court as it "would legal precedent under the common law."[110] They point out that although social science research resembles both fact and law, it is the latter which is more in keeping with the true nature of the social sciences. Both the law and the social sciences "are *general*—both produce principles applicable beyond particular instances. Facts, in contrast, are specific to particular instances."[111] While both law and social science have their beginnings in mere facts, they become "authority" that binds subsequent deliberations "precisely to the extent that [they transcend] the people, situation, and time present in the original case."[112] Consequently, due to these parallels, "it is jurisprudentially *plausible* for courts to treat social science research as they treat prior judicial decisions under the common law."[113]

This suggestion is intriguing in that it addresses two of our immediate concerns. First, were social science research to be treated as social authority pertaining to legislative facts of law and policy considered by the judge, the proper method of presentation for this research would be by brief to the court rather than by testimony to the jury. Swept away are the potential difficulties outlined in the previous section over whether or not anthropologists can pass muster according to *Daubert* factors. Since they are not testifying as to the adjudicative facts specific to the case, they do not aspire to the role of "expert witness." More dramatically, the elevation of anthropological findings to a status equivalent to a precedential legal opinion would immediately fulfill the objective to have law use its prestige to increase the esteem and regard in which anthropology is held by the general public.

In this model, standards would be needed to sort the good social science from the bad, that which warrants regard as "social authority" from that which does not: "Courts should place confidence in a piece of scientific research to the extent that the research (1) has survived the critical review of the scientific community; (2) has employed valid research methods; (3) is generalizable to the case at issue; and (4) is supported by a body of other research."[114] Monahan and Walker believe that these criteria are analogous to those used to assign precedential value to prior judicial decisions, and thus they are not arbitrary or ad hoc determinations.

These criteria present none of the obstacles encountered in the *Daubert* factors. The research is required only to be "valid," not tested.

When experimental testing is not appropriate to the body of research at issue, some other means of validation can be acceptable, leeway not evident on the face of *Daubert*. "Validity" in this context refers specifically to the ability of a study to "rule out, or 'control for,' competing hypotheses that may account for an observed state of affairs."[115] Threats to validity include selection bias, history (the impingement of other influences on the target phenomenon) and maturation (the failure to consider the phenomenon longitudinally, that is, as it develops over time). The opinion of Monahan and Walker is that case studies are "close to useless as a method for drawing any valid conclusions."[116] Since much of the corpus of anthropology is the cultural case study, not all anthropological research would benefit from this new perspective. That negative outcome, however, would not be unique to anthropology. Some comfort may be taken from the authors' own assessment that were all of their criteria rigorously applied, "much of the research cited by courts today would be easily dismissed."[117]

Good anthropological research can handily satisfy the four social authority criteria as outlined in the Monahan and Walker model. Especially insightful is the preference for research whose conclusions converge with other, independent authorities. If a datum fits into a theoretical gap outlined by other research, we may have confidence in that result even if it derives from unconventional (but still valid) methodology.

The "Culture Defense" as Application of Social Authority

One candidate for the kind of social authority Monahan and Walker describe is the culture defense. "A cultural defense will negate or mitigate criminal responsibility where acts are committed under a reasonable, good-faith belief in their propriety, based upon the actor's cultural heritage or tradition."[118] *State v. Kargar*[119] demonstrated the need for such a defense. In this case a man of Afghani origin who had relocated to the United States was charged with "gross sexual assault" for kissing the penis of his nine-month-old son. Kargar admitted to the action, and under a strict reading of the statute, he was guilty of a crime. However, testimony showed that Kargar's action "was considered neither wrong nor sexual under Islamic law and that Kargar did not know his action was illegal under Maine law."[120] In fact, Kargar explained that "consistent with his Islamic culture, by kissing Rahmadan's penis—a body part that is 'not the holiest or cleanest'—he was showing how much he truly loved his son."[121] Was Kargar criminally liable? More pointedly, *should* he be liable? Ultimately the court said no. It concluded that "the gross sexual assault statute, whatever its technical language, was not intended to criminalize non-sexual conduct [and that] Kargar's conduct [could be] deemed non-sexual by virtue of his cultural background."[122]

In Kargar's case most observers were rooting for the success of his defense. Intuitively it would have seemed an injustice for him to be punished for this act of love toward his son, an act that in no way harmed Rahmadan, however much it contravened conventional American mores. But as the cases gradually depart from this positive example, support for the culture defense wavers because it seems to condone harmful conduct such as rape:

> Kong Moua, then twenty three years old, believed he was following Hmong customary marriage practices when he engaged in sexual intercourse with Seng Xiong. But Seng Xiong, then nineteen years old, apparently rejected this tradition and believed herself to have been raped. Both Kona and Seng were born in Laos and moved to the United States as teenagers.[123]

One of the elements that makes this episode so problematic is that according to the Hmong marriage custom, "the man is required to take the woman to his family home and keep her there for three days in order to consummate the marriage. The woman is supposed to protest, 'No, no, no, I'm not ready,' to prove her virtue."[124] The real protest to a rape therefore looks and sounds exactly like a stylized protest to a marriage consummation.

A further difficulty in assigning culpability in this episode is that it was not merely an alleged case of mixed signals, one where real protests were mistaken for scripted ones. Even if the correct message had been received ("you are raping me"), the problem still would not have been averted. By Hmong standards, this act could not have been "rape" at all, even had the protests been recognized as real:

> Hmong language has no exact equivalent to "rape" and … the Hmong use the English term "rape" to refer to adultery and intra-clan marriage, both of which are violations of the Hmong legal code. In [Ruth Hammond's] article *Call It Rape*, she quotes a David Yang, a police officer of Hmong origin. "They [some Hmong] don't understand the term 'raping' someone. When you have an affair with somebody's wife or with a girl without her parent's permission, [for them] that falls into the category of rape.[125]

The claim is that, among the Hmong, rape is a classificatory infraction (having sex with an inappropriate woman), and not a lack-of-consent crime (having sex with an unwilling woman). Nothing Moua did would have led him to believe he was committing a "rape" as Americans understand the term, even had he realized that Seng Xiong's protests were real. Should a culture defense have been available to him? "After hearing the testimony of the parties and witnesses and reviewing a doctoral dissertation on Hmong marriage rituals, the judge sentenced the defendant to ninety days in the county jail. The defendant was also fined $1,000.00, with $900.00 presented to the woman as reparation."[126]

The question of the appropriateness of a culture defense becomes more difficult still as the conduct at issue becomes increasingly violent or traumatic. Female circumcision (also known as "female genital mutilation," or "FGM") could be argued to be an act of parental responsibility toward young daughters, but it is an act also contended to result in profound physical, psychological, and sexual repercussions.[127] Should immigrant parents be prosecuted for submitting their daughters to this procedure?[128]

And, finally, there are the most extreme cases, those that result in death:

> On September 7, 1987, Dong Lu Chen, who had immigrated from China one year earlier, decided to speak to his wife, Jian Wan Chen, about their sexual relationship. When she admitted to having an affair, he left the room, returned with a claw hammer, knocked her onto the bed, and hit her on the head eight times until she was dead.[129]

Several features of this case demand our attention. First, the trial court heard testimony for the defense from an anthropologist, providing one instance when expert testimony from the discipline was deemed relevant:

> Burton Pasternak, a professor of anthropology at Hunter College, testified on Chen's behalf. Dr. Pasternak explained that in the Chinese culture, a woman's adultery is proof of her husband's weak character and a source of great shame upon his ancestors. A husband often becomes enraged upon learning of his wife's infidelity and threatens to kill her.[130]

Thus far, the outburst sounds like simple uncontrolled rage by an isolated individual. Pasternak's next comments show how the release of such anger had been scripted by Chen's culture:

> However, the close-knit Chinese community usually intervenes and offers help to the family before the husband can carry out his threat. Chen's defense was based on the premise that there was no community to protect Jian Wan Chen.[131]

In other words, Chen's reaction to the revelation of his wife's infidelities was culturally appropriate. The same cultural script that allowed him to threaten his wife also provided interventions that would protect her from real harms. It was the lack of the second component that rendered Chen's reaction tragically dysfunctional. Originally charged with second-degree murder, Chen subsequently received the lightest possible sentence for second-degree manslaughter, largely in response to the introduction of facts outlining the relationship of this crime to his cultural background. Thus, the evidence of culture was used to mitigate the outcome rather than exculpate the defendant.

All of the cited examples involve conduct between culture mates. One could argue that when all participants function within the same set of cultural assumptions, no individual is taken completely by surprise. Jian Wan Chen presumably knew that her husband might react to her infidelities with fatal violence, and was therefore in a position to protect herself before the incident. Outsiders, however, are not afforded even this opportunity to foresee and avoid the confrontation. The polar extreme to the *Kargar* case would therefore occur when a person acts in ways appropriate to his or her own culture, but which result in harm to a person of a different culture:

> Prosenjit Poddar was a member of the Harijan (untouchable) caste, who was attending graduate school in naval architecture at the University of California at Berkeley. He was rejected by a nineteen-year-old woman, Tanya Tarasoff, with whom he believed he had a romantic relationship [because she had accepted his gift of a sari, which in his culture meant that she was prepared to marry him]. Because of cross-cultural misunderstandings, he was convinced that she was committed to him. After she rejected him, he killed her.[132]

Poddar was convicted of second-degree murder, but this conviction was later overturned. Rather than proceed with a second prosecution, the court agreed to allow Poddar to be deported.

The culture defense clearly becomes less attractive the farther one moves away from the *Kargar* case.[133] This gradation of equitability could be tracked by a similar gradation of impact the defense is allowed to have. Minimally, the culture defense could serve the defendant as either a justification or an excuse: "Otherwise unlawful behavior is justified if it causes the lesser evil under the circumstances.... By contrast, conduct is excused if the harm caused is wrongful and thus not socially desirable under the circumstances, but the actor is not fully responsible for his or her conduct."[134] Suppose X kills Z. X can offer a *justification* (such as "self-defense") which, if proven, would garner X a verdict of "not guilty," and he would go free. Or, X can offer an *excuse* or *mitigating circumstance* such as "heat of passion," which could garner X a verdict of guilty, but of a lesser offense (manslaughter instead of second-degree murder).

In *Kargar* the culture defense is a justification. Here the defense vitiates the purported criminality of the act without denying the act itself. Kargar did not deny kissing the penis of his son; rather, he argued that this act was not criminal, and the court agreed. Alison Dundes Renteln argues that the culture defense should function only as a partial excuse.[135] In the Chen case, the culture defense was not used to deny the criminality of Chen's conduct, but only to mitigate the penalty he might suffer. Conceivably, the culture defense could reasonably function as a justification in *Kargar*-like cases, a mitigating circumstance in those like *Moua* (the Hmong marriage by capture case), and not at all in situations of the most extreme kind.

Ironically, this possibility of a new relevance for anthropology, depending as it does upon its expertise in handling the concept of culture, comes at a time when many anthropologists are, unfortunately, "disown[ing]" that same concept.[136] This reaction has its roots in the effects of extreme ideologies of cultural relativism: "Culture as explanation languishes in intellectual exile partly because of guilt by association.... [T]he modern multi-cultural concept of culture and ethnic identity have simply become substitutes for racism."[137] While we believe that "culture" continues to be a valuable and potent explanatory variable, clearly much work will be required not only to clarify its exact content, but also to rehabilitate it in the eyes of its critics.[138] It is urgently critical that anthropologists rise to this challenge by taking preemptive steps to rectify these limitations, lest legal understanding of "culture" drift into an aberration of the anthropological understanding, much as the legal definition of "insanity" today bears no relationship to the construct of mental illness in the medical sciences.[139]

Our goal here has not been to hammer out the details of the culture defense. Renteln's article is an excellent and thorough overview of the issue, and serves that purpose well.[140] We only show that despite much rhetoric to the contrary, there can be a place for this defense in the U.S. legal system,[141] and that anthropology would necessarily be the arbiter of its general appropriateness (although *not* its applicability to any specific case). This responsibility falls squarely within the scope of "social authority" as proposed by Monahan and Walker.

While it shall always be a question of fact for the court whether such a defense should apply to any specific defendant, the prima facie plausibility of the defense itself is a matter for anthropology, not law. By this we mean that anthropology would provide evidence to the court about the prevalence and importance of the specific cultural practices invoked by the defense. Is Hmong "marriage by capture" a vital cultural institution in Moua's homeland, or is it merely a cultural ideal that is never actually performed? Many of our own marriage practices fall closer to this latter category, such as the prospective groom asking the girl's father for permission to marry, or the expectation that the bride's father will pay for the wedding. This may be the cultural ideal, but no one is "shamed" into a murderous rage if the father does not pay.

The defendant's argument must be that certain cultural models have so influenced his individual behaviors that in order to feel himself to be a "real" person he must behave accordingly. Anthropology can ascertain whether this is a valid claim, *culturally* speaking. If an individual has fixated upon a particular model that may be available, but which is not invested with special salience within the indigenous culture, then the problem is not one of anthropology but of psychology and psychiatry.[142] The culture defense is geared not toward aberrant individuals, but to the deeply entrenched cultural practices of ordinary persons.

Some might deny that culture can ever exert this kind of potent force. U.S. law fosters this impression by its frequent reliance upon the "reasonable prudent person" standard. There is a sense in which we tend to perceive "White Americans" as being cultureless; it is the Others who have cultures that make them do weird things.[143] The reasonable, rational person should be able, by dint of will, to overcome any predispositions he or she may possess by virtue of cultural background. Failure to do so is read as a failure of character, and certainly should not serve as either excuse or justification for bad or criminal behavior.

What is missed in this belief is the fact that we are ourselves just as much a product of our own cultural presumptions as are those Others. We find it hard to accept that someone would easily do something we think unimaginable (food preferences are an easy example. How many of us would find live beetle larvae a tasty treat?) or could refuse to do something we take to be "natural." Most Americans, for example, would be repulsed by the ritual performance by young boys of fellatio on older men, a practice among the New Guinea Sambia that is intended to ensure the youths' proper development.[144] Their thinking is that semen is required for normal development, but semen is also a limited resource that must be circulated between the generations.

The point is that culture is a potent force that looms so large in our perspective that we do not even notice it, and our own culture is no exception. Our blindness comes perhaps from our full initiation into the cultural logic explaining any of our own behaviors. With this background knowledge our acts appear "rational." Acts whose logic is hidden from us, however, we tend to regard as capricious or foolish, perhaps even sick or perverted.

The power of culture should never be underestimated. The ability of culture to shape something as "natural" as disease is widely conceded. These are the "culture-bound syndromes" such as *koro* (a severe anxiety associated with the perception that the genitals are retracting into the body), *amok* (an episode of sudden mass assault and indiscriminate homicide), and *arctic hysteria* (a syndrome involving the tearing off of clothes, speaking irrationally, fleeing nude, and senseless acts of aggression), among others.[145] "Culture-bound" refers to the restriction of these illnesses to specific culture groups. If culture can impact so drastically something as well-defined as physical illness, so much the more credible is the claim that it can also impact a person's psychological predispositions affecting the "guilty mind" (*mens rea*) element essential to every criminal act.

Cultural influences are potent formative forces. They are known to shape and create unique illnesses; they can surely impede the formation of the state of mind required under our law to render an act criminal. The anthropologist could address this question of the *mens rea* element, perhaps by informing the court what would be the proper "reasonable person" standard to apply to a defendant of any specific cultural background.

Conclusion

Anthropology has, over the course of its approximately one hundred and fifty years of existence as an independent specialty, accumulated a wealth of data and insight. Despite these accomplishments, the discipline still has not settled upon its identity as either art or science. The very interdisciplinary nature of the field, one of its cardinal strengths, has revealed itself as a double-edged sword. Further complicating the discipline's existential crisis is the fact that society at large seems neither to recognize nor appreciate the work that anthropologists do, nor the contributions they have to offer.

Anthropology would benefit on many fronts from the sponsorship of the better established, more prestigious legal profession. The rest of society already looks to its leaders for cues about what to value and support. If society sees the law appropriately deferring and consulting with anthropology, the hope is that these acts will elevate anthropology in the public esteem.

This chapter identified several obstacles that would complicate any easy and immediate incorporation of anthropology into the legal process. The law is by and large a stable institution, whereas the sciences are necessarily in flux. The law prefers its facts to be clear and unambiguous, whereas a proper anthropological conclusion will be nuanced, offering exceptions and qualifications. Finally, the law dislikes anything that undermines its self-image as the sustainer of universal equality. Since anthropology is in many ways a study of differences, the ideological differences can make law and anthropology incompatible in certain respects.

Despite these hindrances, two avenues by which the law could utilize more effectively anthropological data present themselves. Anthropologists could serve more frequently as expert witnesses, or anthropology could be delegated pertinent areas of social authority that would stand as precedent for future legal actions. Either of these strategies would maximize the proposed practical benefit of the law to anthropology, the seconding by the law of anthropology in the public arena.

Notes

1. We are framing the contrast in polarized terms for didactic purposes. Any specific case will be a more nuanced combination, as our discussion in the introduction indicated.
2. WILLIAM H. DURHAM, COEVOLUTION: GENES, CULTURE AND HUMAN DIVERSITY (1991).
3. ROY A. RAPPAPORT, PIGS FOR THE ANCESTORS: RITUAL IN THE ECOLOGY OF A NEW GUINEA PEOPLE (1984).
4. CLIFFORD GEERTZ, THE INTERPRETATION OF CULTURES (1973).
5. CLAUDE LÉVI-STRAUSS, THE RAW AND THE COOKED (Chicago: University of Chicago Press, 1983) (1969).
6. *See* James Lowell Gibbs, *Stanford Anthropology Department Splits*, 39(7) ANTHROPOLOGY NEWSLETTER 21 (October 1998); Christopher Shea, *Tribal Skirmishes in Anthropology*, CHRONICLE OF HIGHER EDUCATION, September 11, 1998, at A17.
7. Some practitioners, we realize, deny that any such tension exists, believing that the field has "moved beyond" such antitheses. The Stanford case belies that facile illusion, as does the fact that annual meetings of the American Anthropological Association regularly include sessions debating this topic.
8. Judith Shulevitz, *Academic Warfare*, NEW YORK TIMES, February 11, 2001, at G35. This negative appraisal is not limited to outsiders: "Extinction is the imminent threat that faces anthropology, at least in Europe (in other parts of the world anthropology never made it beyond being, at most, an appendix to history or sociology)." Ronald Stade, *A Matter of Relevance*, 42(8) ANTHROPOLOGY NEWS 7 (November 2001). Stade recommends that anthropology, to avoid this fate, must become more relevant to the needs of real people.
9. RUTH BENEDICT, THE CHRYSANTHEMUM AND THE SWORD (1946). The U.S. Government commissioned this study of Japanese people in 1944, with the hope that it would reveal what to expect from them both during the war and afterwards. Subsequent events have shown her insights and predictions to be amazingly prescient.
10. Lee Drummond, *Who Wants to Be an Anthropologist?* 41(8) ANTHROPOLOGY NEWSLETTER 6 (November 2000).
11. Stanley Barrett reaches this same conclusion: "individuals who have experienced some kind of trauma in their teens, such as the break-up of their families and perhaps a move to a new community, are especially attracted to the social sciences. The assumption is that such an experience makes them somewhat marginal, and encourages them to be analytical." STANLEY R. BARRETT, ANTHROPOLOGY: A STUDENT'S GUIDE TO THEORY AND METHOD 77 (1996).
12. These claims should be understood to be comparative, not absolute. For an analysis of the psychological forces stirred up by fieldwork, *see* JOHN L. WENGLE, ETHNOGRAPHERS IN THE FIELD (1988).

13. *See* Robert Borofsky, *To Laugh or Cry?* 41(2) ANTHROPOLOGY NEWS 9 (February 2000) ("For many years now anthropologists have played only a minor, supporting role in the intellectual debates that swirl around the cultural concept.").

14. *See* Richard J. Perry, *Why Do Multiculturalists Ignore Anthropologists?* CHRONICLE OF HIGHER EDUCATION, March 4, 1992, at A52. Perhaps this oversight is due to the (ironic) expectation that our studies of "them" (foreigners, primitives, aliens, "others" generally) could not contribute usefully to discussions about "us."

15. Bryce King II, *Who Do We Think We Are?* 41(4) ANTHROPOLOGY NEWS 11 (April 2000).

16. *Id.*

17. *Speed Wins Fellowship*, 41(8) ANTHROPOLOGY NEWSLETTER 22 (November 2000).

18. About twenty years ago this fact was offered as proof that Earth had been visited and colonized by aliens from outer space. The argument was that they had infiltrated the social sciences and rendered them so completely obtuse that that knowledge could not possibly be widely disseminated. Apparently if the true findings of the social sciences ever got out on a large scale they could be used to render us less malleable and subject to the aliens' domination.

19. William C. Young, *"Knowledge" or "Findings"? The Public Demand for Anthropology*, 41(9) ANTHROPOLOGY NEWSLETTER 63 (December 2000).

20. *See* Mark Nathan Cohen, *The Flat Earth Challenge*, 41(5) ANTHROPOLOGY NEWS 13 (May 2000).

21. The American Anthropology Association dedicated a year of discussion in its organizational newsletter to the topic of the public perception of anthropology, in part for this very reason. *See* George B. Thomas, *Untangle the Beast*, 41(1) ANTHROPOLOGY NEWS 11 (January 2000).

22. The genre of lawyer jokes, and their underlying social implication, is discussed by Thomas W. Overton, *Lawyers, Light Bulbs, and Dead Snakes: The Lawyer Joke as Societal Text*, 42 UCLA LAW REVIEW 1069 (1995).

23. SID BEHRMAN, THE LAWYER JOKE BOOK 23 (1991). In this same vein is this comment from Supreme Court Justice Sandra Day O'Connor: "In society at large—that is among those we would call 'non-lawyers'—lawyers are compared frequently, and unfavorably I might add, with skunks, snakes, and sharks." Hugh Maddox, *Lawyers: The Aristocracy of Democracy or "Skunks, Snakes, and Sharks"?* 29 CUMBERLAND LAW REVIEW 323 (1998-99) (quoting Sandra Day O'Connor).

24. Charles E. Hamilton, *Lawyers' Professionalism: Great (and Historical) Expectations*, *in* IN OUR OWN WORDS: REFLECTIONS ON PROFESSIONALISM IN THE LAW 25, 29 (Roger A. Stetter ed., 1998).

25. *See* Carl T. Bogus, *The Death of an Honorable Profession*, 71 INDIANA LAW JOURNAL 911 (1996) ("The legal profession is dead or dying. It is rotting away into an occupation.").

26. ROBERT F. COCHRAN, JR., & TERESA S. COLLETT, THE RULES OF THE LEGAL PROFESSION 1 (1996).

27. American Bar Association, *Model Rules of Professional Conduct*, *in* PROFESSIONAL RESPONSIBILITY: STANDARDS, RULES & STATUTES 6-7 (John Dzienkowski ed., 2000).

28. *Id.* at 7.

29. Hamilton, *supra* note 24, at 41-42 (quoting Rayman L. Solomon).

30. *See* Jane Easter Bahls, *Standards of Quality*, 29(6) STUDENT LAWYER 23 (2001).

31. For a negative perspective of the prestige of the legal profession, *see* Donald F. Harris, *Prisoners of Prestige? Paternalism and the Legal Profession*, 17 JOURNAL OF THE LEGAL PROFESSION 125 (1992).

32. *See* GEORGE C. CHRISTIE & PATRICK H. MARTIN, JURISPRUDENCE: TEXT AND READINGS ON THE PHILOSOPHY OF LAW 740 (2d ed., 1995) ("The social sciences and empirical data did not prove as useful for law as it might have been thought.").

33. William E. Doyle, *Can Social Science Data Be Used in Judicial Decisionmaking?* 6(1) JOURNAL OF LAW & EDUCATION 13, 18 (1977).

34. Andrew Greeley, *Debunking the Role of Social Scientists in Court*, 7(1) HUMAN RIGHTS 34 (1978).

35. *Id.*

36. This claim is a matter of degree. Several earlier decisions, including the polygamy case of *Reynolds* discussed in the previous chapter, did include some factual assertions from the social sciences. But an argument can be made that *Plessy* is one of the first cases in which such assertions actually made a difference in the outcome, as opposed to being mere token supports for conclusions arrived at by other means. 37.   163 U.S. 537 (1896).

38. "Inappropriate" because the theory does not follow from anything Darwin said, although its proponents believed otherwise.

39. ROSEMARY J. ERICKSON & RITA J. SIMON, THE USE OF SOCIAL SCIENCE DATA IN SUPREME COURT DECISIONS 13 (1998).

40. 494 U.S. 972 (1990).

41. James M. Donovan, *Restoring Free Exercise Protections by Limiting Them: Preventing a Repeat of* Smith, 17(1) NORTHERN ILLINOIS UNIVERSITY LAW REVIEW 1, 2-3 (1996).

42. 478 U.S. 186 (1986).

43. Patrick A. Driessen, *The Wedding of Social Science and the Courts: Is the Marriage Working?* 64 SOCIAL SCIENCE QUARTERLY 476, 477 (1983).

44. ERICKSON & SIMON, *supra* note 39, at 13.

45. *Plessy*, 163 U.S. at 552.

46. *Id.* at 551.

47. J. Braxton Craven, *The Impact of Social Science Evidence on the Judge: A Personal Comment*, 39(1) LAW AND CONTEMPORARY PROBLEMS 150, 151 (1975).

48. 208 U.S. 412 (1908). For the history of ideas, it is important to distinguish between the first *explicit* invocation of social science data, and the first significant invocation *per se* of that data. *Muller* is the former; *Plessy* may or may not be the latter. Historical accounts on this issue tend to conflate the two milestones, erroneously claiming that *Muller* is the first invocation.

49. *See* Lochner v. New York, 198 U.S. 45 (1905).

50. *Muller*, 208 U.S. at 423.

51. *Id.* at 422.

52. ERICKSON & SIMON, *supra* note 39, at 14.

53. *Id.*

54. To see how far we have come since *Muller*, one need only look at *International Union v. Johnson Controls*, 499 U.S. 187 (1991). Johnson Controls wished to prevent exposure of women to high levels of lead, which can cause birth defects in later pregnancies. They restricted fertile women from jobs which involved an exposure greater than that permitted by OSHA. While the lower courts supported this action, the Supreme Court found it facially discriminatory and thus forbidden.

55. *See* Driessen, *supra* note 43.

56. *Id.* at 479.

57. STEVEN E. FIENBERG (ED.), THE EVOLVING ROLE OF STATISTICAL ASSESSMENTS AS EVIDENCE IN THE COURTS 78 (1989).

58. DAVID FAIGMAN, LEGAL ALCHEMY: THE USE AND MISUSE OF SCIENCE IN THE LAW 71 (1999).

59. Sir Henry Sumner Maine explains that the origin of this concept of equality is derived from the juridical axiom formulated by the Roman jurisconsults of the Antonine era, *omnes homines naturâ æquales sunt* (all men are equal in the application of natural law), in contrast with Roman civil law which incorporated many distinctions based on the different classes or statuses of the litigants. *See* SIR HENRY SUMNER MAINE, ANCIENT LAW 76 (New York: Dorset Press, 1986) (1861).

> The rule was one of considerable importance to the Roman practitioner, who required to be reminded that, wherever Roman jurisprudence was assumed to conform itself exactly to the code of Nature, there was no difference in the contemplation of the Roman tribunals between citizen and foreigner, between freeman and slave, between Agnate and Cognate. The jurisconsults who thus expressed themselves most certainly never intended to censure the social arrangements under which civil law fell....

Id. at 76-77. This concept later became incorporated in the European continental tradition as "political dogma" rather than an application of a legal principle. *Id.* at 78. Thomas Jefferson was influenced by and relied on this tradition when writing the Declaration of Independence. *Id.* at 78-79.

60. Judge Melvin A. Shortess, Thomas M. Bergstedt, & Frank X. Neuner, Jr., *Barbarians at the Bar, in* IN OUR OWN WORDS, *supra* note 24, at 69, 75-76. The thesis of "equality before the law" has been articulated by JOHN LOCKE, THE SECOND TREATISE OF GOVERNMENT 73 (J.W. Gough ed., 3d ed., Oxford: Basil Blackwell, 1966) (1690) (Legislatures are "to govern by promulgated established laws, not to be varied in particular cases, but to have one rule for rich and poor, for the favourite at court and the countryman at plough.").

61. Aristotle deals with the question of political equality throughout his *Politics*. One of his conclusions is that revolutions are fomented by beliefs in the wrong kinds of equality.

62. An example of radical egalitarianism if found in the work of philosopher Thomas Nagel. *See generally* THOMAS NAGEL, MORTAL QUESTIONS (1979). Nagel suggests, for example, that economic rewards should not vary by intellectual ability. *See id.* at 91-105. A more immediate example comes in the aftermath of the September 11, 2001, terrorist attacks. Airport security has increased screening for potential hijackers. The issue is whether, as Transportation Secretary Norman Mineta believes, "a young Muslim male and a 70-year-old white American woman should be given equal attention at the security gate," or is that attention better focused on those fitting the profile of persons that experience has shown to be more likely to actually hijack? *See* Michael Satchell, *Everyone Empty Your Pockets? Stopping Only Those Who Fit a Terrorist "Profile" Might Make the Skies Safer,* U.S. NEWS & WORLD REPORT, April 1, 2002, at 18-21. Sometimes a rigid demand for equal treatment before the law can be counterproductive.

63. JESSE CHOPER ET AL., CONSTITUTIONAL LAW 1137 (9th ed., 2001).

64. Kathleen O'Brien, *Sept. 11 Survivors: Treat them Equally,* TIMES-PICAYUNE (New Orleans), March 24, 2002, at B7.

65. Tom R. Tyler, *What Is Procedural Justice? Criteria Used by Citizens to Assess the Fairness of Legal Procedures,* 22 LAW & SOCIETY REVIEW 104, 130 (1988).

66. Peter Westen, *The Empty Idea of Equality,* 95 HARVARD LAW REVIEW 537, 566 (1982).

67. Gregory M. Herek, *Myths about Sexual Orientation: A Lawyer's Guide to Social Science Research,* 1 LAW & SEXUALITY 133, 172 (1991).

68. The eight myths Herek seeks to debunk are: (1) homosexuality is a form of mental illness; (2) because of social stigma, lesbians and gay men are more likely than heterosexuals to manifest low self-esteem, to be depressed, or to be suicidal; (4) homosexuals are more likely than heterosexuals to molest children sexually; (5) being exposed to a homosexual parent or role model is likely to have negative effects on a child; (6) lesbians and gay men are not capable of sustained relationships; (7) gay people are not a minority group; and (8) gay people are detrimental to the morale, discipline, or efficiency of an organization or institution.

69. *See* James M. Donovan, *A Philosophical Ground for Gays' Rights: "We Must Learn What Is True in Order to Do What Is Right,"* 4 GEORGE MASON UNIVERSITY CIVIL RIGHTS LAW JOURNAL 1 (1993-94).

70. NATHAN GLAZER, THE LIMITS OF SOCIAL POLICY 155 (1988).

71. *See* Franz Boas, The Mind of Primitive Man (1916).

72. Margaret Mead, Coming of Age in Samoa (1928).

73. *See* Derek Freeman, Margaret Mead and Samoa: The Making and Unmaking of an Anthropological Myth (1983).

74. The National Institutes of Health first announced its policy encouraging the inclusion of women in research study populations in October 1986. *See* Mark V. Nadel, *Problems in Implementing Policy on Women in Study Populations: Testimony before the House Committee on Energy and Commerce*, U.S. General Accounting Office, June 18, 1990. For a general discussion of sex differences on this issue, *see* Karen Young Kreeger, *Yes, Biologically Speaking, Sex Does Matter*, 16(1) The Scientist 35 (January 7, 2002). A specific example is discussed by Bob Huff, *Sex Differences in Nevirapine Rash and Hepatitis*, 15(1) Treatment Issues: Newsletter of Experimental AIDS Therapies 1 (January 2001).

75. Glazer, *supra* note 70, at 152.

76. Mary L. Tenopyr, *A Scientist-Practitioner's Viewpoint of the Admissibility of Behavioral and Social Scientific Information*, 5(1) Psychology, Public Policy, and Law 194, 197 (1999).

77. Westen, *supra* note 66, at 547.

78. Strickland v. Washington, 644 U.S. 668, 708 (1984) (Marshall, J., dissenting).

79. *See* Laura Mansnerus, *During a Trial, Should Judges Let Sleeping Lawyers Lie?* New York Times, November 5, 2000, at D7. *See also* James M. Donovan, Burdine v. Johnson, *To Sleep Perchance to Get a New Trial: Presumed Prejudice Arising from Sleeping Counsel*, 47 Loyola Law Review 1585 (2001).

80. *See* Marc Lacey & Raymond Bonner, *Reno Troubled by Death Penalty Statistics*, New York Times, September 13, 2000, at A17.

81. *See* Timothy Egan, *War on Crack Retreats, Still Taking Prisoners*, New York Times, February 28, 1999, at A1.

82. *See id.*

83. *See, e.g.*, Andrew J. McClung, *Poetry in Commotion:* Katko v. Briney *and the Bards of First-Year Torts*, 74 Oregon Law Review 823 (1995), in which the celebrated case of *Katko v. Briney*, 183 N.W. 2d 657 (Iowa 1971) is discussed with reference to the possibilities that the plaintiff's attractiveness may have led to a jury verdict in his favor.

    In *Katko*, the plaintiff broke into the defendants' abandoned farmhouse to steal old fruit jars that were considered to be antiques. He was injured when a spring gun that the defendants had rigged to protect their property discharged. Although he was convicted for breaking and entering, he sued the defendants for battery and won a $30,000 verdict, $10,000 of which was for punitive damages. Although property professors use this case to illustrate that the law values people more than property, the author notes that Marvin Katko "had penetrating blue eyes, strong nose, dimpled chin, great head of hair, full lips hinting of a seductive smile," and that the defendant farmers were "not very attractive people." *Id.* at 827. The author further notes that "[Judge] Learned Hand said 'juries are not leaves swayed by every breath' but perhaps a wink from Marvin Katko's limpid eyes to the all-female jury was enough to do the trick." *Id.* at 828.

84. Gordon L. Patzer, The Physical Attractiveness Phenomena 61-62 (1985).

85. *See id.* at 63.

86. Henry F. Dobyns, *Taking the Witness Stand*, in Applied Anthropology in America 366, 368 (Elizabeth M. Edy & William L. Partridge eds., 2d ed., 1987).

87. Faigman, *supra* note 58, at 102-103, 120-121. *See also* Jesse Choper et al., *supra* note 63, at 1172-1173.

88. 406 U.S. 205 (1972).

89. *Id.* at 212.

90. Lawrence Rosen, *The Anthropologist as Expert Witness,* 79 AMERICAN ANTHROPOLO-GIST 555, 564 (1977).
91. *Yoder,* 406 U.S. at 235.
92. Frye v. United States, 293 F. 1013, 1014 (D.C. Cir. 1923).
93. In the words of the later *Daubert,* "The *Frye* test has its origin in a short and cita-tion-free 1923 decision concerning the admissibility of evidence derived from a sys-tolic blood pressure deception test, a crude precursor to the polygraph machine." Daubert v. Merrell Dow Pharmaceuticals, 509 U.S. 579, 585 (1993).
94. *See* FREEMAN, *supra* note 73.
95. 509 U.S. 579 (1993).
96. Extensive background information about the *Daubert* case, and its significance for the use of scientific evidence in federal courts, is available in KENNETH R. FOSTER & PETER W. HUBER, JUDGING SCIENCE: SCIENTIFIC KNOWLEDGE AND THE FEDERAL COURTS (1999).
97. *Daubert,* 509 U.S. at 589.
98. FEDERAL RULES OF EVIDENCE 107 (St. Paul, MN: West, 1998).
99. An interesting question, one that we do not explore here, concerns whether or not the judge is free to undertake independent research to "bone up" on specialized knowledge pertinent to a pending case. Monahan and Walker argue in the affirma-tive: "as courts are free to find legal precedents that the parties have not presented, they should also have the power to locate social science research through indepen-dent investigation." John Monahan & Laurens Walker, *Social Authority: Obtaining, Evaluating, and Establishing Social Science in Law,* 134(3) UNIVERSITY OF PENNSYLVA-NIA LAW REVIEW 477, 497 (1986). Adam J. Siegel adopts the opposite position: "when judges take it upon themselves to independently research the scientific and tech-nological facts in dispute, the parties are no longer afforded the unbiased and impartial gatekeepers that our system both guarantees and depends upon." Adam J. Siegel, *Setting Limits on Judicial Scientific, Technical, and Other Specialized Fact-Finding in the New Millennium,* 86 CORNELL LAW REVIEW 167, 214 (2000).

    The following describes one famous case for which the judge engaged in the kind of independent fact-finding here contested:

    > Justice Blackmun, in preparing to write *Roe* [*v. Wade*], did his own research on the subject by going to the Mayo Clinic in Rochester, Minnesota, to search for scientific and medical data upon which to base the opinion. During the summer before the Court considered *Roe,* he spent two weeks at the clinic virtually clos-eted and speaking to no one about what he was doing. Two things are unusual about Blackmun's initiative: first, Justice Blackmun used extralegal data, and second, he did much of the research himself. The trimester system on which Blackmun based his opinion is unique to his reasoning.

    ERICKSON & SIMON, *supra* note 39, at 41.
100. *Daubert,* 509 U.S. at 593.
101. The beginnings of a small cottage industry can be detected in the efforts to identify additional *Daubert* admissibility factors. The attorney who argued the *Daubert* case before the Supreme Court has offered a fifth:

    > That factor, which I call the "prestige" factor, is whether the expert is not merely minimally credentialed, but instead a highly-placed, highly-regarded specialist in the field about which he or she is testifying. I suggest that judges have neither the competence nor the right to bar the testimony of "prestigious" expert witnesses.

    Michael H. Gottesman, *Admissibility of Expert Testimony after* Daubert: *The "Pres-tige" Factor,* 43 EMORY LAW JOURNAL 867, 869 (1994).

    Suggested by another author are the criterion of explanatory power and the requirement that the scientific theory not "be self-contradictory or logically ill-formed." *See* Michael Freeman, *Law and Science: Science and Law, in* Science in Court 5 (Michael Freeman & Helen Reece eds., 1998).

102. *See* Herbert Barry III, *Description and Uses of the Human Relations Area File, in* 2 Handbook of Cross-Cultural Psychology 445-478 (Harry C. Triandis & John W. Berry eds., 1980).

103. *See* J.W.M. Whiting & I.L. Child, Child Training and Personality (1953).

104. By some accounts the shortfall is greater even than we have depicted it here. Kim Hopper relates Michael Harner's claim that anthropology was "90 percent hearsay." Kim Hopper, *Research Findings as Testimony: A Note on the Ethnographer as Expert Witness*, 49(2) Human Organization 110, 111 (1990). Legal proceedings generally take a dim view of hearsay evidence. The thrust of Hopper's article is not to dispute this characterization of ethnography, but rather to show the legal exceptions that would render admissible hearsay evidence packaged as anthropological data.

105. *See, e.g.*, Allison Morse, *Social Science in the Courtroom: Expert Testimony and Battered Women*, 21 Hamline Law Review 287 (1998). She agrees that social sciences cannot meet the *Daubert* standard. This limitation is not a major problem, however, because *Daubert's* holding pertains only to "scientific" testimony. Rule 702 is broader than this: its scope covers "scientific, technical, or other specialized knowledge." The social sciences are not "scientific" in this sense, and thus fall outside the confines of *Daubert* but within the province of Rule 702. Whatever the merits of this argument at the time Morse wrote, further developments have rendered it moot. *Kumho Tire Co. v. Carmichael*, 526 U.S. 137 (1999), announced that "the reliability standard [of] *Daubert* for scientific evidence applies also to other [702] technical knowledge." Lori A. Van Daele, Logerquist v. McVey: Frye, Daubert, *or "Nonscientific" Expert Testimony*, 42 Jurimetrics 85, 87 (2001).

The narrowness of the four *Daubert* factors, if strictly applied, has also been noted by Gottesman, *supra* note 101, at 875:

> The lower courts are going to find these factors inapposite in many cases.... Consider, for example, psychiatric testimony in criminal cases. Are psychiatrists' assessments of the mental capacity of a defendant at the time of the crime "testable" or "falsifiable" or "refutable"? Plainly not. Can we determine the "error rate" of psychiatric opinion, or utilize standards to control the technique's operation? Again, plainly not.
> But for the "ordinarily" qualifier, the Court's opinion read literally would dictate the end of the receipt of psychiatric and psychological testimony in federal courts.

106. Daniel W. Shuman & Bruce D. Sales, *The Impact of* Daubert *and Its Progeny on the Admissibility of Behavioral and Social Science Evidence*, 5(1) Psychology, Public Policy, and Law 3, 4-5 (1999). *But see* Mark Hansen, *Admissions Tests*, 87 ABA Journal 28 (February 2001) ("Federal judges today are more likely to exclude expert testimony in civil trials than they were less than a decade ago...."). Any rise in *Daubert* exclusions of experts in civil trials might seem drastic, however, because "until 1984, *Frye* was never used to exclude an expert in a civil case." Ned Miltenberg, *Out of the Fire and into the* Fryeing Pan, 37(3) Trial 19 (2001).

107. *Id*. at 7-8.

108. *See* Mark Hansen, *Dusting for* Daubert, 86 ABA Journal 20 (December 2000).

109. John Monahan & Laurens Walker, *Social Authority: Obtaining, Evaluating, and Establishing Social Science in Law*, 134(3) University of Pennsylvania Law Review 477, 483 (1986). This distinction was proposed in 1942 by Kenneth Culp Davis.

110. *Id*. at 488.

111. *Id*. at 490.

112. *Id*. at 491.

113. *Id*. at 494.

114. Monahan & Walker, *supra* note 109, at 499.

115. *Id.* at 502.
116. *Id.* at 504.
117. *Id.* at 510 note 117.
118. Taryn F. Goldstein, *Cultural Conflicts in Court: Should the American Criminal Justice System Formally Recognize a "Cultural Defense"?* 99 DICKINSON LAW REVIEW 141, 143 (1994) (quoting John C. Lyman, *Cultural Defense: Viable Doctrine or Wishful Thinking?* 9 CRIMINAL JUSTICE JOURNAL 87 (1986)).
119. 679 A.2d 81 (Me. 1996).
120. Nancy A. Wanderer & Catherine R. Connors, *Culture and Crime: Kargar and the Existing Framework for a Cultural Defense*, 47 BUFFALO LAW REVIEW 829, 838 (1999).
121. *Id.*
122. *Id.* at 849.
123. Deirdre Evans-Pritchard & Alison Dundes Renteln, *The Interpretation and Distortion of Culture: A Hmong "Marriage by Capture" Case in Fresno, California*, 4(1) SOUTHERN CALIFORNIA INTERDISCIPLINARY LAW JOURNAL 1, 9 (1994).
124. *Id.* at 8-9.
125. *Id.* at 31.
126. Goldstein, *supra* note 118, at 150.
127. *See generally* BETTINA SHELL-DUNCAN & YLVA HERNLUND (EDS.), FEMALE "CIRCUMCISION IN AFRICA: CULTURE, CONTROVERSY, AND CHANGE (2000).
128. FGM is a federal crime under 18 U.S.C. § 116 (2000); *see also* Celia W. Dugger, *New Law Bans Genital Cutting In United States*, NEW YORK TIMES, October 12, 1996, at A1.
129. Goldstein, *supra* note 118, at 151.
130. *Id.*
131. *Id.*
132. Alison Dundes Renteln, *A Justification of the Cultural Defense as Partial Excuse*, 2 REVIEW OF LAW AND WOMEN'S STUDIES 437, 469 (1993).
133. Renteln, a convincing proponent of the culture defense, recognizes that some believe that the culture defense should not be available when the victim is not from the defendant's culture. She does not take a clear position on this issue, claiming that "it is not obvious why the cultural background of the victim should matter." *Id.* at 496. Presumably, this is because the criminal law is only concerned with the defendant's intent.
134. Stephen J. Morse, *The Misbegotten Marriage of Soft Psychology and Bad Law*, 14(6) LAW AND HUMAN BEHAVIOR 595, 602 (1990).
135. *See* Renteln, *supra* note 132, at 490.
136. *See* Richard A. Shweder, *Moral Maps, "First World" Conceits, and the New Evangelists*, *in* CULTURE MATTERS: HOW VALUES SHAPE HUMAN PROGRESS 158, 162 (Lawrence E. Harrison & Samuel P. Huntington eds., 2000).
137. Orlando Patterson, *Taking Culture Seriously: A Framework and an Afro-American Illustration*, *in* CULTURE MATTERS: HOW VALUES SHAPE HUMAN PROGRESS 203, 204-205 (Lawrence E. Harrison & Samuel P. Huntington eds., 2000).
138. The limitations of the concept of "culture" are recognized, and possible solutions discussed, in THE RELEVANCE OF CULTURE (Morris Freilich ed., 1989).
139. "Insanity" is technically a legal concept, not a psychiatric one, which instead diagnoses *specific* disorders. The legal standard is called the "M'Naghten rule," which states that

> a defendant is not entitled to a "defence on the ground of insanity" unless at the time he "was labouring under such a defect of reason, from disease of the mind, as not to know the nature and quality of the act he was doing; or, if he did know it, that he did not know he was doing what was wrong." This is the so-called "right-wrong" test of insanity, or the "M'Naghten rule."

RONALD N. BOYCE & ROLLIN M. PERKINS, CRIMINAL LAW AND PROCEDURE 739-740 (8th ed., 1999). This standard for insanity is not a medical diagnosis, which no longer recognizes "insanity" as an independent category.

140. *See generally* Renteln, *supra* note 132.

141. Not everyone agrees that the culture defense deserves a place in the American legal system. *See* Alice J. Gallin, Note, *The Cultural Defense: Undermining the Policies against Domestic Violence*, 35 BOSTON COLLEGE LAW REVIEW 723, 725 (1994) ("cultural defense should not be used because the United States should not allow other cultures, which do not respect individual liberty and equality in the same manner as American culture does, to subvert the value we place on preventing domestic abuse."), *but see* Farah Sultana Brelvi, *"News of the Weird": Specious Normativity and the Problem of the Cultural Defense*, 28 COLUMBIA HUMAN RIGHTS LAW REVIEW 657, 663 (1997) ("the 'cultural defense,' as modified by the problematization by feminist critics, should be allowed by courts in the examination of a subject's individual circumstances—but the dangerous tendency to extrapolate the defense and arrive at generalized conclusions about communities of 'others' must be checked.").

142. The temptation exists to frame culture defenses in terms of preexisting psychiatric defenses. The culture defense then becomes a species of insanity defense. The availability of the insanity defense is a good analogy serving to support the acceptance of a culture defense. The two defenses are structurally identical: the foundation for the defense is extralegal, and its applicability in any specific instance, a legal determination. It is relevant to note that the legal defense of insanity differs significantly from the medical definition of mental incapacity, but psychiatrists are nevertheless often used as expert witnesses in legal insanity cases.

143. *See, e.g.*, Leti Volpp, *Blaming Culture for Bad Behavior*, 12 YALE JOURNAL OF LAW AND THE HUMANITIES 89 (2000); Jefferson M. Fish, *What Anthropology Can Do for Psychology*, 102 AMERICAN ANTHROPOLOGIST 552, 556 (2000).

144. *See* GILBERT HERDT, THE SAMBIA: RITUAL AND GENDER IN NEW GUINEA (1987).

145. *See* RONALD C. SIMONS & CHARLES C. HUGHES, THE CULTURE-BOUND SYNDROMES: FOLK ILLNESSES OF PSYCHIATRIC AND ANTHROPOLOGICAL INTEREST (1985).

Chapter Three

THEORETICAL BENEFITS OF ANTHROPOLOGY TO LAW

The culture defense discussed in chapter 2 is not formally available to criminal defendants. "Although the rules of evidence now define relevance broadly enough to permit sympathetic judges to consider culture," they are not required to do so.[1] Where the judge is not sufficiently "sympathetic," the defendant's lawyer may try to introduce the basic components of a culture defense under the guise of some other allowable defense. Renteln offers a list of such preexisting defenses: necessity, duress, self-defense, insanity, diminished capacity and partial responsibility, automatism, provocation, and ignorance of the law/mistake of fact.[2] The success of any particular defense would vary from case to case. She worries, however, about the subtext that results from framing a culture defense in the terms of, say, an insanity defense: "Comparing the logic of immigrants with that of the insane is, at the very least, insulting."[3] Even if advantageous in the short run for serving the immediate tactical needs of a particular defendant, the potential for extended negative consequences should concern us.

The final item on Renteln's list of alternative frames for the culture defense includes religious defenses. Articulating the defense in these terms deflects attention away from the novel claim of a culture defense and converts it into the more familiar terms of the First Amendment, raising the question, "When is a 'culture' a 'religion' for the purposes of the Free Exercise Clause"?[4] Renteln admits that this strategy is unlikely to be very successful. From the *Reynolds* polygamy case through to the *Smith* decision, the United States has readily invoked a belief/action distinction whereby the constitutional guarantees extend to the first

---

Notes for this section begin on page 165.

absolutely but only rarely to the latter. Since by definition a criminal charge requiring the culture defense will fall under the "action" side of this distinction, the Free Exercise protections will usually not apply, making them a poor vehicle by which to import cultural arguments.

This particular effort, despite its poor promise, merits our special attention. Even to ask the question, When is a culture a religion? displays a profound misunderstanding about both culture and religion. If "little has been written about when and whether a 'culture' will be viewed as a 'religion' for the purposes of the Free Exercise Clause,"[5] this could well be because the answer is a flat, Never.

Certainly religion is one component of a culture, although it is rarely possible to claim of a complex culture that it has "a" religion. Even nations in which religion is a predominant focus, such as Iran and Israel, have failed to achieve a religious uniformity that warrants a simple claim of this kind. Alternatively, religion can be an effective conduit of cultural ideals, as is the case with American "civil religion." But by no meaningful construal are "culture" and "religion" ever to be understood as synonyms.

This misunderstanding segues into the second phase of our analysis of the asserted relationship of balanced reciprocity between anthropology and law: the respective *theoretical* contribution made by each. Concepts such as "religion" and "culture" are abstract categories serving as the elemental units of intellectual reasoning and argument. Some of these categories of thought are indigenous to a particular specialty. Examples from law might include "tort," "crime," and "contract." Law also uses categories originating in other disciplines. "Culture" and "religion" are examples of this latter kind. Anthropological work brings clarity to these and many similar categories and concepts, which are then imported into legal thinking.

The theoretical benefit bestowed by anthropology onto law that we will highlight is that of conceptual clarification. We shall closely inspect two such cases. First, what, exactly, *is* "religion"? Although a category of considerable constitutional importance in American law, the referent of the term is surprisingly obscure. Where can (or should) the law look to identify the essential elements of members of this category? Second, we examine the concept of the "human right." Contemporary legal philosophy asserts that the "right" should be treated as a primal element of legal thinking. Not all rights are the same, however. Much has been made in past decades of the "human right." As anthropology is the study of what it is to be "human," the legal idea of the "human right" is necessarily parasitic on the outcome of that anthropological inquiry. These terms may not be as easily paired as some might hope.

What is "Religion"?

The Legal Definition of "Religion"

We examine first the way the term and concept of "religion" has been considered by the courts.[6] This section reviews chronologically the forays into this topic by the Supreme Court.

Reynolds through Ballard, 1878-1944: From Theism to Sincerity

No one can doubt the special place that religion occupies in the American constitutional system. This stature is guaranteed by the First Amendment of the United States Constitution, which reads in relevant part: "Congress shall make no law respecting an establishment of religion, or prohibiting the free exercise thereof."[7] The first half of the sentence is referred to as the *Establishment Clause*, and the second is the *Free Exercise Clause*.

Under the Establishment Clause, government cannot single out a religion, or even religion per se, over or against another religion or non-religion for favorable treatment.[8] The issue of religion is, with rare exceptions, essentially to be *ignored*. The Free Exercise Clause, on the other hand, requires that great deference is to be paid to religions so that they can be protected from the noxious effects of governmental actions. The exemption of churches from paying some taxes, and the right of conscientious objectors to decline induction into the armed services are examples of privileges extended to religions so that baneful government interference can be minimized. The Free Exercise Clause requires, in essence, that religions be specially isolated so that their interests can be protected. Already the reader should detect the inherent tension between these two constitutional commandments. For our limited purposes, we observe only that the operation of the clauses presumes "religion" can be reliably identified so that it can be either ignored or protected as the situation warrants.

The U.S. Supreme Court's first attempt to clarify the term "religion" was in a case discussed in the first chapter, *Reynolds v. United States*,[9] which upheld the criminalization of Mormon polygamy. In *Reynolds*, the Court observed that "the word 'religion' is not defined in the Constitution. We must go elsewhere, therefore, to ascertain its meaning, and nowhere more appropriately, we think, than to the history of the times in the midst of which the provision was adopted."[10]

For this guidance the Court resorted to the reconstructed intentions of the Framers of the Constitution, keeping with the common but not universal position that "a word should be defined as it was understood by the legislators who enacted it."[11] Unfortunately, there is no clear idea what the Framers meant when they used the word. The *Reynolds* Court took judicial notice of the intellectual emphasis on duty, stating that each man is best able to judge his duty to, and relationship with, the Supreme Being for himself.[12] Still, religion for these eighteenth-century men was inevitably theistic. Theism, the belief in supernatural entities, could be extrapolated as the constitutionally necessary element that qualified a set of beliefs as being a "religion."

This implicit theistic requirement was made explicit twelve years later in *Davis v. Beason*,[13] another Mormon polygamy case. Yet a third polygamy case, *The Late Corporation of the Church of Jesus Christ of Latter-day Saints v. United States*[14] went further still. Here the Court depicted polygamy as "a crime against the laws, and abhorrent to the sentiments and feelings of the civilized world."[15] The novel conclusion in this case was not that this characterization, if true, rendered polygamy a religious act which the state could justifiably regulate; that had been the argument in *Reynolds*. The new claim of *Late Corporation* was that such a "barbarous" practice could not, by its very nature, be religious at all. Hence the defendant could not appeal to the Religion Clauses of the First Amendment for protection. Religion, according to the Court, was necessarily not merely theocentric, but also "enlightened." Presumably "primitive religion" would have been adjudged an oxymoron.

By the early decades of this century, religious diversity in the United States had increased beyond Mormonism, multiplying the claims for religious protections under the Constitution. The next significant opportunity to shape the legal idea of "religion" arose in *United States v. Ballard*,[16] in which the defendants, accused of mail fraud, swore that they communicated with spiritual entities such as Jesus and George Washington. Through such communication they claimed to be able to cure otherwise incurable diseases. The jury was instructed to address solely whether the defendants had used the sect to defraud their followers of money, or whether they themselves "honestly and in good faith" believed their own stated doctrine.[17] The Court noted that only in the first instance could the defendants be found guilty of mail fraud.

The jury convicted the defendants, but the circuit court later reversed the defendants' conviction, holding that because the defendants' beliefs were a material element of the indictment, it was an error for the lower court to withhold from the jury the issue of the truth of those beliefs. The Supreme Court reversed again on the grounds that religious beliefs could not be examined during a criminal trial to ascertain their truth or falsity.[18] If such inquiry were allowed, the Court reasoned, then "little indeed would be left of religious freedom."[19] Instead, courts should gauge *only* whether individuals are sincere in their beliefs. Even "rank heresy," sincerely believed, could be religious.[20] *Ballard* thus "significantly undermined the view expressed in *Davis* ...

that beliefs that 'offend the common sense of [Christian] mankind' are not religious."[21]

From 1878 to 1944, then, the earlier substantive definition of religion as enlightened theism had transformed into the psychological criterion of sincere belief. This change was sufficient to eliminate the element of "enlightened"; the next series of cases would shed the element of theism altogether.

KAUTEN THROUGH *SEEGER*, 1943-1965: THE CONSCIENTIOUS OBJECTOR CASES

Characterizing the second phase of the attempt to arrive at a legal definition of "religion" are the challenges to the drafts of the Second World War and the Vietnam War. The text of the 1940 Selective Training and Service Act exempted any person from military service who "by reason of religious training and belief" objected to "war in any form."[22] The lower courts disagreed over how to construe this language. *United States v. Kauten*[23] concluded first that atheism did not qualify a person for a draft exemption. Religious beliefs objecting to *all* wars are different from beliefs that are political objections to *particular* wars,[24] and presumably Kauten's atheistic beliefs fell into the latter category.

In reaching this result, *Kauten* appended an epistemological requirement to *Ballard*'s psychological standard of sincere belief. Religion is not delimited by reason and logic, but must go beyond them into the realm of "faith."

> Religious belief arises from a sense of the inadequacy of reason as a means of relating the individual to his fellow-men and to his universe.... It is a belief finding expression in a conscience which categorically requires the believer to disregard elementary self-interest and to accept martyrdom in preference to transgressing its tenets.[25]

Any belief meeting these two criteria would fulfill, in the *Kauten* court's estimate, the definition of the "religion" intended by the Selective Service and Training Act.

Congress responded to these debates by revising the language of the Selective Service Act to include its own definition of "religious training and belief" to mean an "individual's belief in relation to a Supreme Being involving duties superior to those arising from any human relation, but does not include essentially political, sociological, or philosophical views or a merely personal moral code."[26] Many cases challenged the apparent requirement that only believers in a theistic God could claim the religious exemption to the military draft,[27] a requirement that arguably conflicted with the Constitution's Establishment Clause.

With such confusion prevailing in the lower courts, it was only a matter of time before the Supreme Court would find it necessary to resolve the debate. In *Torcaso v. Watkins*[28] the Court determined, for the first time, that religions are not necessarily theistic by definition. Torcaso had been denied a Maryland government appointment because he refused to declare, as that state's constitution required, that he believed in the existence of God. The Supreme Court sided with Torcaso and found this requirement unconstitutional. In this decision the Court observed that "among religions in this country, which do not teach what would be considered a belief in the existence of God ... are Buddhism, Taoism, Ethical Culture, Secular Humanism, and others."[29] This recognition of nontheistic religions was not binding because it was only dicta in a footnote. (Dicta is language in a decision that is not essential to the legal holding, however interesting or powerful it may be rhetorically. Not being part of the holding, dicta has no binding precedential significance, although it can suggest how a court would likely rule on a case in which that point was of central concern.)

The binding precedent severing religion from theism came four years later in *United States v. Seeger*.[30] In *Seeger*, another conscientious objector case, the Supreme Court faced the predicament of either finding section 6(j) of the Military Act unconstitutional for unevenly treating religions, or construing the section to encompass the newly asserted nontheistic breadth of the key term "religion." The Court chose the latter route. The *Ballard* standard of "sincere belief" was narrowed to include only those beliefs that are structurally equivalent to the clearly theistic beliefs of devout adherents to traditional theistic religions.[31] The Court suggests that devout belief in a God occupies specific coordinates within a person's mental space. *Whatever* belief-set resides at these coordinates is parallel to theism and thereby judged "religious."

In support of this decision the Court cited Protestant theologian Paul Tillich's writings on the "ultimate concern." For Tillich, concern about something is more than mere involvement with certain social issues; rather, interests that cause great anxiety are those for which we hold true concern and from which we form the foundation for religious belief.[32] What "concerns one ultimately becomes holy. The awareness of the holy is awareness of the presence of the divine, namely of the content of our ultimate concern."[33] That which is holy to an individual—that which is his religion, his ultimate concern—is completely independent of any specific content of that belief. *Any* statement of belief can be either secular or religious, depending only upon its significance to the speaker. A claimed belief in God would be religious *only* if that belief was an ultimate concern.

The "ultimate concern" standard provides philosophical and theological substance to the "willingness to 'accept martyrdom'" standard suggested earlier by *Kauten*. Jesse Choper, for one, thinks little of Tillich's equation between religion and ultimate concern. He concludes that Tillich's theories are too sophisticated for judges and lawyers.[34] Instead, Choper advocates the regressive position that only beliefs in "phenomenon of extratemporal consequences" should trigger judicial consideration of Free Exercise claims.[35] In other words, he would redirect *Seeger*'s attention away from the believer and back toward what is claimed to be believed, as had been required by *Davis*. He freely admits, and is singularly undisturbed by, the fact that his scheme would exclude many groups currently protected by the Religion Clauses, such as Deists and Universalists.[36] Choper overlooks that the constitutional right at issue lies with the individual to believe, and not with the thing to be believed.

This period from 1943 to 1965 thus began with an understanding of religion as a sincere but theistic belief. At its end, the Court had characterized the object of such belief not by its content but by its unique psychological positioning within the individual. Theism may be a prototypical or modal form of such positioned beliefs, but it no longer claimed a monopoly over them.

YODER TO THE PRESENT

Had the Court gone too far? Did the Justices come to regret the expansive definition they had assigned to "religion" in *Seeger*? Given what came afterwards, we could reasonably believe so.

The next significant case in this history is one we reviewed in chapter 2, *Wisconsin v. Yoder*,[37] in which an exemption from a state compulsory school attendance statute was granted to the Amish. Although the Amish won their case and received the exemption, the standard required of them was much stricter than might have been expected in a post-*Seeger* environment. The Court stated that the Religion Clauses of the First Amendment required something more than the mere beliefs of a Thoreau, because such a loose standard was contrary to the concept of ordered liberty.[38]

What is puzzling about the use by the Court of Thoreau as a counterexample is that under *Seeger* his beliefs undoubtedly would have been deemed "religious," at least had he been seeking conscientious objector status. Yet in *Yoder* the argument is not that Thoreau's religious beliefs are insufficient to defeat a compelling governmental interest, but rather that they are not religion at all.[39]

Instead of the psychological structural approach of *Seeger*, *Yoder* favors the requirement that only those religions with specific organizational or historical dimensions warranted constitutional protection.[40] We repeat here from chapter 2 the relevant words of this decision:

Aided by a history of three centuries as an identifiable religious sect and a long history as a successful and self-sufficient segment of American society, the Amish in this case have convincingly demonstrated the sincerity of their religious beliefs, the interrelationship of belief with their mode of life, the vital role that belief and daily conduct play in the continued survival of Old Order Amish communities and their religious organization, and the hazards presented by the State's enforcement of a statute generally valid as to others.[41]

Whatever the merits of this approach, it incurs high costs. Steven Collier is a strong advocate of the institutional requirement, so we turn to his arguments as a foil.

Collier worries about the many ordinary religious believers who attend services and profess religion without being prepared to die for their faith, contrary to what might be expected of believers of *Seeger*'s "ultimate concerns," and as had been explicitly required by *Kauten*. Ordinary believers, because their religion is not uncompromising enough to qualify as an ultimate concern, would fall outside the *Seeger* definition of religion.[42]

Frankly, if correct, we have no philosophical objection to that outcome. In our view, ordinary (that is to say: weak, extrinsic, convenient, thoughtless) believers may not warrant First Amendment protections. A case from the D.C. Circuit seems to support our position.[43] A lawyer appealed his conviction for violating the "Baby Broker Act" on the grounds that he should have been granted a continuance because the trial extended into his Sabbath. Because "he, a member of the (Reform or 'liberal') Jewish faith, was forced to proceed after sundown on a Friday," his right to religious freedom was violated.[44] When dismissing this objection, the court observed that the defendant was in the habit of going into his office and working on Saturdays. "The religious view that Dobkin professed was not important enough to him to practice, and it was therefore considered by the court as not important enough to warrant protection. If a person does not practice what he professes, he cannot invoke it to protect his conduct."[45]

Unless religious form is to take precedence over religious substance, one's right to go to church merely for social or extrinsic reasons is of a lower order than the same churchgoing behavior for intrinsic motives of "ultimate concern." What Collier identifies as a reductio ad absurdum is for us a tolerable, and maybe even desirable, result. The only reason why we might hesitate to adopt this policy relates to the problem of implementation, not of outcome. Who is to make the determination of whether a religious belief is extrinsic or intrinsic? But since the Supreme Court has already allowed the question of religious sincerity to be submitted to the jury, perhaps the question of motivation is not beyond the ability of a court also to judge.

In any event, while concerned to protect the casually religious, Collier clearly denies protections to "individuals with unique, personal religious beliefs."[46] Under his scheme, the "ordinary, nonmartyr religious believers" are protected, but Jesus the Christ as religious innovator is not.[47] If a choice must be made, religious innovators are more in need of constitutional protections than are mechanical adherents to conventional creeds. The contrary outcome from *Yoder*'s institutional requirement for legal status as a "religion" seems to us to be the truly absurd one.

From this perspective, *Yoder* is a disappointing and confusing step backwards from the more flexible and relevant standard of *Seeger*. It was also the last significant pronouncement from the U.S. Supreme Court on this question of what constitutes a "religion."

Whereas the Supreme Court fears to rule definitively, the lower courts have been more daring. We review here only two of the more interesting positions. The first set of cases questions whether something could be a religion *despite* the believer's protestations to the contrary, or, alternatively, whether it could not be a religion despite the believer's adamant assertions in the affirmative. Can persons be wrong in their own assessments about their religious beliefs?

Apparently so. *Malnak v. Maharishi Mahesh Yogi*[48] has the unique distinction of being "the first appellate court decision ... that has concluded that a set of ideas constitutes a religion over the objection and protestations of secularity by those espousing those ideas."[49] The issue at bar was whether the teaching of transcendental meditation in the New Jersey public schools was an unconstitutional establishment of religion. The Third Circuit decided in the affirmative, even though the members of the program denied that it was a religion. Judge Adams took this opportunity to offer "three useful indicia that are basic to our traditional religions" which should be present in any contested case: (1) the nature of the ideas in question; (2) the element of comprehensiveness; and (3) any formal, external, or surface signs that may be analogized to accepted religions such as rituals and organizational structure.[50]

This same circuit employed these indicia to conclude that the American Christian Movement for Life ("MOVE") was *not* a religion, despite the arguments of the adherents to the contrary. *Africa v. Pennsylvania*[51] considered the demand by a prisoner that he be given a special diet of only raw foods as required by his beliefs. Because the court found these beliefs not to be religious, his request was denied. This decision was justified first by the fact that the organization lacked a "functional equivalent of the Ten Commandments," thus failing the first criterion, and second by the fact that if MOVE qualified on the second element of comprehensiveness, so too would vegetarianism.[52]

Which beliefs are religious is, according to *Malnak*, a conclusion to be judicially determined and not a brute fact to be asserted by the defendant and conceded by the court. Judge Adams stated that "the question of the definition of religion for [F]irst [A]mendment purposes is one for the courts, and is not controlled by the subjective perceptions of the believers."[53] This position seems to be precisely contrary to that of *Seeger*, which held that the status of religion is entirely a subjective determination based upon the hierarchy of beliefs held by that particular person.

The second of our remaining observations concerns the treatment of nontraditional religions. Although couched in language that presumes to address "religion" in the generic sense, the heavy reliance upon Christianity as a prototypical religion to which others must be analogized disadvantages other religious traditions. For example, in an effort to find concrete solutions to practical administrative problems, the Internal Revenue Service (IRS) constructed a fourteen-point test that would determine whether an organization was sufficiently religious so as to be able to claim tax exemptions. The IRS expected a church to have: (1) a distinct legal existence; (2) a recognized creed and form of worship; (3) a definite and distinct ecclesiastical government; (4) a formal code of doctrine and discipline; (5) a distinct religious history; (6) a membership not associated with any other church or denomination; (7) an organization of ordained ministers; (8) ordained ministers selected after completing prescribed studies; (9) a literature of its own; (10) established places of worship; (11) regular congregations; (12) regular religious services; (13) Sunday schools for religious instruction of the young; and (14) schools for the preparation of its ministers.[54]

The complaints of several critics that "each of these criteria is fundamentally flawed"[55] are demonstrably valid. The list probably leaves "no room for unrestricted or loosely structured religious societies, such as the Society of Friends (Quakers) or the Christian Scientists, who undoubtedly enjoy the protection of the First Amendment Religion Clause."[56] Of particular concern to anthropologists is how religious forms likely to be encountered in the field are treated by such a list. For example, Brazilian Candomblé[57] fails on at least eight of these measures,[58] meaning that a *terreiro* (a Candomblé cult house that serves as the center for ritual activity and repository of its spiritual energies, or *axé*) is presumptively not a church—and perhaps, implicitly, that Candomblé would not be a "real" religion as far as the IRS is concerned. This condescension would be censurable but not serious so long as these nontraditional religious forms remained in their indigenous contexts. But they all eventually find their way onto American soil, where real conflicts can result.

Lest we be accused of baseless paranoia, in support of this pessimistic conclusion we point out that as recently as 1980 the federal
courts were called upon to decide whether or not Haitian *voudon* was a
religion. Although clearly wishing to rule in the negative, the Fourth Circuit could only decide that "based on the record presented, we cannot
conclude that Voodoo is not a religion."[59] It would be another decade
before the Supreme Court conceded that Santería, a religion related to
both *voudon* and Candomblé, is inarguably a religion.[60]

This review of the attempt to explicate a legal definition of "religion" could be much extended. Enough has been offered to support the
following conclusions. Despite initial pronouncements to the contrary,
religion is necessarily neither Christian, nor theistic, nor "enlightened."
Beyond this negative result little consensus exists. Religion is at times a
subjective psychological status, at others an objective historical and
organizational entity. Nontraditional religions continue to be disadvan-
taged, probably due more to the general population's unfamiliarity with
them than to any concerted attempt to oppress them. We turn now to
examine how anthropology has tackled this same problem.

The Anthropological Definition of "Religion"

Kent Greenawalt states optimistically that "what is religious for the law
is [not] widely at variance with what otherwise counts as religion."[61] If
true, then the anthropological definition should approximate the legal
definition. Like law, anthropology has its own motivation to control the
term through strict definition. If the goal of a scientific anthropology is
to distill from data cross-culturally generalizable conclusions, then the
variables of interest must be restricted sufficiently to allow meaningful
contrasts and comparisons.

The best method to survey and evaluate the proposed anthropological definitions is not as obvious here as it was in the case of law. There,
two principles converge to identify the proper approach: later decisions
overrule earlier ones, and higher courts bind lower courts. The latest rul-
ing from the highest court is, in most instances, the correct rule of law.
No such sorting principles operate in the social sciences. Instead of
being overruled, theories usually fall in and out of favor upon the weight
of evidence (according to Popper) or to social acceptability (Kuhn's
explanation). Few theories are ever permanently removed from consideration, and the accretion of possible responses to any social scientific
question can be considerable.[62] The present problem is no exception.

The literature generated by anthropologists and other social scientists in the effort to define "religion" shares with the legal field a confusing array of positions. Early attempts to bring order to this chaos
have produced several typologies. For instance, James Leuba offered a

three-part classification of intellectual functions, feelings, and will.[63] An unsystematic survey of the members of the Society for the Scientific Study of Religion yielded six broad definitional groups (plus one inde-terminate category): (1) concepts of the supernatural, spiritual, or non-material; (2) concepts regarding ultimates or the ultimate; (3) definitions involving group concepts; (4) ideas concerning the institu-tional and creedal; (5) ideas emphasizing theology; and (6) ideas of interaction between the inner and outer aspects of life.[64]

More typically, writers have found simple dichotomies most useful. Peter Berger distills the predominant approaches into the "*substantively* defined, in terms of the meaning contents of the phenomenon [and the] *functionally* defined, in terms of its place in the social and/or psycho-logical system."[65] This bipartite scheme contrasts concrete with abstract criteria. Concrete criteria, such as the presence of symbols of supernat-uralisms, are those that can be observed in the real world. Abstract cri-teria reside not in the real world for all to see, but in the minds and subjective experiences of the individual. The investigator must infer the presence of abstract criteria from their presumed relationships to real world observables.

Our discussion preserves the tendency to bifurcate, but will make further distinctions within each of the two primary groups. Concrete definitions are comprised of either content or behavioral/performative criteria. Through concrete definitions, the researcher seeks to identify religion by real world observables, such as what people say or do—for example, going to church or joining nominally religious organizations. The two types of abstract definitions are the mental and the functional, and are identified respectively by the person's emotional or psycholog-ical responses to religion (what it does *to* you), or by the needs fulfilled by religion (what it does *for* you).

Concrete Definitions

1. Content Criteria

Content definitions seek to identify religion based upon the presence of specific symbols, usually supernatural powers or entities. The classic example of this type of definition was offered by Sir Edward B. Tylor: "It seems best … to claim, as a minimum definition of religion, the belief in Spiritual Beings."[66] Theisms (the presence of supernatural entities such as gods and spirits) are not the only conceivable content definitions, but they are the most common, and herein the two will be treated synonymously.

Although we discuss Emile Durkheim more extensively in the fol-lowing section, his influential distinction between the sacred and the profane is applicable here. According to Durkheim, all "known religious beliefs, whether simple or complex … presuppose a classification of all

... things ... into two classes or opposed groups ... [the] *profane* and *sacred*."[67] Two readings of "sacred" are possible. First, it can be assigned a content with the result that it functions as a synonym for "supernatural." William Paden seems to use the word in this sense.[68] Durkheim himself would probably eschew this reading.

The second possible reading assigns "sacred" not to the content category, but to an emotional one. According to Marvin Harris's interpretation of Durkheim, "all the basic concepts associated with religion ... originate in the recurrent experience by which human beings feel the force and majesty of the social group."[69] Here the "sacred" is identified by its emotional impact, not by its content, becoming synonymous with Rudolf Otto's "numinous."[70] The word "sacred" is therefore itself an ambiguous concept lacking the clarity necessary to serve in a definition of "religion."

Rodney Stark offers the best defense of content definitions. In an early work, Stark regarded religions as one type of value orientation. Value orientations are "over-arching and sacred systems of symbols, beliefs, values, and practices concerning ultimate meaning which men shape to interpret their world."[71] (We will set to one side the problematic use of the concept of the "sacred" in this definition.) These systems are of two general types (called "perspective realms"), the *religious* and the *humanist*.[72]

It is possible to accept Stark's distinction between the religious and the humanist perspectives while still referring to both as religions, distinguishing between the supernatural and the secular. In a later work, however, Stark expressly argued against this interpretation. The religious and the humanist perspectives, Stark now argued, are not merely variant value orientations; rather, the former is hierarchically superior to the latter.[73]

Introducing new terminology, Stark defined "religion" as "systems of general compensators based on supernatural assumptions."[74] By "compensator," Stark refers to the substitutes "for rewards that are unavailable to many, and for those not directly available to anyone."[75] Immortality is an example of such a reward; it is not directly available to anyone, so we might be willing to accept a compensator in the form of a promise of such an afterlife in exchange for certain behavioral observances. Stark argued further that although not all compensator systems need be supernatural, and thereby religious, those that are not supernatural are demonstrably inferior. Failure to make this distinction by refusing to restrict religion to supernaturalisms, he suggests, prevents one from observing the many patterns of involvement real people have with value orientations. He adamantly asserts that "a religion lacking supernatural assumptions is no religion at all."[76]

If content definitions of "religion" are to be criticized, Stark at least allows the criticism to occur on meaningful ground. The chief weakness of his theory is that by venturing as far as he does, he has left his original emphasis far behind. He intended to claim that real religions are only those with a basis in the supernatural. What he actually asserts is that real religions are *effective* religions; that is, religions that provide the maximum compensators to the believer. *Belief* then becomes the critical variable determining whether a value orientation qualifies as "religion," because it is one's willingness to accept the compensators that renders the religious benefit. Supernaturalisms are important not in themselves, but only because Stark believes they are inherently more believable and acceptable as compensators for postponed rewards, perhaps because they are less refutable.

Most of the phenomena Stark discusses[77] can be accounted for by a continuum of religious efficacy *independent* of any specific content. His defense of the definition of religion as necessarily supernaturalistic fails, not because it is wrong, but because it is superfluous to his more substantial and valuable suggestions. In the context of advocating a content definition, he speaks in terms of functions and beliefs. This transition should immediately suggest the inadequacy of his initial assertion that content is the crucial element distinguishing religion from nonreligion.

2. Behavioral/Performative Criteria

The second type of concrete definition is the behavioral/performative. These definitions identify "religion" by what people do. An emphasis on ritual activity is typical. This attention is understandable because whatever else is entailed by "religion," behaviors are its most salient features to observers. Religion would have little need for legal protection if actions were not a part of its essence. The anthropologist, who is nothing if not an observer, also tends to emphasize behaviors, and thereby to reduce religion down to ritual. As Mary Douglas observed, "Now we have got to the position in which Ritual replaces Religion in anthropologists' writings."[78]

Durkheim again offers an example of this kind of definitional strategy. In his 1915 masterwork, *The Elementary Forms of the Religious Life,* he concludes that in "all history, we do not find a single religion without a Church"—"church" having been previously defined as "common practices."[79] In his ongoing search for a useable definition of "religion," Durkheim would have very much liked to rely on external behavior. Unfortunately, as he rightly points out, ritual, even if it is typical of all religion, does not characterize *only* religion.[80] Looking for something distinctive about religious rituals, Durkheim is drawn toward their compulsory nature. While morality and law are said by Durkheim to compel obligatory *practices*, religious rituals demand

obligatory *beliefs*:[81] "phenomena held to be religious consist in obligatory beliefs, connected with clearly defined practices which are related
to given objects of those beliefs."[82]

Durkheim's approach is flawed in much the same way as was
Stark's. In an effort to be thorough, Durkheim takes with one hand
what he has given with the other. He concedes that not all religious
phenomena are of the character he has specified.[83] While he seeks to
minimize individualistic religion when compared to his socially cohesive and obligatory religion, Durkheim does not shirk from naming the
former also a "religion." Indeed, having warned that individualistic religion can be only a "secondary consideration," he amends his definition
so that in "addition, the optional beliefs and practices which concern
similar objects ... will also be called religious phenomena."[84]

The combined effect is that religion for Durkheim consists of those
beliefs and practices, both optional and obligatory, which are directed
toward sacred objects. In other words, any belief, and any practice, so
long as it is directed toward the sacred, is religious. By overspecifica-
tion, Durkheim's defining criteria cancel themselves out, leaving an
unintended emphasis upon the object of religion, the ambiguous and
problematic "sacred."

Like Stark, Durkheim unintentionally changed focus. He states initially that "only the exterior and apparent form of religious phenomena
is immediately accessible to observation; [and that] it is to this therefore
that we must apply ourselves."[85] Applying this method, Durkheim constructs his definition by examining ritual and isolating "obligatoriness"
as its defining attribute. The quality of being obligatory, however, is *not*
"external and apparent," nor is it "immediately accessible to observation." This change in emphasis probably indicates, as it did in the previous section, that the original definitional strategy is ill-conceived.

ABSTRACT DEFINITIONS

1. Mental Criteria

Unlike concrete definitions, abstract criteria do not claim that unmedi-
ated sensory perception can provide the basis for a determination
whether or not one is in the presence of religion. These empirical indicators, such as symbols or behaviors, are important only to the extent
that they signify the operation of unobservable variables and processes.
The first of these abstract types is the mental definition.

Although encompassing a wide variety of elements, mental definitions have in common the assumption that what makes religion "religion" exists in one's mind. The particulars of the definition of course
vary, but they fall into three major categories: the emotional, the cognitive, and the psychodynamic.

(a) Emotions

Foremost among those who regard religion essentially as an emotion are Erich Fromm, who dissects the religious experience into wonder, concern, and an attitude of oneness,[86] and William James, who defined religion as an apprehended "relation to the divine."[87] James clarifies that what is divine is whatever "the individual feels impelled to respond to solemnly and gravely, and neither by a curse nor a jest."[88]

Rudolf Otto's *The Idea of the Holy* epitomizes this strategy of emotion. He attempted to analyze "the *feeling* which remains where the *concept* [of 'religion'] fails."[89] The concept of the deity, he explained, is partly rational, partly irrational. The rational deity usually receives the emphasis because language is designed to convey rational meanings.[90] Hence, "expositions of religious truth in language inevitably tend to stress the 'rational' attributes of God."[91] The core of religion, however, resides not in the rationalizations, but in the ineffable "holy" shorn of its intellectualized content.[92] Otto invented "a special term to stand for 'the holy' *minus* its moral factor or 'moment', and ... minus its rational aspect altogether."[93] For that "special term" he chose *numinous*.

The advantage of emotional definitions such as Otto's is that they underscore the importance that people attach to their religions. Any theorizing that does not allow, much less account for this affective dimension has missed something vital. That lack would correctly qualify as a fatal omission for any proposed definition of religion.

As early as 1912, however, James Leuba isolated the flaw in the emotional approach to defining "religion." "The truth of the matter is ... that each and every human emotion and sentiment may appear in religion, and that no affective experience as such is distinctive of religious life."[94] There exists, in other words, no emotional experience that is evoked only within the religious context. To the extent that this definitional strategy is at all viable, it will depend upon the identification of otherwise mundane emotions in lesser or greater degrees than normally associated with other beliefs or institutions. This kind of precise analysis has thus far been absent in the anthropological literature.

(b) Cognition

The second category under the broad heading of mental definitions is the cognitive, and refers to those propositions in which one "believes," "has faith," or to which one is "committed." While many writers imply the presence of beliefs, few formally advocate belief as the defining element of "religion."[95]

Serious obstacles would frustrate a more common exploitation of belief as the central element distinguishing religion. The most obvious is that were believing or having faith restricted to religion, then other sets formally defined by the social sciences must exclude this variable. This possibility is unlikely. In 1931, Kurt Gödel "showed that [Whitehead and Russell's] *Principia*, or any other system within which arithmetic can be developed, is *essentially incomplete*. In other words, given *any* consistent set of arithmetical axioms, there are true arithmetical statements that cannot be derived from the set."[96] These problematic statements fall outside the system, and must be accepted on a kind of "faith."

Necessary incompleteness is an attribute of any formal system. But since "all sciences other than mathematics are so remote from a complete formalization ... [Gödel's] conclusion remains of little consequence outside mathematics."[97] Yet that degree of formalization is the ideal toward which the sciences aspire (a contested claim, we know, but one that we assert for anthropology nonetheless). The implication is that all such systems necessarily have some degree of a belief component, even if the particular discipline is too underdeveloped to distinguish those theorems that are inherently based on faith from those that simply lack adequate data (that is, the unprovable from the unproven).

Few people today would regard mathematics as a religion simply because it contains inherently unprovable assumptions that must be taken on faith. Any attempt to apportion cultural reality into those parts that necessarily include tenets of faith, and those that do not, must fail since the latter would be an empty set, meaning literally everything is religious.

The most that can be ventured is that, if beliefs are organized hierarchically, religious beliefs are the cognitively superior. Assuming that all beliefs lower in the hierarchy than belief *X* cannot overtly contradict *X* (a rule that, when joined with actual behavior, necessitates concepts such as *cognitive dissonance*, or the ability to entertain simultaneously two or more mutually exclusive propositions), then "religion" is that belief which, by being at the top of the hierarchy, forces every lower belief to conform. This view is perhaps one way of capturing the dimension of "commitment."

(c) Psychodynamics

Like the first two mental definitional strategies, the third type emphasizes the mind-set of the individuals. This strategy does not deny the importance of emotions and beliefs, but instead looks to their underlying psychodynamics for their uniquely religious elements. Sigmund Freud's *The Future of an Illusion* is the prototype for this approach. Freud concluded this essay with his famous statement that religion would "be the universal obsessional neurosis of humanity."[98]

Among anthropologists, Melford Spiro in particular has amassed an impressive body of work in this category. At first glance he might appear to be a classic representative of the content strategy because he defines "religion" as "an institution consisting of culturally patterned interaction with culturally postulated superhuman beings."[99] Spiro credits this emphasis upon a superhuman dimension to the legitimate respect that must be paid to "the criterion of intra-cultural intuitivity; at the least, [the definition] should not be counter-intuitive."[100]

It is unclear whether Spiro's definition passes his own test. According to William Herbrechtsmeier, "the 'superhuman' concept wreaks havoc within the belief system of Buddhism, emphasizing the wrong thing in Mahayana versions and relegating Theraveda schools out of religion altogether, both results going against the grain of 'intracultural intuitivity.'"[101] Even more perplexing is the impact of Spiro's standard on Protestant theologians like Paul Tillich.[102]

Spiro did not arrive at his formulation unmotivated. The psychodynamic edifice he constructs is possible only if religion is restricted to those belief sets professing an acceptance of superhumans. A broader definition would have rendered his explanatory model inadequate.

In attempting to explain "why religious actors believe in the reality of the mythicoreligious world," Spiro first notes the benefits that can flow from participation in the system. He states that "religion is the cultural system *par excellence* by means of which conflict-resolution is achieved [and that it serves as] a highly efficient culturally constituted defense mechanism."[103] Not just any system will elicit the necessary emotional reaction from the participant, however. The cultural system must reflect a "correspondence between the symbols in which cultural doctrines are represented and their representation as beliefs in the minds of social actors."[104] In other words, a match must exist between the institution and some level of the person's psychology. The benefits rendered by participation in the institution motivate the individual to seek out such a match.

Spiro argues that our earliest experiences as helpless infants interacting with seemingly omnipotent parents have developmentally equipped us with a symbolic vocabulary for superhuman beings. This symbolic vocabulary is used later to provide the necessary match between the person and the social institution via the former's projections. He or she will seek out religious institutions whose portrayals of superhuman beings resonate with those early experiences. Cultures with differing modal childrearing practices will therefore tend to have different kinds of god-figures. In some sense, the experience of being a helpless child "causes" religion, or is at least conducive to specific religious forms. Religion is thereby explained, at least in part, as the culturally appropriate outlet for the ambivalent emotions one experiences toward one's parents during infancy and childhood.[105]

There is much that is commendable in the psychodynamic approach. For example, it allows Spiro to predict accurately that "religious beliefs will vary systematically with differences in family (including socialization) systems."[106] This relationship may, however, be merely correlational and not causative: "The weight of the argument supports no conclusion further than that religion often serves as a matrix within which the displaced fantasies of infantile residues find expression. It is another matter to say that such projections serve an originative function."[107] If the psychodynamics identified by Freud and adopted by Spiro do not, in fact, generate religion, their necessary presence in "religion" is unestablished, rendering their utility as definitional criteria dubious.

2. Functional Criteria

Functional definitions include terms that are reminiscent of emotion or behavior definitions. Despite this apparent similarity, the category differs in that it stresses religion as a solution to a problem, fulfilling some need that, if ignored, would harm the organism.

As a class, functional definitions are "ipsative." An ipsative definition is

> one in which the ... substantive content and label for a social phenomenon are predicated on the basis of a function identified and categorized by the investigator. The investigator categorizes and labels a function, and the function "ipsatizes" the labeling of the phenomenon.... Thus, *whatever* specific substantive content the investigator locates as performing that function is religion.[108]

Any belief-set doing the work of religion *is* religion. As Clifford Geertz points out, even the game of golf can be religious if approached in the right way.[109] This observation, first written in 1966, was given truth in 1972 by the appearance of Michael Murphy's *Golf in the Kingdom*,[110] in which Murphy recounts the metaphysical lessons embodied within golf and as purportedly imparted by a mythical pro he met at a Scottish country club. The New Age spin offered by Murphy is later countered with a specifically Christian interpretation of golf on the December 12, 1997, broadcast of the evangelical *700 Club*. That show featured Wally Armstrong and Veronica Karama, both of whom extolled the transcendent truths hidden in golf. According to Karama, God's truth is the mechanics of the golf swing, while God's grace is the motion of the swing. As with golf, so with anything. There is no limit to what can be drafted to perform the work of religion.

The proper question, then, to ask is, What is the unique religious task? In response, Bronislaw Malinowski writes that "religious faith establishes, fixes, and enhances all valuable mental attitudes, such as reverence for tradition, harmony with environment, courage and confidence in the struggle with difficulties and at the prospect of death."[111] While religion augments positive mental states, its more profound effect is in minimizing the negative ones.[112]

Many cults and rituals embody and maintain anxiety-reducing beliefs. These beliefs are immensely beneficial to the organism.[113] As Clyde Kluckhohn observes, Malinowski's model would explain religious adherents' "unremitting toil and steadfastness of purpose," despite the lack of *obvious* benefits. Those "individuals whose lives and work are ostensibly devoid of reward in the usual sense of the term are nevertheless reinforced and sustained by the gratification that comes from reduction of conscience-anxiety, or guilt."[114]

Although not usually included within the functionalist school, Clifford Geertz's basic position on this issue falls within the ambit of that term as it is used here. Geertz categorizes the conscience-relief definitions as "confidence theories,"[115] and goes on to propound a sophisticated definition of "religion" focusing on the creation of moods through a system of symbols.[116] These moods provide a perception of reality and general order to human existence. In other words, in "religious belief and practice a people's style of life, which Clyde Kluckhohn called their '*design for living*,' is rendered intellectually reasonable."[117] Critical to our argument is that this work should be imperative, and not merely desirable.

Geertz's essay has been acclaimed as "perhaps the most influential, and certainly the most accomplished, anthropological definition of religion to have appeared in the last two decades."[118] Yet despite its intellectual attractiveness, his definition provides a practically useless standard by which to identify religion. Having elaborated at great lengths as to what "religion" is conceptually, and what it does psychologically and socially, Geertz never tells us how to recognize it in the field. In theory, swinging a golf club for one person can be a fulfilling religious experience, but for his partner the same activity is merely a diverting sport. How, then, are we to know whether golfing is or is not "symbolic of transcendent truths" for any particular player?

While not without its limitations, the functional definitional strategy at present seems superior to the alternatives; its shortcomings are ones of practical implementation that might be overcome in the future, and not of internal inconsistency or counterintuitiveness that cannot be eliminated by any amount of future work. In short, the functional definitional strategy is admittedly incomplete, but it shows promise, a claim that cannot be made for the others.

Lessons Learned

We have reviewed in some detail both the legal and anthropological attempts to define "religion," a key term for both these intellectual activities. This section concludes with some brief observations.

First, it is troubling for our long-term objective of effecting mutually profitable relationships between anthropology and law to note that the legal discussions of the definition of "religion" rarely mention the parallel endeavor in any of the social sciences, much less anthropology. The Supreme Court *never* takes notice of this literature, and only a few lower courts seem aware of it. This oversight is unfortunate. If, as claimed earlier, the legal definition of "religion" should not vary too greatly from that generally accepted elsewhere, this can occur only if the law informs itself as to that wider understanding. Since religion is, for anthropology, an explicit object of intense scrutiny, common sense dictates that law should defer to anthropology (and other relevant social sciences) on this issue. That the law is not even aware of these efforts, much less deferential to them, suggests that this goal of mutually beneficial interaction will not be achieved anytime soon, and that therefore "religion" will remain for the law a term of art rather than a reflection of the common understanding, with serious repercussions upon the perceived reasonableness of the law.

Should the law decide to break its self-imposed intellectual isolation, the results of the anthropological attack on this same problem could be enriching. Anthropology can *ratify* the independently evolved legal trend toward a functional, rather than a substantive definition of "religion." However reasonable a result might appear to be in isolation, there would always remain the suspicion that it could be attributed to idiosyncratic disciplinary biases and not to the essential features of the focal phenomenon. A perfectly logical outcome can still be very wrong if the initial premises are flawed. Law can take comfort from the fact that anthropology has also transcended the limitations of the strictly theistic (content) understanding of religion, tending toward the more functional one. In essence, anthropology provides a second sighting of the target concept, allowing an intellectual triangulation of its true dimensions.

Any settled conclusion to this vexing problem will not—cannot—come from law because of the already-noted constraints: law does not itself study religion, and the acceptable legal definition should resemble the extralegal definition.[119] The law can "champion" its favored candidate definition, but the nominations will most credibly come from extralegal sources, particularly anthropology.

What Are "Human Rights"?

Law benefits from an infusion of anthropological thinking on concepts besides religion. Some concepts that appear to be wholly legal in nature will, upon closer scrutiny, reveal themselves to be dependent upon anthropological ideas and research. This section examines one example: the "human right."

The concept of the "human right" lies at the interface between anthropology and law. Each discipline provides one term in the combination, to produce a new idea. Anthropology specializes in the investigation of what it means to be human, while law is specially equipped to articulate the nature of the right. The conjunction of the two generates a powerful, if not unproblematic, category of thought. Our intention here is not to resolve all of the idea's attendant difficulties, but only to demonstrate how anthropological insights (in this case mainly from the subfield of physical anthropology) are required to properly understand the term.

The concept of "human right" is relatively recent, but one that has become quickly entrenched in international law. Prior to World War II, individuals had no standing to bring any kind of claim under international law. If an individual was aggrieved in some fashion and international law did provide a remedy, the state of which that person was a citizen would have to assert that right on behalf of the individual. With the aftermath of World War II and the revealed Nazi atrocities, courts in different countries began to recognize an exception to the previous practice in international law. Thereafter, an individual could assert a cause of action in the courts of a third state for the actions of another state, or one state could prosecute the citizen of another state for crimes committed in yet a third state. It is the theory of the human right that provides the basis for this new legal standing.

As an area of legal practice, human rights are an ongoing concern. But the devil, as they say, is in the details. The unanimity surrounding the general proposition of human rights cracks under any overly specific discussion about what constitutes those human rights, or even more fundamentally, what is the justification for the category in the first place, much less how the rights are to be enforced. Are they, for example, universal, or, as some claim, a projection of ethnocentric assumptions of Western civilization onto other cultures?[120]

The international recognition of human rights has lead to a plethora of new venues in which it is possible to bring a claim.[121] There are two permanent courts, the Inter-American Court of Human Rights and the European Court of Human Rights, as well as three permanent commissions with quasi-juridical powers, including the European Commission on Human Rights, the Inter-American Commission on Human Rights, and the African Commission on Human Rights. Whether the International Criminal Court can become a functioning organization remains to be seen, given the U.S.'s objections to the court's jurisdiction. Additionally, there are several United Nations Committees involved with human rights, including the Committee on Economic, Social and Cultural Rights, the Committee against Torture, and the Human Rights Committee. Many of these courts, commissions, and committees have overlapping jurisdictions with respect to subject matter, and the binding effect of their decisions, rulings, and opinions varies significantly among member and nonmember nations.

Human rights are set apart from other kinds of rights by more than the venues that have been created to enforce them. Paul Sieghart identifies three features that set human rights apart from mundane legal rights. Unlike the latter, human rights are characterized by inherence, inalienability, and equality.[122] We have earlier critiqued the ideal of legal equality (see chapter 1); the emphasis below will be on the attributes of inherence and inalienability.

What Is a "Right"?

To examine this question, we must first clarify the central concept of "right." Americans particularly are prone to use the word "right" with much ease and little thought. As demonstrated long ago by Wesley Newcomb Hohfeld, the term "right" is frequently used when other legal ideas are intended.[123] For instance, when people claim they have a right to such-and-such, they often mean only that they have a privilege to such-and-such. Because the terms are not synonymous, the claims are not equivalent; hence, the assertions not interchangeable. The term "right" is also used indiscriminately when what is meant are powers or immunities.[124]

Hohfeld, whose writings have been extraordinarily influential on modern discussion of the fundamental elements of legal ideas, held that

> Strictly fundamental legal relations are, after all, *sui generis*; and thus it is that attempts at formal definition are always unsatisfactory, if not altogether useless. Accordingly, the most promising line of procedure seems to consist in exhibiting all of the various relations in a scheme of "opposites" and "correlatives," and then proceeding to exemplify their individual scope and application in concrete cases.[125]

In other words, the elemental units of judicial thought are best highlighted not by isolated definitions of each, but by observing the structural relations between them. This is the conceptual background against which one must ask, What is a right?

What clue do we find, in ordinary legal discourse, toward limiting the word in question to a definite and appropriate meaning? That clue lies in the correlative "duty," for it is certain that even those who use the word and the conception "right" in the broadest possible way are accustomed to thinking of "duty" as the invariable correlative.[126]

To assert a *right* to such-and-such is necessarily to claim that somebody else has a *duty* to make certain that you have such-and-such, or at least a duty to clear away any impediments under his control to the exercise of your right. A *privilege*, in Hohfeld's scheme, is the opposite of a duty; it is the correlative of a no-right. If I have a privilege to such-and-such, you have no right to interfere, but also no duty to see that I succeed.

Examples from ordinary life might be helpful here. Americans have a right to the free exercise of religion. This right imposes a duty on others, such as the government and employers, to avoid infringing upon this right except for serious reasons. In contrast, Americans only have a privilege, not a right, to drive a car. No private person has a right to impede my driving my car, but neither can anyone be held accountable if I am unable to drive a car for whatever reason (perhaps I cannot afford to buy one): there being no right, there is no duty—hence, no breach of duty. But because the general police powers allow the State to regulate safety, a licensing requirement is permissible as a threshold to driving. The only imposition is that, to the extent driving opportunities in the form of licenses are offered by the government, they must be offered to everyone on a nondiscriminatory basis. I cannot be denied my license because of my race, although I can be denied a license if I am blind.

The assertion of a right is a very strong claim indeed. It places upon others the burden to help you actualize that right when the circumstances warrant (and not merely that they refrain from blocking your access). If you have a right to medical treatment (as many currently argue), and you are unable to access that treatment by your own efforts (perhaps there are no adequate facilities in your area), your right to that treatment would entail that someone, somewhere, make it available for you. The government, for example, might have an obligation to offer or construct such resources.[127] My right to vote means that others must make certain that I am able to vote; my privilege to vote means that others cannot block my ability to vote, but neither are they not obliged to smooth the path. In other words, they may not make it more difficult for me to exercise my privilege, but they are not required to make it easier. Despite this marked distinction, we hear voting described as both a "right" and a "privilege" (often in the same sentence) when it can only be one or the other.

One conclusion we should immediately draw is that, by this standard, the list of genuine rights will be short. If there are so few genuine general rights, and because "human rights" must be a subset of those general rights, we should anticipate that if there are any human rights at all, they are very few. One author concludes that although some will draw up long lists of human rights (the UN's Universal Declaration of Human Rights contains thirty articles, and many of these contain more than one explicit right), there are only four negative rights that are today uncontroversial: freedom from slavery, freedom from genocide, freedom from racial discrimination, and freedom from torture.[128]

No one contests that "rights" as generally understood are something that a group recognizes among its own members. These are the rights created and designated by positive law. Positive laws can be enacted either formally or informally. Literate societies typically attempt to delineate these rights in a formal document. Americans, for example, turn to the U.S. Constitution (as amended) to identify their basic rights; other rights will be found in statutory decrees. Other, nonliterate societies may depend upon custom and tradition to identify what duties and responsibilities are possessed by which categories of persons. Literate societies can have these kinds of rights as well; in American society, we generally accept that there is a right to a public education, although this right is nowhere to be found in the Constitution.[129]

Not all rights are considered to have their source in positive enactments. There is a sense in which some rights require no formal recognition, written or traditional, to be asserted. Again, in American society, these are termed by the Declaration of Independence as those "endowed by our Creator"—rights citizens possess whether the state recognizes them or not because their source is not one controlled by the state. These are rights the state can only choose to recognize and honor, or not; it cannot create or bestow them. These are the "natural rights." In order to have the universal scope they possess by definition, human rights would seem most sensibly to belong to the set of natural, as opposed to positive, rights.

That, at least, is the argument. On what basis is this claim for such a class of natural human rights defended? As we plunge headlong into this contentious field of debate, we should remind ourselves of one scholar's assessment of the landscape as we find it: "Currently, there is no adequate theory of human rights."[130] Neither of the two formulations we investigate in the next sections, therefore, should be expected to be clearly and obviously superior to the other.

The Natural Arguments for Human Rights

Human rights are rights that inhere in entities belonging to the class of objects called "human" solely by virtue of that class membership. The contrast is presumably between these inalienable rights and the civil rights, that the state can control, bestow, and withdraw. The inherence of rights in these entities is a natural property. The challenge will be to identify the precise material basis generating this inherent property. "Human" is not a legal idea, but rather a philosophical and anthropological one. As mentioned in the introduction, anthropology's designated task is to clarify what it means to be human. Any serious use of the term must therefore draw upon this substantial effort, and conform its use to those anthropological results.

Natural Law

Although an immensely powerful theoretical model, natural law involves the problem we have already discussed and again must invoke: the relationship between the "is" and the "ought."

But first, a short summary of what is implied by appeal to a theory of natural law:

> [Natural law] is a self-evident law, grounded in the innermost nature of things, independent of historically produced institutions, conventions, and ideologies, absolute, immutable, and universal in the sense that it is unaffected by barriers between peoples and nations, autonomous in the sense that its validity derives from values inherent in itself, and it is the ultimate test of validity for that which is posited by man. Norms of human conduct are, accordingly, derived either from religious articles of faith or from primary postulates of reason.[131]

In the Western world, natural law theory is synonymous with the name of Thomas Aquinas.

This definition underscores one problem for natural law theory. Many wars have been waged over just which postulates are "self-evident." This fatal flexibility of the principle of natural law can be illustrated by a history of the social opprobrium for homosexuality. It could be criminalized as a breach of natural law because, as the saying goes, "God created Adam and Eve, and not Adam and Steve." Heterosexual procreativity arguably being the clear intent of God by virtue of the "fit" between the penis and the vagina, any willful deviation therefrom must be sinful hubris (and the step from sin to crime is small indeed). That conclusion would be for many people "self-evident." But the argument can take just the opposite form: given the widely cataloged occurrence of homosexual behavior in the natural world,[132] the natural law conclusion must be that human homosexuality is not at all "unnatural," and is, therefore, permissible. Given the facts, this conclusion is also "self-evident," even though it contradicts the first one.

Which option one prefers will vary with one's preconceived worldview. The natural world can be variously depicted as the moral standard of humans, since it is untouched by sin, or as a condition of base degradation because it has not been redeemed. The point, in other words, is that there is nothing of moral relevance that is "self-evident" in the natural world. Brute facts entail no moral conclusions, as we saw in chapter 1. Although natural law claims to be deriving moral conclusions from empirical (natural) facts, in actuality, it cannot be doing this logically impossible feat. A closer look shows it to be doing just the opposite: it uses moral premises to identify supportive facts in the natural world.

Against that introductory background we can discuss a preeminent attempt to justify natural law theory. John Finnis's *Natural Law and Natural Rights* is credited with singularly "revitaliz[ing] the natural law tradition in the English-speaking world."[133] His model, however, is the inversion of that of his predecessor, Aquinas. Whereas Aquinas *posited* an essential human nature that one then examined in order to ascertain the good, for Finnis, "human nature or essence is the conclusion of a natural law ethical inquiry ... not the starting point."[134] Finnis will always be at pains to minimize the significant differences between his argument and those of his predecessors in whose tradition he sees himself working: Aristotle and Aquinas. Therefore, his own description of Aquinas's work minimizes the role of the natural in Aquinas, producing a sketch that sounds very much like the product Finnis fashions:

> [F]or Aquinas, the way to discover what is morally right (virtue) and wrong (vice) is to ask, not what is in accordance with human nature, but what is reasonable. And this quest will eventually bring one back to the *underived* first principles of practical reasonableness, principles which make no reference at all to human nature, but only to human good.[135]

This statement is true only as far as it goes. What Finnis obscures is that Aquinas's application of reason is *against the background* of what is natural. It is the kind of reasoning that a person would do given the possession of an essential human nature of Aquinas's description. Excise this background criterion of the ontological primacy of the natural, and the result makes Aquinas sound very similar to Finnis, despite the fact that his process is quite the opposite.

Finnis's thesis begins with the assertion that the basic goods of human living are immediately discernible to "any sane person."[136] He supports this bold claim with a discussion about the conditions of self-evidency. A proposition is "self-evident [when] people (with the relevant experience, and understanding of terms) *assent* to it without needing the proof of argument."[137] A self-evident principle "needs no demonstration"[138]—a claim Finnis buttresses by presenting seven such principles.[139] *Any* argument against such self-evident principles is *necessarily* self-defeating.[140]

Using this standard of self-evidency, Finnis cursorily reviews the relevant anthropological literature,[141] from which he extracts seven basic human goods: (1) Life; (2) Knowledge; (3) Play; (4) Aesthetic experience; (5) Sociability (friendship); (6) Practical reasonableness; and (7) Religion.[142] These seven goods are exhaustive: any other good proposed as a candidate to be added to the list "will be found, on analysis, to be ways or combinations of ways of pursuing (not always sensibly) and realizing (not always successfully) one of the seven basic forms of good, or some combination of them."[143] Finnis completes this sketch of his theory by clarifying the sense in which these seven goods are "basic":

> First, each is equally self-evidently a form of good. Secondly, none can be analytically reduced to being merely an aspect of any of the others, or to being merely instrumental in the pursuit of any of the others. Thirdly, each one, when we focus on it, can reasonably be regarded as the most important. Hence, there is no objective hierarchy amongst them.[144]

The remainder of Finnis's book serves to elaborate in detail the "basic requirements" of the sixth of his basic goods, practical reasonableness, and how these requirements function to elucidate concepts such as *law*, *justice*, and *human rights*.

Finnis's concept of what constitutes natural law also diverges from that of Aquinas. For Aquinas, natural law was the participation by rational creatures in divine law, as instantiated in our natural inclinations; in theory, any motion caused by an unperverted natural inclination was interpretable as the actualization of natural law. For Finnis, however, natural law is much narrower: it is "the set of principles of practical reasonableness in ordering human life and human community."[145] Of the seven basic human goods, natural law is intrinsic to only one.

Finnis devotes one chapter to the analysis of human rights. Analyzing the concept of human rights that emerges from a study of the core United Nations documents on this matter, he concludes that human rights "is simply a way of sketching the *outlines of the common good*, the various aspects of individual well-being in community."[146] Without doubt, his discussion lands Finnis in some strange territory. Paternalism is desirable in his view: it is acceptable to judge another as "mistaken," and to act on that judgment. "[I]t would certainly be wrong to suggest that any individual is bound or even permitted in justice to show everyone equal *concern*."[147] At most, one can expect "respectful consideration," but not "equality of treatment."

Still, Finnis does identify some *absolute* human rights. Absolute human rights are rights that are not conditioned by any cultural circumstances. Other rights, for instance, might be reasonably abridged during times of national emergency, or contingent upon a particular level of technological development (as is the UN identification of paid vacations as a human right). Absolute human rights residing beyond the reach of even Finnis's permitted paternalistic intervention include

> the right not to have one's life taken directly as a means to any further end;
>
> the right not to be positively lied to in any situation (e.g., teaching, preaching, research publication, news broadcasting) in which factual communication (as distinct from fiction, jest, or poetry) is reasonably expected;
>
> the right not to be condemned on knowingly false charges;
>
> the right not to be deprived, or required to deprive oneself, of one's procreative capacity; and
>
> the right to be taken into respectful consideration in any assessment of what the common good requires.[148]

Assuming that Finnis's theory of natural law is internally consistent and philosophically cohesive, it could function to ground a theory of human rights, and is even sufficiently refined to generate a list of some specific human rights it would support.

Finnis's approach to natural law contains much that merits criticism. Many of those comments would spring from a disagreement about his fundamental assumptions (such as his dependence upon the dubious method of self-evidency) and specific applications. That kind of criticism would demonstrate why we might hope that Finnis is wrong, but not really show that he is in fact wrong. For that purpose, we will instead focus on the points where Finnis appears to fail to meet his own standards of evaluation. We will look at the flaws that, although not the most exciting in this text, are perhaps the most damning. Specifically, the list of seven basic goods is neither basic nor nonarbitrary, nor self-evident, as he requires. If the list of human goods is other than he composes it, then most of what follows in the remainder of his argument is shorn of its philosophical anchor. That surviving discussion might remain appealing, and even correct, but it will no longer have been developed from first principles such that, having accepted the latter, we are logically compelled to concede the former. As such, Finnis's reformulated natural law theory, being more ideology than philosophy, would be inadequate to ground a theory of human rights.

In Finnis's terms, the basic goods are basic in three senses, one of which is that "there is no objective hierarchy amongst them." His own analysis, however, refutes this claim. The sixth good, practical reasonableness, is more important than the other six in at least two ways. First, it is the only one that he analyzes in any depth at all, suggesting that this category is intrinsically richer conceptually than the others. The closest he comes to discussing any of the other goods is in the chapter on knowledge. But the purpose of that chapter was not to discuss knowledge, but to defend his criterion of self-evidency with what he perhaps believed was the least controversial of his listed goods.

The conclusion that the basic goods are not equally basic, however, is more plainly demonstrated by Finnis's own words:

> For amongst the basic forms of good that we have no good reason to leave out of account is the good of practical reasonableness, which is participated in precisely by shaping one's participation in the other basic goods, by guiding one's commitments, one's selection of projects, and what one does in carrying them out.[149]

By this description, practical reasonableness is the precondition for the achievement of the other named goods. This dependency is not reciprocal. In other words, the relationship between practical reasonableness and the other goods is not dialectic, suggesting that the dependency Finnis here describes is not attributable to present emphasis, but to actual structure. If true, then practical reasonableness is fundamentally prior to, and thus *more* basic than the other six goods, refuting Finnis's own condition that the seven basic goods are all equally basic.

The seven anthropologically derived goods Finnis lists are deemed elemental to the whole of possibly imagined human goods. Any other potential candidate human good can be parsed into some combination of these seven. This requirement assigns a certain necessity to each of the seven goods. But the list is arbitrary in at least three ways.

First, scrutiny finds the seven items to be a hodgepodge of incommensurables; it is unclear what qualifies something as a good. Most frequently, Finnis characterizes goods as goals "to-be-pursued."[150] An examination of the list, however, reveals them to have another character altogether, the virtue of being "worth having."[151] So while he speaks of human flourishing as the pursuit of the basic goods, clearly that flourishing is the *consequence* of prior possession of those goods. If the list were restricted only to the criterion he emphasizes ("to-be-pursued"), then most likely only knowledge (and religion as a species of knowledge) would qualify as a good, the pursuit of which constitutes flourishing: we flourish to the extent that we pursue knowledge in and of itself, not necessarily to the extent to which we *have* knowledge. For example, Einstein's store of possessed knowledge was significantly greater than Aristotle's, yet Aristotle and Einstein both equally flourished *qua* rational humans in their pursuit of knowledge. The other goods, on the contrary, are such that flourishing depends not upon the pursuit of the good, but rather upon the actual possession, even being a function of the amount possessed. It is, in Finnis's analysis, the *exercise* of practical reasonableness that constitutes human flourishing, not its pursuit. This inconsistency over the quality of a basic good makes the list ad hoc—hence, arbitrary.

Second, Finnis's basic goods are arbitrary in the sense that he has expanded the scope of the categories beyond his original justifications. The good of "life" serves as the example here. Reasoning from the observed "drive for self-preservation," Finnis proposes as his first good the "value of life," and reasonably includes within it "bodily (including cerebral) health, and freedom from the pain that betokens organic mal-functioning or injury."[152] But then he wonders whether "[p]erhaps we should include in this category the transmission of life by procreation of children." We see immediately why Finnis wants to do this: procreation is one of his "absolute human rights," a stature it enjoys only because of its alleged relationship to a basic human good. He will also, else-where, want to use this association to argue that heterosexual procre-ativity is morally normative, and that all other kinds of sexuality are immoral.[153] These are all, in themselves, not utterly irrational asser-tions. Yet the introduction of procreation into the good of "life," which is founded upon the instinct of *self*-preservation, is not (to use Finnis's term) "self-evident." Even if defensible (and there are arguments to the effect that procreation is one strategy to achieve personal immortal-ity[154]), the linkage must still be argued. To introduce such controversial propositions in with these "indemonstrable" basic claims undermines the philosophical structure of his categories. Finnis's ploy, it seems, is to construct the category upon some initial concession the reader is likely to allow, but then to furnish that category with ad hoc elaborations. Sig-nificantly, it is the ad hoc additions that will play the greater role in his philosophical musings. In this sense, the basic goods are arbitrary.

The list is arbitrary in a third and more obvious sense. Other writ-ers have proposed other lists. For example, Stephen Reiss, based upon his experience as a psychiatrist, offers a list of sixteen basic human goods.[155] Although ostensibly based upon anthropological cross-cul-tural data, Finnis's list is nonempirical (being ultimately "self-evident"); he offers no means by which to choose between competing lists. The choice between all such lists is therefore arbitrary.

Finnis advances his list of basic human goods without any defense. His conclusions, he maintains, are self-evident, discernible to any "sane" person. Certainly, some propositions are self-evident in the sense that they contain the terms of their own verification. Aquinas offers these examples: Every whole is greater than its part; Things equal to one and the same are equal to one another (Q.94, a.2). Some propo-sitions require special knowledge to recognize their self-evidency, but the difference is of degree, not of kind, from the propositions self-evi-dent to everyone with ordinary knowledge. Lon Fuller's tale of Rex and

the identification of the eight ways to fail to make law[156] are one attempt
to isolate self-evident rules for a working legal system.

Unfortunately, many of Finnis's own examples of self-evident propositions are anything but. He offers seven such propositions (besides the
seven basic goods). At least two are not self-evident as the term is normally understood. His sixth proposition is "that a method of interpretation which is successful is to be relied upon in further similar cases until
contrary reason appears."[157] In other words, the inductive reasoning
David Hume discredited in his *An Enquiry Concerning Human Understanding*[158] is self-evidently valid. It is hard to know what to do with
Finnis's claim, since Finnis also asserts that another self-evident proposition, one he takes from Aquinas, is that "Man is a rational being."[159]
The joint claim, then, is that rational beings reason irrationally, and that
this state of contradictory affairs is self-evident and valid.

Another problematic example is found in Finnis's seventh proposition: "theoretical accounts which are simple, predictively successful, and
explanatorily powerful are to be accepted in preference to other
accounts."[160] Here he is restating Ockham's razor, which is, indeed, a
prevalent principle in scientific theory choice: a theory with fewer
explanatory entities is to be preferred to one with more, when both are
of equal explanatory power. However, the principle is *heuristic*, not rational. Ockham's razor is an aesthetic preference that may be wrong in any
particular case. As such, it holds by convention only, not because of any
intrinsic correctness to be discerned self-evidently, contrary to Finnis's
explicit denial that any of his examples are "a matter of convention."

Finnis's own attempt to identify uncontroversial examples of self-
evident propositions is uneven at best. This performance does not
inspire confidence in his ultimate claim, then, to be able to identify the
self-evident goods of human flourishing. As an example, we can doubt
that knowledge, as he defines it, is a human good:

> [T]he knowledge we have here in mind as a value is the knowledge that
> one can call an *intrinsic* good, i.e., that is considered to be desirable for its
> own sake and not merely as something sought after under some such
> description as "what will enable me to impress my audience" or "what will
> confirm my instinctive beliefs" or "what will contribute to my survival."[161]

The question we must ask is whether anything fits this description.
While many people pursue knowledge without any practical benefit,
they do so because it renders psychological rewards. But by Finnis's definition, because such knowledge is therefore not sought "for its own
sake," it is not the kind of knowledge which constitutes a human good
to pursue. Only knowledge one did not *want* to acquire could be
acquired for its own sake. So either Finnis is wrong in his character-

ization of knowledge, or there is no such knowledge which fits the description frequently enough to render it a universal human good—as opposed to the good for some very unusual individuals. The latter would founder on his requirement that the human goods "can in principle be pursued, realized, and participated in by any human being," leaving us with only the first possibility.[162]

Finnis attempts to defend the concept of human rights by deriving them from his revived theory of the natural law. As these comments have demonstrated, this theory fails by his own criteria that the elemental components of his theory be basic, nonarbitrary, and self-evident. At the least, it is too problematic to provide a sound philosophical ground for a theory of human rights.

For these and many other reasons not herein discussed, natural law theory seems unable to provide a satisfying justification for the existence of human rights. At the very least, any theory of natural law up to the task will have to be drastically different from Finnis's, which is regarded as the superior version available today. Yet even if we conclude that human rights are not "natural" in the sense of natural law theory exemplified by Finnis, there is at least one other sense in which human rights may still be "natural."

BIOLOGICAL NATURE

With the historical decline (until recently) of natural law[163]—at least in the sense of a self-evident moral order—the dependent concept of natural rights also fell into disfavor. To fill this gap, the concept of the "human right" arose around the time of World War II. Instead of finding these fundamental rights in the natural order, they were now attached more narrowly to the status of being human.

The argument runs that human rights are beyond the reach of the state because it is not within the state's power to deprive us of our humanity. An example of this kind of reasoning is the following:

> The very term *human rights* indicates both their nature and their source: they are the rights that one has simply because one is human. They are held by all human beings, irrespective of any rights or duties one may (or may not) have as citizens, members of families, workers, or parts of any public or private organization or association.... [Because] being human cannot be renounced, lost or forfeited, human rights are inalienable.[164]

If this argument is to serve as more than a policy statement, the term "human" must be assigned positive content. What are the definitional criteria by which membership in the class of "human" is to be determined? If that word lacks specific meaning, it is hard to imagine how it could attach to anything as substantive as a right. Rights are the claims and privileges of concrete entities, and some means are needed to determine who belongs to the class of rights-bearers in order to determine whether the invoked claim should be honored. As we explore this question, it should become obvious that this is the anthropological problem par excellence.

What is it to be human? The primary work of this term is usually to distinguish "us" from nonhuman "animals." The demarcation between animal and human is philosophically and scientifically vague.[165] Still, most educated persons begin with the assumption that humans are a product of the evolutionary process and assign them membership in the Animal Kingdom. Whatever they may be in addition to this, humans have their origin here, and are thereby animals with the name *Homo sapiens*. To contrast animals with humans is therefore disingenuous from the outset.

This broad caveat can be elevated to the level of high principle. Perhaps "animal" is equivalent to "non-*Homo sapiens*." Those organisms belonging to the species *Homo sapiens* are therefore "humans." That is, to be *Homo* is to be human; to label someone *Homo* is also to find him to be human.

There is a strong sense in which we do take these terms to be synonyms. We have two reasons, though, to reject the equation "human = *Homo sapiens*." First, if "human" and *Homo sapiens* are synonymous, we should be able to employ them identically. That is, the two should be linguistically interchangeable. But this is not the case. Consistently we find that the criteria for "human" are behavioral, while those for *Homo* are biological.

This point can be illustrated by considering what we mean when we discuss "human nature":

> *Human nature*, in general terms, denotes the nature of man, with more especial reference to his personality and/or character *as acquired in the course of socialization* and often with further reference to aspects of human potential and powers of development.[166]

This definition of "human nature" is typical; that which is "human" results from the organism's socialization into a culture. "Philosophies of human nature reflect beliefs about what people are like *after* they have moved through a lengthy socialization process. The concept does *not* attempt to reflect beliefs about inherent or innate qualities."[167] Work in this area does recognize forces that are biological rather than social, but these are not collected under the category of "human nature" but instead within "psychic unity." This perspective holds that the organism left to develop in isolation might survive but would never be quite human, regardless of its genotype.[168] That is, *Homo* is not human where it lacks enculturation.

Alternatively, again regardless of the genotype, an enculturated organism may be definitionally human. If culture and being human are strictly correlated,[169] "then some chimpanzees may be human or human-like."[170] Recent fieldwork has turned up evidence that this primate species displays behaviors that are unmistakably cultural.[171] The force of this fact has become so strong that "a growing number of scientists argue that [chimpanzees] belong in our own genus *Homo*."[172] If human rights are tied to our humanness, which in turn is definitionally equated with our status as *Homo*, and further, if the higher primates are embraced by that genera either literally or proximately, then by conclusion we will have to accept that these animals are entitled to the full panoply of human rights. This outcome will please some more than others.

These facts in combination force the conclusion that although *Homo* and human are highly correlated, they are not equivalent; even if in practice they are largely co-occurring, they are nevertheless distinctively different categories and cannot be defined in terms of one another. This logical conclusion that the extensions of "human" and *Homo* are nonequivalent can be historically illustrated. The criteria for judgments about whether a particular token of *Homo* qualified as human have ranged widely.

Prior to the Middle Ages, humans and animals were viewed as biologically permeable categories, meaning that individuals could just as easily move in one direction as the other: humans become animals (werewolves, vampires), and animals become humans (the characters of Aesop's fables). Later, however, behavioral category markers allowed the possibility that even certain members of *Homo* routinely failed to qualify as human. If being "rational," for example, is the definitional human trait (Joel Feinberg identifies this as "the capability most commonly favored for this role";[173] in the next chapter we offer our own candidate) then persons who act in ways judged "irrational" (e.g., women in general,[174] peasants in French folk tales) may come off as less than human.[175] This trend can so overexercise itself that by tighter and tighter constriction, no actual humans exist. If true rationality is the possession of only the theoretical philosopher, only he might be human. But in the last analysis, true knowledge is an impossible goal that no one achieves, so no one at all is human.[176]

"Human" is obviously a fuzzy category, and not merely at its boundaries. But suppose, despite the problems outlined above, we stipulated for practical reasons that the referent of "human" shall be the species *Homo*. Would advocates of human rights approve?

Most would have no difficulty accepting some of the readily apparent practical benefits of this position; it does, for example, have the

attractive virtue of seeming to definitively resolve the abortion controversy. *Homo* is a status conferred by genetic code; a fetus is consequently *Homo* and by this version also human. By this reasoning, the
fetus possess all human rights from conception, including the right to
life. But such parsimony in some areas is not without costs in others.
Some advocates for animals imply that human rights are such that they
should embrace animals in some way or other. Feinberg at least believes
that "a human right held by animals is not excluded by definition."[177]
Those who think it *should not* be so excluded (that is, those who
believe that animals should have human rights) cannot therefore be
friends of the stipulation that "human = *Homo*"; otherwise we are put
in the position of having to identify an independent source for any
human rights animals may possess.

The most attractive aspect of the equation between "human" and
Homo is that it does seem to answer clearly to whom human rights
should be assigned. Or does it? This clarity may be illusionary. Even if
we restrict ourselves to the biological criteria implied by the term *Homo*,
what *exactly* earns someone that label? The number of chromosomes?
Some people have extras: are they therefore not sufficiently *Homo* to
deserve human rights? If not chromosomes, what? Particular genes?
What, then, of the differing alleles? Odds are that whatever biological
trait is identified, here, too, some presumptive bearers of human rights
will be found to be disqualified as they were when we considered cultural and psychological variables.

Our primary problem is not only to identify to whom human rights
apply, but also what are the grounds for any human rights. There are
difficulties in requiring that the "human = *Homo*" equation perform
this work. How can biological species membership confer moral status?
Recall that the claim is not that the human rights are perfectly correlated with *Homo* status, but the stronger claim that *Homo* status generates the human rights. The naturalistic fallacy (see chapter 1) says that
we cannot derive an *ought* from an *is*. Human rights are, by definition,
statements of what *ought* to pertain; biological species is a description
of what *is* the case. Unless a way is found to bridge this gap, *Homo* can
never serve as a ground for human rights.[178]

The anthropological perspective reveals that the category "human"
is richer and more subtle than generally supposed by political and legal
theorists. Our illustration above highlights that whatever trait is identified as essential to being human—be it achieved enculturation or
endowed biology—some members of *Homo* will lack that trait. The
fetus, for example, has achieved nothing, and hence, cannot be contained by any definition of human as encultured.[179] When an offspring
acquires human status can vary cross-culturally. For first-century

Romans, the child became human only when he or she could walk and talk.[180] Similarly, the brute fact of biological variability means that whatever psychological, behavioral, or genetic criterion we select as the marker for "human," some specimens of *Homo* will lack this trait (and, depending on the trait, some non-*Homo* might possess it).

So anthropological insight into the nature of being "human" does allow us to assign positive content to "human rights." However, when the category is restricted adequately to assign meaning to the term, it generates outcomes that are not easily reconciled with our intuitive expectations about who should possess human rights. Our choices are these: either the term "human rights" is to remain undefined, in which case it is meaningless, or at least a wisp too insubstantial to generate duties in others; or it is defined, in which case it fails to demarcate rights-holders from nonrights-holders in a way compatible with our intuitions. There either are no human rights at all, or what rights as might follow from a sophisticated understanding of the term "human" are hugely different from the popular idea.[181]

The Legal Argument for Human Rights

The attempt to identify the source for human rights in our natural condition fails, regardless of whether "natural" refers to the self-evident state of affairs or the biological substrate of our existence. If the category of "human rights" as ordinarily conceived is at all legitimate, its authority must reside outside the category of the natural.

If the rules of standard English apply, "human rights" are a subset of the larger class of rights. The essence of such hierarchical categories is that what is true about the class as a whole must be true of the subsets therein. The relationship *between* the subsets, however, is an open question.

Judith Thomson discusses this broader category of rights in general.[182] One of her many projects is to sever moral (human, natural) rights generally from the specific class of legal rights. The issue arises because of the influence of early theorizing by Hohfeld reviewed above. While Hohfeld made a general contribution to the theory of rights in his discussion of duties and claims, he specifically limited his concerns to *legal* rights. The question then turns to the relationship of legal to moral rights.

Positivists claim that moral rights are only legal rights. Just as there are no crimes other than those acts statutorily criminalized, so too are there no rights except those legislatively granted. Thomson disagrees. Her aim is to demonstrate that legal and moral rights are neither synonymous (that is, the set of legal rights is not identical to the set of moral rights), nor is one a subset of the other (all moral rights are not legal rights; neither are all legal rights moral rights). She dramatizes her point with the following scenario:

> For suppose a law is passed in our community which declares that there is henceforth no penalty attached to murdering Jews, and moreover that there is henceforth a penalty attached to attempting to prevent the murder of Jews. Here is Bloggs, who hates a certain Jew, namely Smith. Does Bloggs now have a legal privilege as regards Smith of murdering Smith? Does Bloggs now have a legal claim against me that I not attempt to prevent his murdering Smith? If Positivism is correct, the answer to both questions is yes. But then at least legal rights are not members of the genus rights. No doubt Bloggs has a *legal* privilege of murdering Smith, on this understanding of legal privileges; but he has no privilege of murdering Smith. No doubt I infringe a *legal* claim of Bloggs' if I attempt to prevent him from murdering Smith, on this understanding of legal claims; but he has no claim against me that I not do this—I infringe no claim he really has if I proceed to do it.[183]

Thomson believes that this hypothetical brings into relief the difference between moral rights and legal rights. We can be granted the legal right to do something (kill Smith) without thereby acquiring the moral right to do that thing:[184] *lex injusta non est lex* (an unjust law is not a law). Because some legal rights are obviously not moral rights, the relationship between the two is neither of the two possibilities mentioned above, but instead a third. Legal rights and moral rights are independent but intersecting categories.

Whatever this example accomplishes, it is not as much as Thomson hopes. She has shown that not all moral rights are legal rights, and that not all legal rights are moral rights. We can grant her this. She is concerned to deflect the positivistic interpretation of law, and we can stipulate that she has succeeded.

But she frames her conclusions in overly broad terms. It is one thing to conclude that there are extralegal sources for rights. That result does not force upon us the conclusion that there exists a natural source for rights. Thomson has adequately demonstrated that "our rights have different sources."[185] But her proof is framed in purely dichotomous terms, the legal versus the natural, so that, if some rights are nonlegal, there must be natural rights: she holds that we have natural rights "just in case [the claim] is not a pure social claim."[186] But her conclusion is valid only if legal claims exhaust the kinds of social claims that can exist.

Unfortunately for her argument, there can be nonlegal social claims that can function as a source for rights. Perhaps all rights are even reducible to social claims of this kind. That opens the possibility that, despite the case of Bloggs, natural rights do not exist; human rights exist only to the extent that they are grounded in social premises.

Thomson specifically is vulnerable to this argument because for her, unlike Finnis, natural rights are a merely residual category; they are those claims that are nonsocial—they have no positive definitional attributes of their own. If that category is empty, there are no natural claims, even by her estimate. Thomson only arrives at the conclusion that natural rights exist because she equates "legal" with "social," and having demonstrated that nonlegal rights exist, she feels justified in asserting that natural rights necessarily exist.

In seeming support of Thomson's dichotomous categories of natural and legal rights, Feinberg makes the following distinction:

> A man has a legal right when the official recognition of his claim (as valid) is called for by the governing rules. This definition, of course, hardly applies to moral rights, but that is not because the genus of which moral rights are a species is something other than claims. A man has a moral right when he has a claim, the recognition of which is called for—not (necessarily) by legal rules—but by moral principles, or the principles of an enlightened conscience.[187]

But Feinberg makes explicit what is hidden in Thomson's text. Moral rights are legitimated by "moral principles, or the principles of an enlightened conscience." Whence the source of moral principles or those principles of an enlightened conscience, if it is not one's social environment? Can anyone, even a detached philosopher, claim to be other than a product of his or her time and place? If moral rights are chartered by socially derived principles, then they are themselves social products, and the distinction between legal and moral rights does not hinge on the assertion that one is social and the other not.[188]

This problem becomes obvious in Thomson's text through her examples of moral data. These are her private intuitions that she thinks are sufficiently obvious and inarguable (again displaying the resort by natural law theorists to claims of self-evidency) that they constitute the prima facie evidence for the existence of a nonsocially grounded moral right. As she says, "I take much of the stuff of morality as given."[189]

One example of this kind of bald assertion is her claim that "One ought not torture babies to death for fun" "is surely a necessary truth."[190] We can concede that it is indeed a true statement about public morality without agreeing that it is a necessary truth. Aristotle, for example, claimed that babies are like animals; and Descartes believed that animals are like machines. Surely we have no necessary repugnance against breaking our machines for amusement. That we do not have this attitude toward babies is therefore a contingent truth, not a necessary one.[191]

An appeal to the universality of such an "ought" is no help to Thomson either. Human society is such, for instance, that it could not exist if internal members were free to kill one another. The universal claim against murder by others is therefore derivable as a social claim. All moral imperatives are arguably reducible in similar ways.

The outcome is this: Our initial question was whether moral rights are reducible to legal rights. Thomson has shown adequately that this is not true. Thomson invalidly uses this result to claim that rights exist that are not social, and that by implication *natural* rights exist. Her conclusions do not follow from her argument. In fact, given her position that natural rights, if they exist, are a residual category, the conservative result of this discussion is the same as in the previous section: there is no logical requirement that human rights exist. Since all rights are grants by society, human rights cover only those social grants of rights that are universal because some brute facts of social living, in any culture or time, are likewise universal.

As claimed earlier, whatever is true of rights generally must be true of human rights specifically. If rights generally are better seen to be social rights (whether legal or not) then so, too, must this be said of human rights. If there are any human rights, they exist as grants from society, not as the natural endowments of organisms. The anthropological review shows that there is no material feature supporting the generation of those rights, or even the rational retrospective assignment of them. Thompson tries to circumvent this outcome by making human rights a negative, residual category. But her magnificent effort trips over another anthropological fact: that morality is as much a social product as is law.

The result that rights, including human rights, are social grants has implications. For one, there can be no such thing as an inalienable right. What society gives, it can take away. This would be harder to argue were the question whether the state can deprive the individual of a biological endowment, or a supernatural gift. But that is not the case of rights; the sole source of rights is society. Some rights might be so fundamental to the healthy functioning of any human society that any such society would be unwise to eliminate such rights. The charge to anthropology should be to identify these core rights essential to a healthy society of whatever political form.

If the nonexistence of inalienable rights seems extreme, we can take comfort in the fact that others have reached the same conclusion. Thomson seems largely sympathetic to this claim in her later chapters. And, by entirely different arguments, Francis Lieber (discussed in the context of polygamy in chapter 1) arrives at the same result:

> The rights which I have called primordial, or some of them, have been termed by others absolute rights. This is not a very apt term, for ... there are no absolute rights, if this term mean either that they cannot be abridged, or that men cannot agree to give them up.... Blackstone says, absolute rights

are "such as would belong to their persons merely in a state of nature, and which every man is entitle to enjoy, whether out of society or in it." There is a strange confusion of ideas—rights in a state of *nature!*[192]

Legal philosopher Jeremy Bentham, generally regarded as the first major utilitarian, expressed the view that "'natural rights' were simple nonsense, and 'natural and imprescriptible' (that is, inalienable) rights were rhetorical nonsense, 'nonsense upon stilts.'"[193]

The Prospect for Human Rights

Sieghart distinguished human rights by three characteristics: inherence, inalienability, and equality. In chapter 2 we concluded that legal equality was a fiction. Differences are the rule, with the associated responsibility to sort the relevant from the irrelevant ones in any given situation. In the sections above we failed to isolate any material foundation upon which such rights could reasonably inhere by nature. The attempt to assign positive content to "human" by equating it to biological *Homo* leads to inconsistencies and undesirable outcomes. Thomson's negative approach fared little better, resulting as it did in an empty set. Finally, the reasonable outcome of our investigation is that no rights are inalienable, a result in which we are supported by other writers.

If no right has the qualities of equality, inherence, and inalienability, then perhaps there are, after all, no human rights, at least as ordinarily understood. That conclusion would comport with that from philosopher Alasdair MacIntyre:

> The best reason for asserting ... that there are no [human] rights is indeed of precisely the same type as the best reason which we possess for asserting that there are no witches and the best reason which we possess for asserting that there are no unicorns: every attempt to give good reasons for believing that there are such rights has failed.[194]

Some anthropologists have reported societies that share Macintyre's negative conclusion. The argument is that moral obligations inhere not in persons but in relationships:

> There is [among New Guinea societies] no concept of universalist moral obligation, as in the official ethic of the Western state. Moral obligation tends to exist only where there are recognized and effective relationships, and hence potential exchanges of goods and services, between persons. Where no such relationships exist—as outside a man's tribe, phratry, clan, or kindred—there is no sense of moral obligation and hence no formally prescribed rules of behaviour. The individual does not have value to all other individuals purely as human being but only in respect of social ties—that is, the social services he can render.[195]

We have now answered the preliminary question about the prima facie sensibility of the concept of "human rights." The term "human" in this context may be infelicitous, since it carries implications that are not necessarily compatible with or helpful to the legal gap this category of rights was designed to fill.

We should rush to reassure the reader that our conclusion that there are no human rights per se does not mean that we believe that it is permissible, for example, to torture people. The right to be free from torture can be asserted on its own terms. It does not need to justify itself by asserted membership in a wider group of rights, and may even lose something of its potency by that effort. No longer should it suffice to justify the assertion of any right by labeling it a "human right" and leaving it at that.

That the term "human rights" should be regarded as a mere category label, absolutely devoid of theoretical implications or justifications for the category, is actually a good result for the advocates of this class of rights, whatever it may be called. They will no longer be forced to expend their intellectual capital attempting to explain why the right to paid vacations (Article 24 in the United Nations Universal Declaration of Human Rights) is a human right and not a workers' right. The possibility of a paid vacation, much less the perceived right to one, is relevant to only a small portion of contemporary peoples, and hardly speaks to a need inherent in our biological condition as humans. The justification for this category of rights need only rest on the virtue of being valued in our world today, and not on whether or not they are dubious conclusions arising from questionable premises.

Conclusion

Anthropology can clarify for law other concepts besides human rights. Religion, as we saw, is another. Law could also benefit from an anthropological understanding of "race." Although much administrative policy treats race as a meaningful biological concept that divides the population along natural fault lines, anthropology has concluded that "race" in this sense is not simply overemphasized or simplified; it is patently false. Most (but not all) uses of the word could be replaced with another—perhaps "ethnicity." But this change, running deeper than a mere change in terminology, would impact legal arguments that have heretofore presumed a biological essentialism. As a final example paralleling that of race, law has only the loosest conceptual grasp on the terms "sex" and "gender," inconsistently treating them as synonyms. Some anthropological housekeeping in the areas using these terms—such as employment discrimination—would greatly clarify the state of our laws.

Many are the ways in which anthropology can confer theoretical benefits to the law.[196] We have mentioned but a few.

Notes

1. Alison Dundes Renteln, *A Justification of the Cultural Defense as Partial Excuse*, 2 REVIEW OF LAW AND WOMEN'S STUDIES 437, 496 (1993).
2. *See id.*
3. *Id.* at 461.
4. Nancy A. Wanderer & Catherine R. Connors, *Culture and Crime:* Kargar *and the Existing Framework for a Cultural Defense*, 47 BUFFALO LAW REVIEW 829, 860 (1999).
5. *Id.*
6. The arguments in this section first appeared in James M. Donovan, *God Is As God Does: Law, Anthropology, and the Definition of "Religion,"* 6(1) SETON HALL CONSTITUTIONAL LAW JOURNAL 23 (1995).
7. U.S. CONST. amend. I.
8. *See* Epperson v. Arkansas, 393 U.S. 97, 104 (1968) (stating that government cannot advance nonreligion or be hostile to religion as a whole, nor can it promote a particular religion).
9. Reynolds v. United States, 98 U.S. 145 (1878).
10. *Id.* at 162.
11. Comment, *Defining Religion: Of God, the Constitution and the D.A.R.*, 32 UNIVERSITY OF CHICAGO LAW REVIEW 533, 539 (1965).
12. *See Reynolds*, 98 U.S. at 163-164.
13. 133 U.S. 333 (1890).
14. 136 U.S. 1 (1890).
15. *Id.* at 48.
16. 322 U.S. 78 (1944).
17. *See id.* at 82.
18. *See id.* at 86.
19. *Id.* at 87.
20. *See id.* at 86.
21. Steven D. Collier, *Beyond* Seeger/Welsh: *Redefining Religion under the Constitution*, 31 EMORY LAW JOURNAL 973, 979 (1982).
22. Public Law No. 73-783, ch. 720, 54 Stat. 885 (repealed 1955).
23. 133 F.2d 703 (2nd Cir. 1943).
24. *See id.* at 708.
25. *Id.*
26. Selective Service Act of 1948, Public Law No. 80-759, ch. 625, § 6(j), 62 Stat. 604, 612-613 (current version at 50 U.S.C. app. § 456(j) (1976)).
27. *See, e.g.*, George v. United States, 196 F.2d 445 (9th Cir. 1952).
28. 367 U.S. 488 (1961).
29. *Id.* at 495 note 11.
30. 380 U.S. 163 (1965).
31. *See id.* at 166.

32. *See, e.g.,* PAUL TILLICH, THE ESSENTIAL TILLICH 33 (F. Forrester Church ed., 1987).
33. *Id.* at 19.
34. Jesse H. Choper, *Defining "Religion" in the First Amendment,* 1982 UNIVERSITY OF ILLINOIS LAW REVIEW 579, 595. Choper's skepticism about the abilities of judges in this matter can be interestingly compared with the demand upon judges to ascertain the reliability and relevance of scientific and technical theories required by *Daubert.* Why so capable in one context, but hopelessly befuddled in the other?
35. *See id.* at 599.
36. *See id.* at 600.
37. 406 U.S. 205 (1972). A thorough presentation of the history of the attempts to contrive a legal definition of "religion" would here consider *Welsh v. United States,* 398 U.S. 333 (1970). *Welsh* minimally reinforced *Seeger,* and in some senses extended it even further by apparently equating "religion" with "conscience." Plus, the procedural effect of *Welsh* was to shift the burden from the individual to prove that he was entitled to the exemption from the draft, to the government to prove that he was not.
38. *Yoder,* 406 U.S. at 215-216. The full statement in which Thoreau is offered as a non-religious comparison follows:

> Although a determination of what is a "religious" belief or practice entitled to constitutional protection may present a most delicate question, the very concept of ordered liberty precludes allowing every person to make his own standards of matters of conduct in which society as a whole has important interests. Thus, if the Amish asserted their claims because of the subjective evaluation and rejection of the contemporary secular values accepted by the majority, much as Thoreau rejected the social values of his time and isolated himself at Walden Pond, their claims would not rest on a religious basis. Thoreau's choice was philosophical and personal rather than religious and such belief does not rise to the demands of the Religion Clauses.

39. Justice Douglas also noted this contradictory treatment of Thoreau by the *Yoder* Court. *Id.* at 247-248 (Douglas, J., dissenting in part).
40. Even before *Yoder,* anthropologist Walter Goldschmidt had noticed this tendency for law to prefer to protect the organized forms of religion. *See* WALTER GOLDSCHMIDT, COMPARATIVE FUNCTIONALISM: AN ESSAY IN ANTHROPOLOGICAL THEORY 63 (1966) ("In some states the law, in practice, distinguishes between the leaders of a religious cult and a psychopath by specifying some minimum number of acceptors of his system; i.e., a social definition of his private symbolic world.").
41. *Yoder,* 406 U.S. at 235.
42. *See* Collier, *supra* note 21, at 995.
43. Dobkin v. District of Columbia, 194 A.2d 657 (D.C. App. 1963).
44. *Id.* at 659.
45. Ray Jay Davis, *Plural Marriage and Religious Freedom: The Impact of* Reynolds v. United States, 15 ARIZONA LAW REVIEW 287, 299 (1973).
46. Collier, *supra* note 21, at 1000.
47. *See id.* at 995.
48. 592 F.2d 197 (3rd Cir. 1979).
49. *Id.* at 200 (Adams, J., concurring).
50. *Id.* at 207-209.
51. 662 F.2d 1025 (3rd Cir. 1981).
52. Eduardo Peñalver, *The Concept of Religion,* 107 YALE LAW JOURNAL 791, 818-821 (1997), argues that MOVE, by his criteria, should have been found to be a religion. However, he argues that Marxism would not qualify, despite the existence of a con-

siderable literature adopting the contrary view. *See, for example*, JOHN E. SMITH, QUASI-RELIGIONS: HUMANISM, MARXISM, AND NATIONALISM (1994).

53. *Malnak*, 592 F.2d. at 210 note 45. A different case reaches a similar conclusion: "the mere labeling of something as coming within a 'religious' area by theologians does not serve to make that area 'religious' for purposes of invoking First Amendment protections." Women Services, P.C. v. Thone, 483 F. Supp. 1022 (Neb. App. 1979).

54. Jerome Kurtz, *Remarks of Jerome IRS Commissioner Jerome Kurtz before the PLI Seventh Biennial Conference on Tax Planning (Jan. 9, 1978), in* FEDERAL TAXES (P-H) P54, 820 (1978); *see also* Treasury Regulation 1.501(c)(3)-1(d).

55. Bruce J. Casino, *"I Know It When I See It": Mail-Order Ministry Tax Fraud and the Problem of a Constitutionally Acceptable Definition of Religion*, 25 AMERICAN CRIMINAL LAW REVIEW 113, 139-140 (1987).

56. Edward McGlynn Gaffney, *Governmental Definition of Religion: The Rise and Fall of the IRS Regulations on an "Integrated Auxiliary of a Church,"* 25 VALPARAISO UNIVERSITY LAW REVIEW 203, 209 (1991).

57. Candomblé is an African-derived spirit possession trance cult, genetically related to other New World religions such as *voudon* (voodoo) and Santería. A recent ethnographic description of Candomblé is available in JIM WAFER, THE TASTE OF BLOOD: SPIRIT POSSESSION IN BRAZILIAN CANDOMBLÉ (1991).

58. Specifically, numbers 3-4, 6-8, 13-14.

59. Barringer v. Garrison, No. 80-6120, slip opinion (4th Cir. June 16, 1980), *quoted in* Jon Gelberg, *Inmate Wins Voodoo Appeal: Remand over Whether "Cult" is Religion*, NATIONAL LAW JOURNAL, July 21, 1980, at 4.

60. *See* Church of the Lukumi Babalu Aye, Inc. v. City of Hialeah, 508 U.S. 520 (1993).

61. Kent Greenawalt, *Religion as a Concept in Constitutional Law*, 72 CALIFORNIA LAW REVIEW 753, 757 (1984).

62. If methodology is the selector of theories, what are the criteria to select the method? The best answer to this question may differ according to whether it is asked of the individual scientist or the scientific community. *See* HUSAIN SARKAR, A THEORY OF METHOD (1983).

63. *See generally* JAMES H. LEUBA, A PSYCHOLOGICAL STUDY OF RELIGION (1912).

64. *See* Walter Houston Clark, *How Do Social Scientists Define Religion?* 47(1) JOURNAL OF SOCIAL PSYCHOLOGY 143 (1958).

65. Peter L. Berger, *Some Second Thoughts on Substantive versus Functional Definitions of Religion*, 13(2) JOURNAL FOR THE SCIENTIFIC STUDY OF RELIGION 125 (1974).

66. Edward B. Tylor, *Animism, in* READER IN COMPARATIVE RELIGION: AN ANTHROPOLOGICAL APPROACH 9-10 (W.A. Lessa & E.Z. Vogt eds., 4th ed., 1979).

67. EMILE DURKHEIM, THE ELEMENTARY FORMS OF THE RELIGIOUS LIFE 37 (New York: Free Press, 1965) (1915).

68. *See* WILLIAM E. PADEN, RELIGIOUS WORLDS: THE COMPARATIVE STUDY OF RELIGION 11 (1988).

69. MARVIN HARRIS, THE RISE OF ANTHROPOLOGICAL THEORY 478 (1968).

70. *See generally* RUDOLF OTTO, THE IDEA OF THE HOLY (2nd ed., London: Oxford University Press, 1950) (1917).

71. CHARLES Y. GLOCK & RODNEY STARK, RELIGIONS AND SOCIETY IN TENSION 9 (1965).

72. *See id.* at 10-11.

73. *See* Rodney Stark, *Must All Religions Be Supernatural? in* THE SOCIAL IMPACT OF NEW RELIGIOUS MOVEMENTS 159, 161 (Bryan Wilson ed., 1981).

74. *Id.* at 162

75. *Id.* at 160-161.

76. *Id.* at 159.

77. Stark examines several phenomena such as declining hurch membership, geographic patterns, and other social trends that have led to the creation of nontraditional religious (i.e., nonsupernatual) religious forms. *See id.* at 163-175.
78. Mary Douglas, Purity and Danger: An Analysis of the Concepts of Pollution and Taboo 65 (London: Ark, 1984) (1966).
79. Durkheim, *supra* note 67, at 44.
80. *See id.* at 88, 91.
81. *See id.* at 90.
82. *Id.* at 93.
83. *See id.* at 96.
84. *Id.* at 98.
85. *Id.* at 87.
86. *See* Erich Fromm, Psychoanalysis and Religion 94-95 (1950).
87. *See* William James, the Varieties of Religious Experience 31-32 (New York: Longmans, Green, 1916) (1902).
88. *Id.* at 31, 38.
89. Otto, *supra* note 70, at xxi.
90. *See id.* at 3.
91. *Id.* at 2.
92. *See id.* at 4-5.
93. *Id.* at 6.
94. Leuba, *supra* note 63, at 37.
95. One exception is found in Peñalver, *supra* note 52, at 819. He claims that "The refusal to submit a belief system to scientific or philosophical standards of reason and evidence can be highly indicative that the system is a religion." Peñalver fails to grasp what a faith is. The mere "refusal" to submit is irrelevant; the essence of faith is that the proposition *cannot* be evaluated by scientific or philosophical (logical) standards, but is accepted as true nonetheless. Faith is not a substitute for rational thought; rather, it begins where rationality has exhausted itself.
96. Ernest Nagel & James R. Newman, Gödel's Proof 58-59 (1958).
97. J. van Heijenoort, *Gödel's Theorem*, 3 The Encyclopedia of Philosophy 348, 356 (1967).
98. Sigmund Freud, The Future of an Illusion 43 (New York: W.W. Norton, 1961) (1927).
99. Melford Spiro, Culture and Human Nature 197 (1987).
100. *Id.* at 192.
101. *See* William Herbrechtsmeier, *Buddhism and the Definition of Religion: One More Time*, 32 Journal for the Scientific Study of Religion 1 (1993).
102. *See id.* at 9.
103. Spiro, *supra* note 99, at 159.
104. *Id.* at 183.
105. *See* Sigmund Freud, Civilization and Its Discontents 20-21 (New York: W.W. Norton, 1961) (1930).
106. Spiro, *supra* note 99, at 203.
107. W.W. Meissner, Psychoanalysis and Religious Experience 60 (1984).
108. Andrew J. Weigert, *Whose Invisible Religion? Luckmann Revisited*, 35 Sociological Analysis 181, 184 (1974) (emphasis added).
109. Clifford Geertz, The Interpretation of Cultures 36 (1973) [hereinafter Interpretation].
110. Michael Murphy, Golf in the Kingdom (1972).
111. Bronislaw Malinowski, Magic, Science and Religion and Other Essays 89 (1948).
112. Malinowski's functional explanation of religion is described in more detail in James M. Donovan, *Implicit Religion and the Curvilinear Relationship between Religion and Death Anxiety*, 5 Implicit Religion 17 (2002). This article also recounts the con-

trast between Malinowski's approach and that by Radcliffe-Brown. If for Malinowski the function of religion was the mitigation of death anxiety, for Radcliffe-Brown religion was the *cause* of that anxiety, not its cure.

113. *Id.* at 89-90.

114. CLYDE KLUCKHOHN, MIRROR FOR MAN: THE RELATION OF ANTHROPOLOGY TO MODERN LIFE 214 (1985).

115. Clifford Geertz, *Religion: Anthropological Study*, 13 INTERNATIONAL ENCYCLOPEDIA OF THE SOCIAL SCIENCES 398, 401 (1968) [hereinafter *Anthropological Study*].

116. Geertz writes that religion is "(1) a system of symbols which acts to (2) establish powerful, pervasive , and long-lasting moods and motivations in men [and women] by (3) formulating conceptions of a general order of existence and (4) clothing these conceptions with such an aura of factuality that (5) the moods and motivations seem uniquely realistic." GEERTZ, INTERPRETATION, *supra* note 109, at 90.

117. Geertz, *Anthropological Study*, *supra* note 115, at 406.

118. Talal Asad, *Anthropological Conceptions of Religion: Reflections on Geertz*, 18 MAN 237 (1983).

119. Given the weight we place upon this criterion of conformity, we should point out that we do not depend solely upon Greenawalt's authority. Were it necessary, a separate argument could be marshaled that would reach the same result. Two prongs of that argument would be (1) since the average citizen believes that he or she already understands what "religion" is, an excessively jargonistic legal definition would be patently unacceptable, and would undermine the social authority of law in general; and (2) since the constitutional protections afforded religion are meaningful only if every citizen understands the terms, and the collateral duties and responsibilities attached to that term, the constitutional and legal definition of "religion" must conform, in the main, to the lay conception. The technical definition can be *deeper* than the common understanding, but it cannot significantly *diverge* from it without negating the intended benefits. JACK DONNELLY, INTERNATIONAL HUMAN RIGHTS 35 (1993).

Most writers deny that the international conventions on human rights exhibit this bias. De Bary, for example, argues at length that the presumed incompatibility of Confucianism with Western human rights ideals is greatly overblown. *See* WM. THEODORE DE BARY, ASIAN VALUES AND HUMAN RIGHTS (1998). But just as the ideological differences should not be exaggerated, neither should they be glossed over. *See* ALISON DUNDES RENTELN, INTERNATIONAL HUMAN RIGHTS: UNIVERSALISM VERSUS RELATIVISM (1990). Some tension does exist. Immediately after insisting that it would be "wrong to content, as some do, that the [human rights] code insists on imposing 'Western' or 'First World' structures of government on peoples who have different traditions," Sieghart rather sheepishly goes on to admit that "the code does have a subtle bias in favour of democracy." PAUL SIEGHART, THE LAWFUL RIGHTS OF MANKIND 160 (1985).

121. *See generally* Laurence R. Helfer, *Forum Shopping for Human Rights*, 148 UNIVERSITY OF PENNSYLVANIA LAW REVIEW 285 (1999).

122. SIEGHART, *supra* note 120, at 43. Were we to pursue this inquiry in greater depth, we would have to apply the results of our discussion above and excise Sieghart's third element of "equality" as being conceptually redundant and possessing no substantive content of its own.

123. Wesley Newcomb Hohfeld, *Some Fundamental Legal Conceptions as Applied in Judicial Reasoning*, 23 YALE LAW JOURNAL 16 (1913).

124. *Id.* at 30.

125. *Id.*

126. *Id.* at 31.

127. *See, e.g.,* Jeanne M. Woods, *Justiciable Social Rights*, 38 Texas International Law Journal (forthcoming 2003).

128. Sieghart, *supra* note 120, at 60. As contrasted with these four, Sieghart tallies from the relevant international documents a much longer list of "forty or fifty distinct rights and freedoms." *Id.* at 81.

129. In American society, conservative Republicans frequently question the justification for governmental involvement in education, at least at the federal level, for just this reason—the Constitution fails to assign this task to the federal government. At the international level, Article 26 of the United Nations' Universal Declaration of Human Rights declares that "Everyone has the right to education." The argument could be made that, if nowhere else, our federal government has acquired the duty to provide education for all its citizens through the recognition and adoption of this instrument.

130. Michael Freeman, *The Philosophical Foundations of Human Rights*, 16 Human Rights Quarterly 491, 495 (1994).

131. S. Prakash Sinha, *Why and How Human Rights*, 10(6) International Journal of Legal Information 308, 309 (1982).

   For an example of an argument favoring natural law as the basis for human rights, *see* Jean Rhéaume, *Human Rights and Human Nature*, 28 Revue Générale de Droit 523 (1997). Typical of this position, Rhéaume argues that (1) human rights exist even when denied by positive law, because (2) they are always recognized by a natural law discernable by correct human reasoning, and (3) this reasoning is an element of our human nature. This same reasoning also reveals our condition as beings "endowed with a spiritual immortal soul and a physical mortal body [who are] destined to eternal happiness and temporal well-being." *Id.* at 528-529. He is wrong to say that this belief is one supported by reason. *See* James M. Donovan, Reconciling Arguments regarding a Self-Preserving Soul with Evolutionary Theory (2000) (M.A. thesis, Louisiana State University). Even were this belief reasonable, it is not universal, and hence is a poor basis for the concept of human rights to the extent that we expect nations outside of our specific religious tradition to endorse and protect them.

132. *See* Bruce Bagemihl, Biological Exuberance: Animal Homosexuality and the Natural World (1998).

133. George C. Christie & Patrick H. Martin, Jurisprudence: Text and Readings on the Philosophy of Law 193 (2d ed., 1995).

134. Anthony J. Lisska, Aquinas's Theory of Natural Law: An Analytic Reconstruction 147 (1996).

135. John Finnis, Natural Law and Natural Rights 36 (1980) [hereinafter Natural Rights].

136. *Id.* at 30.

137. *Id.* at 31.

138. *Id.* at 65.

139. *See id.* at 68-69.

140. *See id.* at 73-75.

141. Although Finnis claims to be basing his list of basic goods upon an inductive reading of the anthropological literature, he directly cites very little of that literature at all, and almost none in this specific discussion of the basic goods. *See id.* at 18-19.

142. *See id.* at 86-90.

143. *Id.* at 90.

144. *Id.* at 93.

145. *Id.* at 280.

146. *Id.* at 214.

147. *Id.* at 223.

148. *Id.* at 225.
149. *Id.* at 100.
150. *Id.* at 85.
151. *Id.* at 30.
152. *Id.* at 86.
153. *See, e.g.*, John Finnis, *Law, Morality, and "Sexual Orientation,"* 69 NOTRE DAME L. REV. 1049, 1065 (1994).
154. *See* Leon R. Kass, *L'Chaim and Its Limits: Why Not Immortality,* 113 FIRST THINGS 17, 24 (May 2001).
155. *See* STEVEN REISS, WHO AM I? THE 16 BASIC DESIRES THAT MOTIVATE OUR BEHAVIOR AND DEFINE OUR PERSONALITY (2000).
156. *See* LON L. FULLER, THE MORALITY OF THE LAW 33-41 (1964).
157. FINNIS, NATURAL RIGHTS, *supra* note 135, at 68-69.
158. DAVID HUME, AN ENQUIRY CONCERNING HUMAN UNDERSTANDING (Antony Flew ed., La Salle, IL: Open Court, 1988) (1772); *see also* Robert J. Fogelin, *Hume's Scepticism, in* THE CAMBRIDGE COMPANION TO HUME (David Fate Norton ed., 1993).
159. FINNIS, *supra* note 135, at 32.
160. *Id.* at 69.
161. *Id.* at 62.
162. *Id.* at 106. The same difficulty attaches to his description of practical reasonableness, which includes the value of authenticity. Authenticity is a Heideggerian concept, which by definition is achieved by only the exceptional, existentially heroic individual. By no stretch of the imagination is authenticity a value that can be realized by just any human being, even if he or she works diligently to achieve it.
163. *See* PETER FITZPATRICK, MODERNISM AND THE GROUNDS OF LAW 92 (2001) ("the sustaining ethos of the common law was that it merely 'declared' an order subsisting elsewhere."). According to one analysis, it was the deconstruction of the belief that the common law tradition rested on external foundations such as the natural law that led to the increased reliance on other devices, such as *stare decisis*, to limit the freedom of judges to make law. *See* Caleb Nelson, *Stare Decisis and Demonstrably Erroneous Precedents,* 87(1) VIRGINIA LAW REVIEW 1, 22 (2001).
164. DONNELLY, *supra* note 120, at 19.
165. One recent attempt to explore the boundary between humans and animals is DOUGLAS KEITH CANDLAND, FERAL CHILDREN & CLEVER ANIMALS: REFLECTIONS ON HUMAN NATURE (1993); *see also* TIM INGOLD (ED.), WHAT IS AN ANIMAL? (1994).
166. E.H. Volkart, *Human Nature,* A DICTIONARY OF THE SOCIAL SCIENCES 306 (1964) (emphasis added).
167. L.S. WRIGHTSMAN, ASSUMPTIONS ABOUT HUMAN NATURE 46 (2nd ed., 1992).
168. An early articulation of this position is to be found in Aristotle's POLITICS:
an individual *incapable* of membership of a *polis* is not, strictly speaking, a human being, but rather a (non-human) animal, while one who is self-sufficient apart from the *polis* is superhuman, or, s Aristotle puts it, a god.... [One] cannot be a human being except in the context of a *polis*.
C.C.W. Taylor, *Politics, in* THE CAMBRIDGE COMPANION TO ARISTOTLE 233, 239 (Jonathan Barnes ed., 1995).
169. *See, e.g.*, STANLEY R. BARRETT, ANTHROPOLOGY: A STUDENT'S GUIDE TO THEORY AND METHOD 16 (1996) ("most anthropologists, including social anthropologists, would probably agree that what distinguishes *Homo sapiens* from other primates is culture.").
170. WILLIAM NOBLE & IAIN DAVIDSON, HUMAN EVOLUTION, LANGUAGE AND MIND 83 (1996). A description of the growing consensus that chimpanzees possess a true, if rudimentary, culture is given by Andrew Whiten and Christophe Boesch, *The Cultures of Chimpanzees,* 284(1) SCIENTIFIC AMERICAN 61 (January 2001).

171. *See* W.C. McGrew, L.F. Marchant, S.E. Scott, & C.E.G. Tutin, *Intergroup Differences in a Social Custom of Wild Chimpanzees: The Grooming Hand-Clasp of the Mahale Mountain*, 42 Current Anthropology 148 (2001); Frans de Waal, The Ape and the Sushi Master (2001). Similar claims have been made for other species. *See* Bruce Bower, *Whales and Dolphins Strut Their Social Stuff for Scientists*, 158 Science News 284 (October 28, 2000).

172. Joseph Hart, *Chimps Are People Too: But Should Their Rights Ape Our Own?* 99 Utne Reader 20 (May-June 2000); *see also* Jared M. Diamond, The Third Chimpanzee (1993).

173. Joel Feinberg, Social Philosophy 91 (1973). Feinberg's magnum opus, The Moral Limits of the Criminal Law (1984-88), is highly regarded. "In its impact on contemporary analytic philosophy, few works can compare. Practically everyone who thinks or writes about liberalism, legal moralism, autonomy, paternalism, coercion, and a host of other concepts in moral, legal, and political philosophy owes a debt to Feinberg's *Moral Limits*." Stuart P. Green, *Introduction to* Symposium, *The Moral Limits of the Criminal Law*, 5 Buffalo Criminal Law Review 1 (2001).

174. This historical observation shall stand as representative for the many arguments about the diminished capacities of women: "Some Elizabethans revived the Platonic doubts whether a woman could be considered as a reasoning creature; others questioned whether she had a soul." Lawrence Stone, The Family, Sex and Marriage in England, 1500-1800, at 137 (1979).

175. *See* Joyce E. Salisbury, *Human Beasts and Bestial Humans in the Middle Ages, in* Animal Acts: Configuring the Human in Western History 9, 15 (Jennifer Ham & Matthew Senior eds., 1997).

176. *See* Gregory B. Stone, *The Philosophical Beast: On Boccaccio's Tale of Cimone, in* Animal Acts, *supra* note 175, at 23.

177. Feinberg, *supra* note 173, at 86.

178. Judith Thomson claims that she has solved this problem. *See* Judith Jarvis Thomson, The Realm of Rights 1-33 (1990). We are unconvinced, however, by her argument that she has successfully found a way to argue from facts to values.

179. That the fetus lacks the qualities definitionally required of rights-holders seems, for example, to be one of the undiscussed implications of Paul Ricoeur, The Just 1-10 (David Pellauer trans., 2000).

180. Lewis Lord, *The Year One*, U.S. News & World Report, January 8, 2001, at 38, 41. John Locke also believed that children below the age of reason were not yet fully human. *See* Thomas de Zengotita, *The Functional Reduction of Kinship in the Social Thought of John Locke, in* Functionalism Historicized 10, 20 (George W. Stocking, Jr., ed., 1984).

181. Falling between this consideration of any natural source of human rights and that in the following section, the social attribution of rights, is the curious assertion that "human rights" are not the rights we need for health, economic security, and so forth, but are rather the rights we need to live lives of human "dignity." *See* Donnelly, *supra* note 120, at 21. It is unclear what such a claim means, and in any event it would advance our argument not at all, having only changed the terms of the debate, leaving us to ascertain the source and content of "dignity."

182. *See* Thomson, *supra* note 178. Although many books address the topic of the legal argument for rights, Thomson's work comes particularly well recommended. She has earned serious attention in both philosophy (*see* Shelly Kagen, Normative Ethics 317 (1998)) and law (*see* Book Note, *Talking about Rights: The Realm of Rights by Judith Jarvis Thomson*, 104 Harvard Law Review 1955 (1991); Richard J. Mooney, *1992 Survey of Books Relating to the Law; VI. Legal Philosophy: The Realm of Rights by Judith Jarvis Thomson*, 90 Michigan Law Review 1569 (1992)). *The Realm of Rights* is especially useful for our purposes because it picks up where Finnis leaves off. Whereas Finnis attempted to ground human rights in natural law by detailing

the *positive* content of the latter, Thomson attempts the same project via a different tactic—by *negative* implication. By critiquing how rights cannot be the result of positive law, she expects natural law to win by default.

183. THOMSON, *supra* note 178, at 75.

184. *See also* KAGEN, *supra* note 182, at 9:

> [T]he substantive moral claims of normative ethics should not be confused with descriptive claims about what people actually do, or about what various groups (or individuals) think people should do. But there is something else normative ethics should not be confused with: the law. Determining what people morally should do is not the same thing as determining what the *law* says they should do. For the law may permit some particular act, even though that act is immoral; and the law may forbid an act, even though that act is morally permissible, or even morally required.

185. THOMSON, *supra* note 178, at 76.

186. *Id.* at 274.

187. FEINBERG, *supra* note 173, at 67.

188. A recent invocation of this principle was made by the Vatican. In its buildup toward an apology "for the Roman Catholic Church's historical failings," the document entitled *Memory and Reconciliation* pointed out that "many acts of earlier centuries cannot be judged solely by contemporary moral standards." *Pope Releases Preface to Coming Apology*, TIMES-PICAYUNE (New Orleans), March 2, 2000, at A13. Moral principles are temporally relative in this way if they are based upon something that is itself temporally relative, like society. However this claim comports with the Vatican's broader stance on human rights, here they are depending upon the belief that they are *not* grounded in immutable features. Otherwise, what is immoral to our eyes today would have been necessarily immoral at the time they were committed, a charge the Vatican would prefer to avoid.

189. THOMSON, *supra* note 178, at 4. Thomson has here fallen victim to the weakness noticed by Simpson:

> The mass of people usually find that their own introspective judgment of right and wrong, the edicts of the authorities accepted by them, and the conventions of their society coincide rather closely. They coincide because their sources are related and because the individuals in society tend to modify them or to ignore their discrepancies so as to produce the illusion, at least, of coincidence.

GEORGE GAYLORD SIMPSON, THE MEANING OF EVOLUTION 295 (1950).

190. THOMSON, *supra* note 178, at 18.

191. Similarly, Thomson claims that "Isn't it obvious that *X*'s throwing a child into the water is something bad, and that *Y*'s jumping into the water to save it is something good? How could anyone think otherwise?" *Id.* at 131. Here's how:

> There is no Merit in saving an innocent Babe ready to drop into the Fire: The Action is neither good nor bad, and what Benefit soever the Infant received, we only obliged our selves; for to have seen it fall, and not strove to hinder it, would have caused a Pain [to ourselves], which Self-preservation compell'd us to prevent.

1 BERNARD MANDEVILLE, THE FABLE OF THE BEES 56 (Indianapolis, IN: LibertyClassics, 1988) (1732). This counterexample does not mean that Thomson is wrong, but only that what she assumes needs no supportive argument actually does need supportive argument.

192. 1 FRANCIS LIEBER, MANUAL OF POLITICAL ETHICS, DESIGNED CHIEFLY FOR THE USE OF COLLEGES AND STUDENTS AT LAW 200 (2nd ed., Philadelphia: J.B. Lippincott, 1876).

193. Quoted in SIEGHART, *supra* note 120, at 31.

194. Quoted by Freeman, *supra* note 130, at 498.

195. Peter Lawrence, *Law and Anthropology: The Need for Collaboration*, 1 MELANESIAN LAW JOURNAL 40, 44 (1970).

196. Another possible direction for our discussion could have concerned methodology, and the contribution that anthropological research techniques can make toward the untangling of legal problems. *See, e.g.*, William M. O'Barr & E.A. Lind, *Ethnography and Experimentation—Partners in Legal Research, in* THE TRIAL PROCESS (B.D. Sales ed., 1981). O'Barr, in partnership with John M. Conley, has authored many pieces demonstrating the beneficial application of ethnographic technique to courtroom and other legal contexts. *See, e.g.*, William M. O'Barr & John M. Conley, *Lay Expectations of the Civil Justice System*, 22 LAW & SOCIETY REVIEW 137 (1988); JOHN M. CONLEY & WILLIAM M. O'BARR, RULES VERSUS RELATIONSHIPS: THE ETHNOGRAPHY OF LEGAL DISCOURSE (1990); JOHN M. CONLEY & WILLIAM M. O'BARR, JUST WORDS: LAW, LANGUAGE, AND POWER (1998).

Chapter Four

THEORETICAL BENEFITS OF LAW TO ANTHROPOLOGY

The thesis of balanced reciprocity demands that law make theoretical contributions to anthropology. At first, this expectation may seem easily fulfilled given the success of the specialty of legal anthropology. But that study does not satisfy the criteria for balanced reciprocity, since in legal anthropology the anthropologist treats law as a subordinate object of study rather than as a coordinate disciplinary peer.

Just as anthropology intimately informs important concepts within law, law performs the same service for anthropology. We have already seen an example of this: although anthropology should be required to give content to the legal idea of the "human right," legal premises are the basis for the concept of the "right," which anthropology uses frequently.

Only a little reflection is required to realize how seminal the legal idea of a "right" is for anthropological inquiry. A plethora of other taken-for-granted analytic categories are but elaborations of this basic legal concept. For example, "property" is a special kind of right: a material thing becomes the "property" of whomever acquires the exclusive right to possess, use, and enjoy that particular thing. A prominent theory in law—the labor theory of value—holds that common material becomes personal property to the extent labor has been exerted over that material. Traditional ethnographic studies endeavor vigorously to identify who possesses what property, how these rights are transferred to whom, and by what means. A man in a matrilineal society can expect to inherit from his mother's brother; from a patrilineal society, from his father.

Notes for this section begin on page 198.

Kinship became the quintessential topic of study for social anthropology.[1] This dominance can be traced directly "to the 'comparative jurisprudence' practiced by [law trained] disciplinary founders like Maine and Morgan."[2] Kinship also contains within it the legal idea of a right: what claims, including property claims, can you make upon other persons by virtue of kin ties? Although seemingly an obvious biological fact, who you count as relatives is a complex sociocultural determination. From the biologically nominated persons, a culture will ignore some, emphasize others, and add in altogether new ones through the creation of fictitious kinship (e.g., adoptions, godparents). The kind of kinship bond you share with another person will dictate important elements of that relationship, especially in the more traditional societies. Who you can eat, sleep, laugh or war with, or from what group an acceptable partner for marriage may be found, can all be influenced, or even determined by, the ties of kinship shared by the participants. Some of these cultural options may be strongly colored as duties, both those you can claim from others, and those that can be claimed from you. Unraveling and understanding these threads of intermeshing kinship ties have occupied the careers of anthropologists for at least a couple of generations. And at the heart of this massive undertaking are pure legal concepts.

This kind of analysis alone, however, is too much like legal anthropology to satisfy our present needs. It uses legal ideas as one tool among many to achieve the anthropological goal of understanding culture. Even if they are superior tools, the implication is that the ends could, at least in theory, be attained without the benefit of those particular means. Balanced reciprocity requires a more intimate dependency between the two disciplines.

In anthropologists' ordinary practice, law has been regarded as a useful perspective on two of anthropology's most elemental concepts, society and culture. Law, the common view goes, may be an important part of those categories, but at the end of the day, it is only one part among many. It is possible, if not necessarily wise, to devote one's entire professional life to the study of society and culture without giving serious attention to law. Most anthropology departmental curricula easily demonstrate this observation: whereas courses on religion, for example, are routinely available, formal exposure to even the rudimentary distinctions in legal thought are rare.

In countermeasure, we assert here a strong claim. Law is not, as ordinarily supposed, merely one component among many of society and culture. Instead, law is uniquely necessary to both those concepts in a way that even religion is not. Specifically, law is originative of society, and the key to culture. By this statement, the claim to an understanding of either society or culture without a command of the law of that culture is self-refuting. We expect disagreement. The present chapter constitutes the most risky section of this book. However, we hope to defend our claim at least well enough to garner concession that law holds the position and performs the function we identify, leaving the most likely remaining objection that other institutions may hold an identical position and perform that same function. If we are successful even to this degree, however, we will have at least satisfied the immediate demand of balanced reciprocity.

Law as Originative of Society

Recall the concept discussed in chapter 3 of the "human right." One feature of that concept that attracted our attention was that the special relationship between law and anthropology is obvious in the term itself. "Human" is the anthropological object of study, while "right" is, at least in American legal thought, the legal concept par excellence. The goal of that discussion was to consider how these terms interact when conjoined into a single idea.

A similar term applies to the present discussion for exactly those same reasons. Consider the "social contract." Again, a purely anthropological idea is connected to a quintessential legal concept, one that is intimately involved in the origins of the American constitutional republic, as evidenced by statements about its moral authority arising from "the consent of the governed."[3] The effect of this word combination is to invoke a theory that has law and society mutually generating one another. The simple claim we make is that to the extent that the hypothesis of the social contract is valid or useful, to that same extent law and anthropology are dependent upon each other for the full explication of their own central concepts. Instead of law being merely one tool among many that anthropology invokes to understand society, law would be the privileged perspective to illuminate, if not the actual origin of social organization, at least its organizing principles.

Although the general theme of social contract theory has a longer intellectual history, it rose to special prominence in Western thought in the seventeenth century with Hobbes' *Leviathan*.[4] After further articulation by Rousseau and Locke, social contract theory fell into general neglect until its revival by John Rawls in his classic *A Theory of Justice* (1971). These theories "seek to legitimate civil authority by appealing to notions of rational agreement."[5] Social contract theories share in common (1) a depiction of humankind in a natural, presocial condition or "state of Nature"; (2) an identified lack or failing of that natural condition; and (3) a solution to that failure in the coming together of persons to form a new condition of society whereby each person sacrifices some of the benefits of the natural condition so as to gain the means to solve the greater problems of that condition. Each rendition of social contract theory puts its own spin on each of these accounts. Its depiction of the natural condition will necessarily contain the elements of the alleged shortcoming, and thereby the kind of contractual agreement required as a solution.

For Hobbes, the initial condition is a state of constant war, one against another, requiring a social contract that cedes near absolute power to the "mortal god" of the monarch. Locke takes a different view. Although the state of nature was not so brutal as Hobbes imagined, it inadequately protected private property. The state arose from the social contract with its primary purpose to protect property and to allow for the accumulation of capital. The state sanctioned by this contract is much more restricted in its legitimate powers than that required by Hobbes. Finally, Rawls imagines an initial condition of the original position behind a veil of ignorance, where persons are unaware of what traits they will hold in the world. Will they be male or female, black or white, rich or poor? Ignorant of their final positions, these persons negotiate to identify principles that would be fair to anyone in any position. These imaginary negotiations purportedly result in a social contract of "justice as fairness," and a liberal democratic welfare state.

Few today require the social contract to refer to an actual historical event. Instead, the social contract is a way of modeling the transition into organized group living from a more atomistic condition. But one does not have to consider too deeply the myth of the social contract before some perplexing tensions emerge. For the contract to command any deference, there must already exist the idea of obligation; for the participants to draw up the terms for the contracted society, they must already be familiar with what such a society might look like. In other words, if the social contract is to make any sense, even as an ahistorical explanatory device, it must presuppose what it intends to explain. The transition it purportedly marks, therefore, is not from the other to the new, but from a condition that already prefigures and contains the outcome. In that case, the significance of the social contract seems minimal.

The difficulties of the social contract are discussed in detail by Peter Fitzpatrick in his *Modernism and the Grounds of Law*. Fitzpatrick critiques a social contract text by an author other than those already mentioned. Instead of Hobbes or Locke, Fitzpatrick analyzes Freud's *Totem and Taboo* (1913). Freud, writing his own version of the anthropological origin tale, identified the origins of law and society in the primordial horde, when the sons rose up against the father and then murdered and consumed him. Besieged by guilt for their act of parricide, the sons denied themselves the fruits of this murder—sexual access to the father's women—and committed themselves to ritual reenactment of the original crime through cyclic killing and eating of the totem.[6] Of all the themes contained within this ambiguous tale, the one most important to our immediate interest is the conclusion that within the totem we find "the first society [and] the perfection of law."[7] Law and society are, in their most fundamental origins, coequal.

The result, Fitzpatrick claims, is that "elements of modern society provide grounds of law but these elements become socially effective when brought together by law."[8] Law does not emerge out of or within a prior society; law and society come into existence simultaneously. Law is constitutive of society in a way that other institutions, even religion, are not. It can be odd, but not inconceivable, to speak of a religion-less society. But a lawless society is by its own terms a contradiction: that which is without law is, by that fact alone, not a society. To ascertain the actual mechanisms of society, therefore, one must look to its true law (i.e., not simply its overt codes). To study society is necessarily to study law; otherwise one enters several scenes after the play has begun. That belated admission can cause one to be misled by surface appearances that mask the deeper relationships.

One can miss, for example, the opposition between law as a determining force in society, and law as "integrally responsive to possibility."[9] Too much of the former signals a "return to the total order of the primal horde";[10] too much of the latter, and law cannot fulfill its primary function to regulate society, failing to provide the necessary "certainty, predictability, and order" to ground a rule of law.[11] To mediate this balance[12] "law not only stands distinctly apart from, say, society, but also orders, shapes, or even creates society."[13]

Fitzpatrick's analysis is intriguing and exciting. If valid, he points out a critical symbiosis between the study of law and the study of society. Properly done, the one cannot outpace the other. The result warrants an initial admonishment to both law and anthropology to attend to what the other has to contribute. But law is less needful of a reminder to consider the impact of society on its subject matter, although it might be unaware of how deeply that impact strikes. The practice of anthropology, however, is more likely to expect that it can fruitfully study society without necessarily considering the role of law. We suggest that this assumption is an error, and that one of the benefits that law can render to anthropology in a relationship of balanced reciprocity is a theory of law that informs the study of society at the most basic level.

Law as the Key to Culture

Fitzpatrick contributed a chapter[14] to a collection edited by another Commonwealth law professor, Desmond Manderson. That collection, *Courting Death: The Law of Mortality* (1999), functions as the exemplary text for the second part of our demonstration: just as an understanding of society requires a command of law, so too does a grasp of culture uniquely profit from the lens of law.

Consider again the anthropological inquiry into kinship patterns. Anthropologists do not study kinship patterns simply for the joys of constructing arcane classification systems (or rather, they shouldn't). The real motivation is that if you follow the thread of a kinship tie closely enough through all of its points of social contacts, you will, in the end, have traced at least a rough outline of the whole of the culture:

> In any discussion of kinship some mention must be made of religion, politics, education, and other facets of culture. One simply cannot describe fully the kinship practices of any society without reference to most other aspects of culture.[15]

The purpose of kinship analysis is merely to afford an initial foothold into the structure of a target society. Even limited success in the endeavor will identify for the fieldworking anthropologist most of the major organizing principles, worldview tenets, and unspoken assumptions known to every culture participant and used daily to guide ordinary behaviors.

This same result can be achieved from almost any starting point. The ethnological assumption is that the parts of a sociocultural complex intimately interlock, so that a deep analysis of practically *any* selected behavioral pattern will eventually take you through the round of culture: To know *A*, you must first understand *B*, which requires knowledge of *C*, which presumes familiarity with *D*, and so forth, back all the way around again to *A*. To achieve knowledge of anything specifically, the anthropologist must first acquire a great deal of familiarity with everything generally.

By this research model, the initial point of entry into cultural analysis is irrelevant. Although that choice will obviously influence the form of the argument and its development, the final outcome—an accurate account of the target culture—should not be seriously affected. Many anthropologists choose the classic topics of religion or economics as their starting point; others achieve comparable success with more innocuous initial data. One of our acquaintance, for example, chose bicycle accidents on urban Chinese streets.[16]

The technical name for this approach is *functionalism* (or the closely related *structural-functionalism*), and it has been variously characterized:

> The functional view attempts to study the interrelation between the various elements, small and large, in a culture. Its object is essentially to achieve some expression of the unities in culture by indicating how trait and complex and pattern, however separate they may be, intermesh, as the gears of some machine to constitute a smoothly running, effectively functioning whole.[17]

For A.R. Radcliffe-Brown, the principle figure associated with this school, the parts of a social system are analogous to the organs of a body. Each performs its specialized task (its "function"), which contributes to the survival and health of the whole—in this case, the maintenance of the structural continuity of the society.[18]

The critical insight for our purpose is that a society is not an aggregate of independent institutions: law, religion, economics, agriculture, and so forth, which are somehow clumped together into a "culture." The parts are presumed to fit together to form a single whole, the society. The boundaries between these institutions are highly permeable, if they can be said to exist at all. Moreover, they work cooperatively to achieve a specific goal, to hold the society in equilibrium irrespective of extrinsic events.[19] A sociocultural system is, according to functionalists, normally homeostatic (like a thermostat in a room). To achieve this result, each component of the system must be responsive to changes in every other. If one becomes more or less, the others must compensate so that the net result is the same as before.

Although functionalism would seem to make sense, it does have its limitations as a complete anthropological theory. Its emphasis on stability makes it difficult to explain culture change except as an aberration or system failure.[20] On the contrary, conflict of some kind is now taken to be the normal condition for a culture; it is homeostasis or stability that is aberrant. Another shortcoming of functionalism is that since it is designed to explain the continuation of a sociocultural system, it cannot account for that system's origins. These limitations do not detract from the original premise that sociocultural elements are interconnected. Even if useful only heuristically rather than theoretically,[21] functionalism still serves as an invaluable organizing principle for the gathering of data.

Below we will argue that law constitutes not merely one among many available entry points into the culture round; it is, in fact, a uniquely effective one. This privileged stature derives from its special ability to inform on the motivational impetus that spurs cultural development in the first place. In what follows we veer closer to "doing" anthropology than to merely "reviewing" the received findings of that field. We should immediately put the reader on notice that our example is far from the received consensus of either anthropology or law. While some may disagree with our particular example, we hope that it serves to underscore the flow of theoretical benefit from law to anthropology.

Law as Revelator of Attitude

Fundamental to our approach is the proposition that law grants unique access into the round of culture. An easy example concerns homosexuality. A detailed understanding of a society's stance toward homosexuality would be an important component of other issues, such as sexual stereotypes generally, their relative rigidity, and thence onto all matters regarding interactions between the sexes.[22] How could one reliably plumb this posture? Religious proclamations would be pertinent, but not directly. Not all religions represent core social values; others are peripheral in their emphasis. Our primary interest would be in actual attitudes, which religious rules do not always reflect. Religion tends to be a conservative institution, with the result that its positions on such matters as sex lag behind those of the wider culture of which it is one part.

Another approach might be to conduct a survey of a representative cross section of respondents. Although this method will yield the desired result, it is expensive, time-consuming, and may again only elicit socially acceptable responses rather than a person's true attitudes. Perhaps an even larger obstacle to the routine enlistment of this method among anthropologists is that responding to standardized surveys, while so commonplace in our own culture as to be unremarkable, is still relatively new in others. This unfamiliarity brings with it a raft of complications, from the impact upon the respondents' perception of the anthropologist as a participant-observer to the unreliability of survey responses, either of which defeats the larger purpose of the data-gathering enterprise.

In contrast, legal actions are an excellent, and perhaps the best single means of assessing a society's attitudes on a controversial subject. Opponents are given the opportunity to present their views and have them debated, to the end that some definitive conclusion is reached, perhaps a law or a court decision. These outcomes cannot routinely diverge drastically from what would be acceptable to the majority of the involved constituencies without undermining the legal institution itself. So while not everyone will be happy with any specific determination, neither will it be completely idiosyncratic or wholly unrepresentative of the major opinions, tastes, and preferences of the population at large.

So, returning to our example, a very good handle on the American attitude toward homosexuality can be obtained by reviewing only a few laws and court decisions. For example, a Louisiana case held that to question someone's sexual orientation (i.e., to publicly call someone a homosexual) is not merely "susceptible of a defamatory meaning," but is defamatory "per se."[23] Malice and falsity, normally elements needing to be proven by the plaintiff, are, in this situation, to be presumed. The clear implication is that to be a homosexual is so horrible that there could never be a nondefamatory significance to such an accusation. The United States government had earlier adopted a similar stance in an amicus curiae brief to the Supreme Court. In *Linn v. Plant Guard Workers*[24] the government argued to limit liability to "grave" defamations; its own list of offenses rising to this level included criminal, treasonous, infamous, and (of course) homosexual conduct.

Other informative highlights would include the debates surrounding the attempt by Colorado to remove fundamental political remedies from its homosexual citizens in its ill-fated "Amendment 2," which was ruled unconstitutional by the U.S. Supreme Court.[25] The passage of the "Defense of Marriage Act" by the Congress,[26] and the roiling, ongoing confrontations about hate crime legislation round out the short list of specimen debates. Finally, we could note that even in the impassioned aftermath of the terrorist attack on the World Trade Center on September 11, 2001, and the response of public and private agencies to assist the families of the victims, diminished concern is extended to the same-sex partners of the killed gays and lesbians. The government's Victim Compensation Fund, for example, will dispense aid to survivors in compliance with state inheritance laws, which uniformly ignore the gay partner of the deceased. A command of all these materials would enable one to accurately place homosexuality within the cultural schema of contemporary America. Alternative methods would either be less accurate, or require much more effort to achieve the same results.

Our claim that law is a unique revelator of culture has thus far been argued pragmatically. It seems, in other words, to work better. We now offer theoretical justifications for this posture as well. In short, because culture develops as a response to our existential needs, and because law is also a development from those same existential needs, law is inherently attuned to culture in a way that other of our intellectual achievements are not. But that is where we will end up. We must first provide a basis for this claim.

Death and Humanity

We begin with a thumbnail sketch of our major example: (1) a central element of our "humanness" is our consciousness of our own mortality; (2) our grappling with this inescapable knowledge is what generates the psychological motivation that results in the building of cultural institutions; and (3) law offers an especially apt lens through which to view our collective attitudes toward death. If successfully argued, then we would be justified in asserting that (4) law is a privileged revelator of cultural meanings.

DEATH ANXIETY AS THE CRITERION OF HUMANNESS

Anthropology, we have said, is the study of what it means to be "human." The emphasis of this new problem requires that we expand "human" into its more complex compound "human being." The problematic term in that appellation is normally presumed to be "human," and in chapter 3 that was indeed the case. This section, however, argues that it is our grappling with the second term, "being," which provides the ground from which we rise into our humanity. Chapter 3 demonstrated that humans are something over and above *Homo sapiens*, that the former category cannot be delineated in mere biological terms. That shortfall, we saw, was the reason why the status of being "human" is a poor peg upon which to hang substantive claims such as claims to rights.

We now offer a more positive conclusion about what separates humans from the other members of the Animal Kingdom. The difference is not merely our self-consciousness, but particularly our consciousness of the mortality of that self. In other words, we are human not simply because we know that we *are*, but because we know that we will *die*.[27] The realization of this single existential fact sets us qualitatively apart from any other species on the planet. Thus, the plethora of new studies suggesting that animals may have a sense of self do not impinge upon the intuitive conviction that humans are still qualitatively different.

Despite the fact that few disagree that death constitutes a problem for human beings,[28] it has been surprisingly understudied. Not always a respectable topic within psychology, death-related studies have, however, been part of anthropology since its inception.[29] But recognizing the special problematic nature of death addresses only part of the issue. The real challenge entails analysis and explanation of that problematic nature. Certainly, the knowledge that we shall die can be disturbing, but so too are other bits of information. Some may minimize this fact, as when Batson lists the fear of death as just one among several important existential dilemmas.[30] Our challenge is to demonstrate that the more accurate assessment characterizes death anxiety as the protean psychological experience of the species, that the achievement of *sapiens* status comes at the price of inescapable anxiety.[31]

A glimmer of the magnitude of this death problem reveals itself in our very status as human *beings*, for then death, or *non*-being, becomes the antithesis of what we claim to be. This glib analysis, however, does not take us very far on the specifics, and unsurprisingly less agreement prevails on the magnitude of this death problem than in the attempts to account for its peculiar intractability.

Members of contemporary American society are not well positioned to recognize the power of the idea of personal mortality. We have raised the avoidance of death to a high art. Where once death was an element of everyday life, we now relegate the process to the hospital and the nursing home, and the remnants to the funeral parlor.[32] Entire institutions have as a primary purpose the masking of death from our view. These endeavors have not removed the problem of death, but they have allowed us to bury it away from our conscious thoughts. Carl Jung addressed this façade of nonchalance:

> Naturally we have on hand for every eventuality one or two suitable banalities about life which we occasionally hand out to the other fellow, such as "everyone must die sometime," "one doesn't live forever," etc. But when one is alone and it is night and so dark and still that one hears nothing and sees nothing but the thoughts which add and subtract the years, and the long row of disagreeable facts which remorselessly indicate how far the hand of the clock has moved forward, and the slow, irresistible approach of the wall of darkness which will eventually engulf everything you love, possess, wish, strive and hope for—then all our profundities about life slink off to some undiscoverable hiding place, and fear envelops the sleepless one like a smothering blanket.[33]

To find out how death anxiety affects us when we do allow ourselves to think about it, we must look elsewhere.

Writing about his fieldwork among the Nuer, Evans-Pritchard observed that these African peoples "regard [death] as the most dreadful of all dreadful things."[34] The price for leaving this anxiety unresolved can be high:

> Procreation of the Australian aborigines ... diminishes or ceases altogether if their unconscious mental life is disturbed. Far more than among ourselves, their biological productivity seems also to be dependent upon their mental balance.
>
> Disturbances of the subconscious have the effect of reducing the number of children. The aborigines express the inadequate mental disposition to procreation by saying: "We cannot dream any more children."[35]

According to Margaret Mead this pattern is common:

> Faced with any sort of new situation—the coming of the white man in the Pacific, the disappearance of the buffalo on the American plains, the introduction of firearms, even simply the need to cope with a river when a group had formerly been a bush people—a group may find its social arrangements so altered that it is impossible to keep the population moving in a stable or desirable direction. Many small South Seas populations, without any new contraceptive practices, began to die out in the face of the white man's advance....

Such reductions in the birth-rate may be an accurate measure of despair, but we still know very little about the mechanisms that are involved. Very often they cannot be referred to such simple social conditions as a later age of marriage or a lower marriage rate, or to overt practices like contraception, abortion, and infanticide. Behind all of these age-old devices there lies a subtler factor, a willingness or an unwillingness to breed that is deeply imbedded in the character structure of both men and women.[36]

These observations by anthropologists make two points. One is the seriousness of the problem of unrelieved death anxiety. The second is that it is not the simple death of the body that is of primary importance, but rather the death of the self and the systems of meaning defining that self. The death that is feared may or may not involve the destruction of the body.

In *The Denial of Death* Ernest Becker, an anthropologist by training, powerfully asserts the unique impact that our awareness of death inflicts upon our human existence. The "idea of death, the fear of it, haunts the human animal like nothing else; it is a mainspring of human activity—activity designed largely to avoid the fatality of death, to overcome it by denying in some way that it is the final destiny for man."[37] Having described the stupefying terribleness of this reality, Becker seems to rely upon our intuitive recognition of its seriousness. This concession we readily grant, but we demand more in the way of understanding the contours of this obsession. But Becker fails to develop explicitly and in detail, or at the least in any way convincingly, *why* death should be so especially problematic. To address this issue we need to consider what Becker envisions as experiencing death.

His riveting depiction of the horrifying thought that God made man, a creature of sublime complexity and transcendent moral potential, to be nothing more than "worm food," suggests that he most usually understands death to be what the body experiences. For Becker, the body as container for the self is the object of the fear. This approach is fully in keeping with the Enlightenment assumption that the self must be taken as one object among innumerable others. The self and the body form a unit (an Aristotelian perspective), and it is this unit that dies. Consequently, the threat of death is necessarily the threat to bodily continuance. The genesis of the fear is that since the body and the self are a unit, and since we know beyond all doubt that the body does die, the idea inescapably arises that the self must also die at that same moment. We fear physical death only because we fear existential death, and the first entails the second.

Yet only a moment's reflection shows our anxieties about death to be empirically broader than concerns about mere corporeal endurance. One can actually whittle away significant chunks of the physical body without incurring death. Organs can be replaced with mechanical devices without compromising either life or sense of self. Even the brain need not be intact to preserve life, and its viability depends less upon the preservation of any specific organic isolate than upon some minimal structure. As Kierkegaard (a significant influence on Becker) noted, "there is much [a person] can lose without losing the self."[38] Against this background of nonspecific physicality, where, then, does the self reside? Not, apparently, with the body, even if it is in some sense centered on that body.

If the death problem were solely, or even primarily, reframeable as a problem of bodily continuance, then as we master techniques that extend that continuance, to that same degree our anxiety over death should decrease.[39] Since we have yet to achieve immortality, we expect some amounts of death fear to remain; but also since our medical technologies have vastly extended life expectancies, we should expect that our death fears would be observably less than they are. As our life spans extend into the seventh or eighth decade, we should experience long periods when we can comfortably convince ourselves that personal death is not a daily possibility. But two bodies of data demonstrate that this negative correlation between death anxiety and technology does not seem to be the case.

First, levels of death anxiety as they are currently quantified do not seem to vary according to the technological achievements of the culture group.[40] Second, we have no reason to believe, as this position would require, that death anxiety was greater in less technologically advanced eras. On the contrary, some historical reviews suggest that earlier societies that lacked our scientific advantages were, if anything, *less* vulnerable to excessive death concerns.[41]

One explanation for this inversion of our initial expectations readily presents itself. As medical improvements have extended bodily continuance, we have noticed that this accomplishment has *not* noticeably mitigated our death fears. This experiential outcome directly refutes the reigning ideology that holds that, if only we could live longer, we might grow more confident in our ability to cheat death. Whatever the prospects of attaining this immortal ideal, at the very least it afforded the psychological comfort of presuming to know where lay the antidote to death. But the successful manipulation of that variable has not rendered the expected relief; we have longer lived bodies but no less death anxiety. Consequently, we have as much anxiety as before, but now we lack the comforting thought that we know what to do about it, if only we could. The net outcome may be that without this presumed solution to buffer our raw experiences, we endure more anxiety than ever before.

These considerations converge to force the conclusion that the living self is not a property of the body in the sense usually assumed, such that it is the death of the body that presents the existential problem. The problematic death may well be coterminous with the body, so that when the body dies this other thing dies also. But even if co-occurring (and we doubt that they are), the outcomes would be distinguishable.

We should thus all be agreed that although the death of the body is an obstacle, this is not the death that obsesses our thoughts. Where, then, should we look?

Becker's philosophical charter for his analysis comes from Søren Kierkegaard. As a Christian determined to defend Christianity from Christendom, Kierkegaard acknowledged the death of the body, and was one of the first philosophers to isolate the individual's confrontation with death awareness as formative for her moral maturity. But he denied that the spirit suffered the body's fate: "In natural death a kind of once-for-all annihilation occurs when a man's body ceases to be animated, but in spiritual death there is no such annihilation. If the sickness [unto death] does not heal, the man is destroyed, yet he lives on; he is reduced to nothing, yet he remains. He does not experience annihilation, but the process of annihilation. The reason is in the spiritual ontology. Ontologically, the spirit is eternal and does not expire."[42]

Shorn of its particular religious adornments, Kierkegaard resolves the anxiety over physical death by positing the existence of an immortal soul or spirit distinguishable from the physical body, a classic Cartesian dualism framed by the specific context of our problem. The self previously associated with the body is now whisked away by the spirit when that body expires, the spirit moving on to experience nonmaterial realities. The assertion of such spirits was, as chapter 3 discussed, the essence of Tylor's minimal definition of "religion." In that formulation, the institution of religion becomes vested with the responsibility to manage our species' anxieties about death by rendering the spirit hypothesis a reasonable proposition to believe. Our worries now allayed by this religious belief in enduring spirits, the idea of personal physical death becomes tolerable.

The spirit hypothesis has a great appeal, evidenced by its almost universal appearance cross-culturally. But this solution to the death problem has serious flaws. Even if Becker and those who share his perspective adequately disambiguate the natural or physical death from the spiritual "sickness unto death," by thinking in terms of "spirit" at all, the very dilemma they claim to be resolving has become a straw man. How awful can death really be if there is an enduring spirit? Answer: Not very. To assert the existence of an immortal soul in which the self survives intact is to deny the initial premise—that death is a uniquely "mortifying" psychological and philosophical conundrum. In retrospect, they do not argue that death *is* a problem, but only that it *would be* a problem were it not for this enduring spirit. They have answered a completely different question than the one we began with.

We should accept Becker as sincere in his characterization of death as a genuine problem, and not as using that depiction as a rhetorical strategy to bolster other metaphysical claims. But to recognize sincerely the profound problem that is death is necessarily to concede a psychological state that *precedes* recognition (or creation) of the idea of a soul. In other words, the spirit or soul is at least a cognitively more recent acquisition than is death anxiety—at least developmentally, and perhaps even evolutionarily.

If death anxiety is a problem of the magnitude Becker and other authors suggest—and few serious thinkers on the human condition would contest this observation[43]—then logically it must precede the cultural institution with which it is most closely associated, religion. At the very least, this temporal succession leaves open the real possibility that the one *causes* the other. We see here an early glimmer of our major point, which is that awareness of our own mortality drives the subsequent development of culture.

Before moving on to consider that proposition, one further argument needs to be presented here. The claim is not simply that death is a problem for human beings, but that it is the problem that ultimately *makes* us human beings. At the least, this means that other members of the Animal Kingdom are spared this particular anxiety. This conclusion is Becker's own opinion,[44] but it can be a close call.

Awareness of personal death is possible in *Homo* by virtue of specific cerebral endowments that permit future awareness and the imaginary acting out within those possible futures. The same cognitive ability that permits us to plan for next month's birthday party has the inevitable, if unfortunate, side effect of also thrusting before our mind's eye our own deaths. Therefore, death can only be a problem for animals with (a) a sense of self that (b) they can imaginatively project into the future.

Some animals apparently possess self-recognition, which is the prerequisite to death anxiety.[45] David Premack muses that "until I can suggest concrete steps in teaching the concept of death without fear, I have no intention of imparting knowledge of mortality to the ape."[46] They may not need his instruction. Primatologist Alison Jolly refers, albeit with skepticism, to reports that gorillas are capable of discussing "abstract ideas such as death."[47] Similar reports come from Frans de Waal, a noted ethologist, who writes that "chimpanzees may respond emotionally as if realizing, however vaguely, what death means."[48]

Roger Fouts recounts this story about Washoe, a chimpanzee taught American Sign Language. One of Washoe's caretakers became pregnant, and missed work for many weeks after she miscarried.

> People who should be there for her and aren't are often later given the cold shoulder—her way of informing them that she's miffed at them. Washoe greeted Kat [the caretaker] in just this way when she finally returned to work with the chimps. Kat made her apologies to Washoe, then decided to tell her the truth, signing "MY BABY DIED." Washoe stared at her, then looked down. She finally peered into Kat's eyes again and carefully signed, "CRY," touching her cheek and drawing her finger down the path a tear would make on a human. (Chimpanzees don't shed tears.) Kat later remarked that that one sign told her more about Washoe and her mental capabilities than all her longer, grammatically perfect sentences. When Kat prepared to leave that day, Washoe did not want her to go without some emotional support. She signed "PLEASE PERSON HUG."[49]

The opinions on the mental abilities of the chimpanzee, our nearest relative, span the extremes. On the one hand, they are said to "have very different minds" from ours,[50] while on the other, the conclusion is that "the chimpanzee and the human mind are essentially the same."[51]

The most that can be said is that these higher primates have a grasp of the implications of the death of *others*. No evidence suggests that they go on to attain an awareness of their own impending mortality. Death anxiety remains the peculiar accomplishment of *Homo sapiens*.

CULTURE AS A RESPONSE TO DEATH ANXIETY

The problem of death anxiety must be resolved lest crushing despair ensue. The counterweight to this anxiety is religion. Religion—and we have seen hints of this throughout the last two chapters—provides the individual with a basis to believe that death has been, if not tamed, at least understood. It may be no less inevitable, but at least it need not be a mystery.

Critical to our discussion is the distinction between religion as a function and religion as an institution.[52] The institutions of religions— the churches, mosques, synagogues, temples, and so forth—may or may not actually serve this function at any given moment for any given person. Moreover, institutionalized religions can vary in their effectiveness of addressing this problem, making it sensible to speak of one religion being "better" than another in this regard. The religious function, however, can be performed by anything, including, it has been suggested, golf.

The ties between death and institutional religion have always been tight. When reviewing the changes that had transpired in a small, conservative Catholic parish in France, Yves Lambert noted many of the

expected signs of secularization. What had been near-unanimous attendance at services fifty years before had severely tapered off, so that, on
any given Sunday, only one-third of the parishioners attended. But even
within this environment of growing religious apathy, there was one—
and within this village *only* one—occasion that could still crowd the
pews: "Death remains the strongest link between the villagers and religion: All Saints is the only occasion on which the church is full."[53]

One of the major debilitating reactions to death is to doubt whether
the struggle to remain alive is worth the effort. Institutional religions
prototypically serve to assign meaning to life in the face of this inescapable defeat. They may do this by asserting that this life is but a
precursor to some other phase of existence (where things have a chance
of being better). Or that we owe this effort to our gods or ancestors simply as a matter of duty. Whatever the answer given, the goal is to give
an answer of some kind that is believable to the individual.

But not all religious functions are fulfilled by institutional religions.
Another way to escape the complete catastrophe of death is to distribute the "self" throughout the social system so that even when our bodies die, we can believe that we yet survive. Unlike other animals, a
human's ego is not bounded by the skin of her body but can extend
throughout the social fabric, incorporating items physically external to
the body into the sense of self, the ego. Through a process of empathic
identification, we invest entities and institutions with parts of our ego.
Our children, our country, our religion—any one of innumerable external foci allow us to bravely face death so long as *they* continue on. Part
of the enduring importance of things like kinship systems, then, is that
membership in a strongly cohesive group provides one way to parcel
out the ego in the hope that even when the personal body dies, these
other bits will survive. When these alternative ego-containers themselves begin to disintegrate, the impact can be disastrous.

The strategy of ego-dispersion is therefore a double-edged sword. In
order to escape the consequences of the personal death event, we
expand our egos beyond our bodies, vesting external entities with a
sense of our own selves. But this means that we are always at risk of
having *some* part of ourselves always dying. The single, catastrophic
death has been evaded at the price of what Salvatore Maddi terms the
innumerable "small deaths" of everyday life:

> A small confrontation with death occurs whenever something ends that you
> did not want to end, or whenever you are overwhelmed by the insufficiency
> of time and energy to do all that you sincerely wish to do, or whenever
> events are monotonous. The mental experience in these events is fear, how-
> ever mild, that things are beyond your control and do not necessarily conform
> to your wishes. Another small confrontation with death that is important
> occurs whenever your conventional values are contradicted by events.[54]

We can see why people can behave so irrationally in the face of social change. Everytime something in which we have invested our ego disappears, that part of us so invested disappears with it. To change is, in a real sense, to die, and unless one has alternative survival strategies, the reaction will be more stubborn than gracious.

The point is that in response to the problem of death, our species has evolved two kinds of cultural responses. The first was to create an institution whose primary purpose was to directly confront and dissipate the fear of death. These are the institutions normally covered by the term "religion." The second response was to elaborate alternative repositories for the individual's ego: extended families, nation-states, secret brotherhoods—any group with which the person could identify, onto which he or she could project some portion of the sense of self. In combination, these cultural solutions allowed the individual to believe that life had meaning despite the inevitability of death, and that in any event, some important part of her would escape the full brunt of death.

If this argument is at all reasonable,[55] then "religion stands as a shorthand for the whole of a given culture; its world view, its culturally constituted behavioral environment, its values (including those involved in human interactions) and its meanings and symbols."[56] We are not surprised to learn that to theologians "culture is the expression of religion,"[57] but this opinion is also shared by many prominent social scientists. Religion is

> not only *the* social phenomenon (as in Durkheim), but indeed *the* anthropological phenomenon *par excellence*. Specifically, religion is equated with symbolic self-transcendence. Thus everything genuinely human is *ipso facto* religious and the only nonreligious phenomena in the human sphere are those that are grounded in man's animal nature, or more precisely, that part of his biological constitution that he has *in common* with other animals.[58]

If culture is largely the expression of religion (taken here as the combination of institution and function), or at least religious concerns, then this must mean that culture, all of culture, is nothing but the accretion through time of death-denying strategies.

> Most, perhaps all, known cultures can be better understood ... if conceived of as alternative ways in which the primary trait of human existence—*the fact of mortality and the knowledge of it*—is dealt with and processed, so that it may turn from the condition of impossibility of meaningful life into the major source of life's meaning.[59]

The stuff of which culture is made, wrote Géza Róheim, is "defence systems against anxiety." Humankind, he says, has evolved culture because of the great danger "of being left alone in the dark."[60]

We agree, in other words, with Franz Borkenau when he writes that "the self-contradictory experience of death is a basic element in shaping the course of human history,"[61] a belief he shared with the philosopher Hegel.[62] Indeed, it is "fascinating to consider what human history would have been like if the representational capacity of man had not been linked so urgently to the solution of one problem—the knowledge and dread of death."[63] In a nontrivial sense, there would have been no *human* history at all, but only an ahistorical account of *Homo sapiens*.

Speculating on origins, beginnings, or first causes is no longer fashionable in anthropology: "What culture depends on is then of course the kind of question no well behaved anthropologist should ask, because looking for origins is 'outmoded,' in fact it is nineteenth century, a truly terrible thing, a word loaded with the worst possible kind of *mana*."[64] But it is hard to escape the obvious conclusion: man is a cultural animal only because he is a religious one, and he is that because he is an anxious one, and of all things he is most anxious about the prospect of his own death. Our entire cultural and individual histories can be—should be—interpreted as cumulative attempts to address, repress, or deny the raw fact of personal death.[65]

The Relationship between Law and Death

Where within this developmental model of death, religion, and culture does law figure? The elements of our response are cogently articulated by Desmond Manderson.[66] He begins by asserting the same point outlined above: "our challenge is not just to accept death but to understand its meaning for us, and to appreciate why our human societies have developed this particular understanding of it."[67] Law, according to Manderson, is especially positioned to bring privileged insight to the contemplation of death because they are both expressions of "the human capacity for responsible action."

> Law is the collective expression of our belief in the human capacity for responsible action. It defines, authorises and enforces responsible conduct. Our responsibility is nowhere more profound than in relation to death, a duty from which noone can relieve us. But these two types of responsibility—one legal, one ethical; one social, one personal—are contradictory. On the one hand, law seeks to control every aspect of our lives, including the manner of our passing; while death is precisely that element which lies outside of our control. On the other, the legal order is constructed around individual action and responsibility, yet death is precisely the moment at which this "I" ceases to be. There are two desires here, Apollonian and Dionysian. The law expresses our desire for individuality and control, while death suggests a desire for dissolution and transcendence.[68]

"Law and death," Manderson concludes, "meet in the crypt."[69]

Just as Becker relies heavily upon Kierkegaard, Manderson's invocation of the concept of responsibility in relation to death is meant to call the reader's attention to the philosophy of Martin Heidegger. The existential analytic of Heidegger's *Being and Time* (1927) has at its center the confrontation of the *Dasein* (for our purposes only, a German term translated loosely as "human being") with death. The importance of death for Heidegger is that it forces a recognition of our finitude: in its face we are compelled to recognize our existential condition as "thrown" and "fallen."

"Thrown" and "fallen" example Heidegger's talent for turning ordinary words into exacting technical jargon. Thrown-ness refers to the conditions into which we are born and over which we have no control: our sex, our parents, our nationality, and so forth. We are each "thrown" into a preexisting cultural world that molds and shapes us. "Fallen" is a negative condition. At critical moments (as in the confrontation with death) we are faced with the choice to either claim our individuality, or to retreat in fear back into the faceless "They" who govern everyday life. The They are the subjects of our statements about common wisdom: They say that.... They always do this…, and so forth. The They are pitiless dictators of everyday life, but by conforming to the dictates of the They, we are relieved of making decisions for ourselves. What is the fashion, what is current, what is popular: these are handed to us by the They.

Those who remain thrown and fallen are "inauthentic." The emergence from this condition into one of "authenticity" requires deliberate choice. We are presented with this choice most clearly in the knowledge of our personal mortality. Anxiety in the face of death moves us out of our complacent existence among the They and into a recognition of our true condition as having possibilities: "The essence of the originally nihilating nothing lies in this, that it brings Da-sein for the first time before beings as such."[70] An authentic person is one who is able to make choices because she recognizes that she has a choice, that the tyranny of the They is not inevitable. Only when we are aware that we have choices can we truly make choices. And only when we have choices can we be held responsible for bad choices. Shorn of its peculiarly Heideggerian setting, the claim is simply that legal liability rests on a presumption of a personal power to choose to act otherwise, which power springs from freedom and authenticity. Where some might argue that this freedom is our natural condition, Heidegger finds it a hard-fought accomplishment.

The moral conditions that the law presumes (personal responsibility, free will) are possible, according to Heidegger, only in an "authentic" existence, and one achieves authenticity by facing death and recognizing it for what it is: the absolute and utter end. In Manderson's words, "In the concept of responsibility, the logic of the law which requires it meets the ethics of death that constitutes it."[71] Without an encounter with the knowledge of personal death, there is no responsibility, and without responsibility, there can be no law.

Manderson further maintains that justice, a goal of much of the law, makes sense only against this background of mortality:

> Death makes justice possible because it provides the horizon or parameters of a life in which freedom and responsibility are not simply functions of obedience or of calculation. But by the same token, injustice and illegality become equally possible choices. Without death there is neither, only a grey insomnia of passivity, a state of suspended animation....[72]

It is only a slight overstatement, he claims, "to say that the concept of immortality governed by a system of punishment and reward renders justice impossible ... One cannot but wonder if there might not be more justice and less arrogance in a world that had a better sense of its own mortality."[73]

In summary, law is possible only because individuals are presumed to possess freedom and power to choose, and may therefore be justly held responsible for their actions. The genuine ability to choose, even to choose unwisely, contrasts with the mere somnambulistic role-fulfillment characteristic of ordinary existence. The emergence of the authentic self, one able to choose, is a consequence of the stark personal encounter with one's own death.

Law, Manderson seems to say, is but the inverted reflection of the significance of death. In any event, the relationship between the two appears to be intimate. This Heideggerian analysis cannot be pressed too far, however. If only authentic persons can choose, and are therefore responsible, then only authentic persons are subject to the law and its retributions. But according to Heidegger, very few persons ever actually achieve true authenticity. Indeed, one could reasonably conclude from reading the body of his writings that the whole universe of authentic persons who ever lived—some German poets and maybe a few ancient Greeks—could be counted on two hands. If true, then the number of persons subject to the law would be small, and that cannot be the point Manderson wishes to make. So while the full philosophical details remain to be thrashed out, the general conclusion remains valid: law and death are specially joined by their mutual participation with other concepts, such as responsibility.[74]

Law as the Privileged Lens on Culture

Combining the results of the previous two sections, we find on the one hand that culture, and especially religion, is one enormous death-deny-

ing project, and on the other, that law, due to its own inherent presup-
positions about human nature, is itself intimately attuned to the death
problem. Law and culture therefore have in common a primordial relationship to death. The details of those relationships are not the same.
Whereas culture is the outcome of the wish to flee from death, law is
the benefit of successful confrontation with death. Despite this difference, we can suppose that law is, nonetheless, sympathetic (to invoke
a Frazerian image) to the cultural whole. This is not to deny that law is
technically only one portion of culture; it is only to claim that it is the
one portion which is most like the whole in terms of its underlying genesis. If true, then for students of culture, law would be the single best
access point.

This claim elicits an obvious retort. Given what has been said—that
man is a cultural animal because he is a religious animal—should not
religion be the superior point of entrance into culture, not law? We
defend our position with two observations. First, religion in the functional sense is almost synonymous with the culture itself. From the perspective of methodology, the use of religion to illume the cultural logic
can approach circularity. For the exercise to be enlightening, we would
almost have to presume the kind of knowledge we are trying to obtain.
Law, on the other hand, emerges from the same elemental existential
stuff that produces religion and culture, but without being identical to
these in its solution. Culture and religion are death-*denying*, whereas
law is death-*affirming*. Given that death is real, an inquiry into the cultural institution of law provides illumination about the realities of the
culture rather than its wishes and fantasies.

Religion in the institutional sense fares little better. The primary
level of efficacy of religion is the individual.[75] Religion as an institution
arises only indirectly, as an efficient means to achieve this kind of private benefit. A society lacking institutional religion would be unusual in
the extreme, but it would not be nonsensical or self-contradictory. If
every individual were capable of arriving at their religious solutions
independently, then there would be no need to construct a religious
institution. But there are economies of scale in this kind of endeavor,
and many persons prefer to believe what they are told to believe, rather
than to ferret out their own answers to disturbing existential questions.
Religious institutions do arise, but they are at one remove from the
source necessitating the religious solution.

In contrast, law is inherently a social institution that is never reducible, even in imagination, to the individual. While it is theoretically
possible to have individualized religion (and there will be some persons
in every society who have, in fact, adopted this strategy), personal law
is a contradiction in terms. A private standard of conduct does not rise

to the level of law because it lacks the threat of enforcement by either man or god.

Law is consequently a purer example of a cultural institution than is religion. If the goal is to research the cultural logic of a given group, the better strategy will be to do it through an institution that is itself necessarily sociocultural rather than one that is only contingently or accidentally sociocultural. While institutional religion may seem to some to be the best access point into the culture round of an unfamiliar society, we conclude that law would be the better choice. Law springs from the same source as does culture itself, and by definition operates at the same level of analysis as does culture.

Conclusion

The purpose of this chapter was to highlight one way in which law bestows important theoretical benefits onto anthropology. These benefits can take many forms. The more obvious exchange concerns the importation of developed legal concepts into anthropological thinking. We briefly illustrated this kind of benefit with the idea of the "right" and the "social contract."

Beneath this expected exchange of concepts, however, lies a more creative benefit. Anthropologists flesh out their understanding of a foreign culture by following the interlocking pieces of everyday life. The functionalist heuristic says that the full outline can be obtained regardless of the initial starting point. Even so, not all such points of entry are equally fruitful. Law, we believe, provides a privileged access to the culture round. This insight derives from the fact that both law and culture receive their "charters" from the same existential dilemma—the confrontation with the knowledge of personal mortality. Because they share this genetic relationship, we conclude that law is more sensitive to the logic of the specific culture, and therefore its study is more conducive to the extraction of insight into the study of culture itself.

If these suggestions seem audacious and fail to persuade the reader as to their correctness, they still serve to accomplish the immediate task of showing how law can throw fresh theoretical light on anthropological work.

Notes

1. *See* WALTER GOLDSCHMIDT, COMPARATIVE FUNCTIONALISM: AN ESSAY IN ANTHROPOLOGICAL THEORY 127 (1966) ("Kinship studies have a special place in anthropology; they have been of particular importance to the structural school of functionalists, who find in them an opportunity to relate one aspect of social behavior—the system of classifying kin—to others, especially formation of corporate groups and the regulation of marriage.").
2. Thomas de Zengotita, *The Functional Reduction of Kinship in the Social Thought of John Locke, in* FUNCTIONALISM HISTORICIZED: ESSAYS ON BRITISH SOCIAL ANTHROPOLOGY 10, 13 (George W. Stocking, Jr., ed., 1984).
3. Although this phrase itself comes from the Declaration of Independence, the idea it encapsulates shows up in the Constitution's use of the word "consent" eleven times.
4. For an overview of the history of social contract theory, *see* Michael Levin, *Social Contract*, 4 DICTIONARY OF THE HISTORY OF IDEAS 251 (Philip P. Wiener ed., 1973). *See also* DAVID BOUCHER & PAUL KELLY (EDS.), THE SOCIAL CONTRACT FROM HOBBES TO RAWLS (1994).
5. Anita L. Allen, *Social Contract Theory in American Case Law*, 51 FLORIDA LAW REVIEW 1 (1999).
6. The more traditional response of anthropology to Freud's "just so" tale of *Totem and Taboo* can be gleaned from the two reviews written by Alfred Kroeber: *Totem and Taboo: An Ethnological Psychoanalysis*, 22 AMERICAN ANTHROPOLOGIST 48 (1920), and *Totem and Taboo in Retrospect*, 43 AMERICAN JOURNAL OF SOCIOLOGY 446 (1939). A more complete historical overview of the impact of Freud on anthropology is available in MARVIN HARRIS, THE RISE OF ANTHROPOLOGICAL THEORY (1968) (*see especially* chapter 16).
7. PETER FITZPATRICK, MODERNISM AND THE GROUNDS OF LAW 52 (2001).
8. *Id.* at 1.
9. *See id.* at 61.
10. *Id.*
11. *See id.* at 71.
12. One device that Fitzpatrick discusses to illustrate the precarious balance that law must strike between flexibility and stability is the "legal fiction." *See id.* at 86- 90. The seminal text of SIR HENRY SUMNER MAINE, ANCIENT LAW (New York: Dorset Press, 1986) (1861), discusses at length the functions of the legal fiction. *See id.* at 17-36.
13. FITZPATRICK, *supra* note 7, at 72.
14. Peter Fitzpatrick, *Death as the Horizon of the Law, in* COURTING DEATH: THE LAW OF MORTALITY 19 (Desmond Manderson ed., 1999).
15. ERNEST L. SCHUSKY, MANUAL FOR KINSHIP ANALYSIS 3 (2d ed., 1983).
16. *See* WILLIAM R. JANKOWIAK, SEX, DEATH AND HIERARCHY IN A CHINESE CITY (1993).
17. M.J. HERSKOVITS, MAN AND HIS WORKS 215 (1948). This use of the term "functionalism" varies from that in chapter 3 when the function of religion was discussed. This word has had many distinct incarnations in anthropological theory. The reader should not attempt to reconcile them here; nor shall we.
18. *See* A.R. RADCLIFFE-BROWN, STRUCTURE AND FUNCTION IN PRIMITIVE SOCIETY 178-187 (1952).
19. *See* JAMES PEOPLES & GARRICK BAILEY, HUMANITY: AN INTRODUCTION TO CULTURAL ANTHROPOLOGY 78-80 (2d ed., 1991).
20. *See* STANLEY R. BARRETT, ANTHROPOLOGY: A STUDENT'S GUIDE TO THEORY AND METHOD 66 (1996) ("Structural functionalism downplayed conflict and almost ignored social change.").
21. *See* John H. Chilcott, *Structural Functionalism as a Heuristic Device*, 29 ANTHROPOLOGY & EDUCATION QUARTERLY 103 (1998).

22. Andrew Koppelman, for example, argues that antigay laws are a function of social attitudes toward women generally. *See* Andrew Koppelman, *Why Discrimination against Lesbians and Gay Men Is Sex Discrimination*, 69 New York University Law Review 197 (1994).

23. Manale v. City of New Orleans, 673 F.2d 122, 125 (5th Cir. 1982).

24. Linn v. Plant Guard Workers of America, 383 U.S. 53, 65 note 7 (1966).

25. Romer v. Evans, 517 U.S. 620 (1996).

26. About DOMA, *see* James M. Donovan, *DOMA: An Unconstitutional Establishment of Fundamentalist Christianity*, 4(2) Michigan Journal of Gender & Law 335 (1997).

27. *See* Leon R. Kass, *L'Chaim and Its Limits: Why Not Immortality*, 113 First Things 17, 20 (May 2001) ("For to argue that human life would be better without death is, I submit, to argue that human life would be better being something other than human. To be immortal would not be just to continue life as we mortals now know it, only forever. The new immortals, in the decisive sense, would not be like us at all.").

28. *See* Ian Wilson, The After Death Experience 197 (1987) ("Death is death_certain, repellent, and degrading. It is sheer deceit and hypocrisy for anyone to try to present it as otherwise."). One writer who does "try to present it otherwise" is E.M. Cioran. In Cioran's opinion the problem is not death, but birth: "We do not rush toward death, we flee the catastrophe of birth.... The real evil is *behind*, not ahead of us." E.M. Cioran, The Trouble with Being Born (1976). Martin Heidegger recognizes that birth does present a dilemma parallel to that of death. If the nothingness after dying presents a conundrum, so too should the nothingness prior to birth. But Heidegger's own emphasis remains on the future death orientation, and not on the historical birth. *See* Martin Heidegger, Being and Time (John Macquarrie & Edward Robinson trans., New York: Harper & Row, 1962) (1927).

29. *See* Robert Kastenbaum & Paul T. Costa, *Psychological Perspectives on Death*, 28 Annual Review of Psychology 225 (1977).

30. *See* C. Daniel Batson, Patricia Schoenrade, & W. Larry Ventis, Religion and the Individual: A Social-Psychological Perspective (1993).

31. *See* Ernest Becker, The Denial of Death (1973). Several points may be acknowledged at this point. First, little harm is done to our thesis if the claims being made about the relationship between death anxiety and our species apply rather to our genus, *Homo*. Since *sapiens* are the only extant member of that genus, the net practical effect is the same. However, that modification would allow for the possibility that other, extinct *Homo* species (such as *erectus*) shared this experience. More detailed work on the archaic psychology is necessary to rule definitively on this issue.

   Second, and somewhat surprisingly, some people find the universality of the experience of death anxiety an alien idea. Given the enormous quantities of data showing otherwise, the burden would be on the contrarians to demonstrate that death anxiety is an existential experience accessible only to certain selected persons, or is characteristic of only a limited number of cultures.

32. *See generally* Donald Heinz, The Last Passage: Recovering a Death of Our Own (1999).

33. Carl Jung, *The Soul and Death, in* The Meaning of Death 3, 4 (Herman Feifel ed., 1959).

34. Quoted by James Lewton Brain, The Last Taboo: Sex and the Fear of Death 71 (1991).

35. Andreas Lommel, Shamanism: The Beginnings of Art 74 (Michael Bullock trans., 1967).

36. Margaret Mead, Male and Female 225 (1949).

37. Becker, *supra* note 31, at ix.

38. Søren Kierkegaard, The Sickness unto Death 55 (Howard V. Hong & Edna H. Hong trans., Princeton, NJ: Princeton University Press, 1980) (1849).

39. *See* Kass, *supra* note 27, at 18-19 ("victory over mortality is the unstated but implicit goal of modern medical science, indeed of the entire modern scientific project, to which mankind was summoned almost four hundred years ago by Francis Bacon and René Descartes.").

40. *See* Richard Lonetto & Donald I. Templer, Death Anxiety (1986).

41. *See generally* Philippe Ariès, The Hour of Our Death (Helen Weaver trans., 1981).

42. George Hunsinger, Kierkegaard, Heidegger, and the Concept of Death 36-37 (1969).

43. One illustration of our unique reaction to death appears in special legal rules. For example, tort claims for the infliction of mental disturbance usually requires a physical manifestation of the alleged harm. Two recognized exceptions to that rule are the "death telegram rule" (recovery for emotional injury arising from negligent delivery of telegram erroneously announcing death) and "negligent interference with death bodies." *See* Victor E. Schwartz, Kathryn Kelly, & David F. Partlett, Prosser, Wade and Schwartz's Torts: Cases and Materials 459 (10th ed., 2000).

44. *See* Becker, *supra* note 31, at 27.

45. The higher primates are known to achieve self-recognition. *See* Dorothy L. Cheney & Robert M. Seyfarth, How Monkeys See the World 242-246 (1990). This accomplishment may exist in other species. *See* Diana Reiss & Lori Marino, *Mirror Self-Recognition in the Bottlenose Dolphin: A Case of Cognitive Convergence*, 98 Proceedings of the National Academy of Sciences 5937 (2001).

46. David Premack, *Language and Intelligence in Ape and Man*, 64(6) American Scientist 674 (1976).

47. Alison Jolly, The Evolution of Primate Behavior 444 (2d ed., 1985).

48. Frans de Waal, Good Natured: The Origins of Right and Wrong in Humans and Other Animals 55 (1996).

49. Roger Fouts, *My Best Friend is a Chimp*, 32(4) Psychology Today 68, 72 (July/August 2000).

50. *See* Rabiya S. Tuma, *Thinking Like a Chimp*, No. 90 HMS Beagle: The BioMedNet Magazine, November 10, 2000; *see also* Willard Gaylin, On Being and Becoming Human 7 (1990) ("the order of change between the chimpanzee and the human being is of such a magnitude as to represent a break, a discontinuity, in this great chain of life. Mankind is that noble discontinuity. We are not the next step, or even a giant leap forward. We are a parallel and independent entity; a thing unto ourselves; in a class of our own; *sui generis*.").

51. Steven Mithen, Prehistory of the Mind 212 (1996).

52. *See* James M. Donovan, *Implicit Religion and the Curvilinear Relationship between Religion and Death Anxiety*, 5 Implicit Religion 17 (2002).

53. Yves Lambert, *From Parish to Transcendent Humanism in France*, in The Changing Face of Religion 49, 58 (James A. Beckford & Thomas Luckmann eds., 1989).

54. Salvatore R. Maddi, *Developmental Value of Fear of Death*, 1(1) Journal of Mind and Behavior 85, 86-87 (1980).

55. A fuller exploration of the problem of death and the religious response it provokes can be found at James M. Donovan, Defining "Religion": Death and Anxiety in an Afro-Brazilian Cult (1994) (Ph.D. dissertation, Tulane University).

56. Erika Bourguignon, *Religion as a Mediating Factor in Culture Change*, in Religion and Mental Health 259, 263 (John F. Schumaker ed., 1992).

57. Paul Tillich, The Essential Tillich 74 (F. Forrester Church ed., 1987).

58. Peter Berger, The Sacred Canopy: Elements of a Sociological Theory of Religion 176-177 (1967).

59. Zygmunt Bauman, Mortality, Immortality & Other Life Strategies 9 (1992).

60. Géza Róheim, The Origin and Function of Culture 81-82, 77 (1943). *See also* Weston LaBarre, The Ghost Dance: Origins of Religion 341 (1972) ("Culture is thus necessarily in part a defense against irrational anxiety....").

61. Franz Borkenau, *The Concept of Death*, 157 Twentieth Century 313, 315 (1955).

62. *See* Bauman, *supra* note 59, at 23.

63. Premack, *supra* note 46.

64. A.I. Hallowell, Contributions to Anthropology 273 (1976).

65. "Na verdade não existe nenhuma conduta individual or coletiva que não seja de alguma maneira investida, amoldada pele experiência da morte." [In truth there does not exist any personal or collective behavior that is not in some manner invested and shaped by the experience of death.] Wilma Costa Torres, Wanda Gurgel Guedes, Therezinha H. Ebert, & Ruth Costa Torres, *Morte como Fator de Desenvolvimento*, 39 Arquivos Brasileiros de Psicologia 146 (1983).

66. Desmond Manderson is director the Julius Stone Institute of Jurisprudence for the Faculty of Law at the University of Sydney, Australia.

67. Desmond Manderson, *Introduction: Tales from the Crypt—A Metaphor, an Image, a Story, in* Courting Death, *supra* note 14, at 1, 2.

68. *Id.*

69. *Id.* at 3.

70. Martin Heidegger, *What Is Metaphysics, in* Pathworks 82, 90 (David Farrell Krell trans., Cambridge: Cambridge University Press, 1998) (1929).

71. Manderson, *supra* note 67, at 6.

72. *Id.* at 12.

73. *Id.* at 13. Given the discussion of the preceding section, one is hard pressed not to add to Manderson's statement the thought that, if more justice requires a better grasp of mortality, and we lack that grasp because of the work of death-denying religion, then justice and religion become, at points, mutually exclusive aspirations.

74. A similar conclusion is expressed by Fitzpatrick, *supra* note 7, at 100. Fitzpatrick's brief discussion identifies other philosophical textual authorities besides Heidegger, such as Derrida.

75. *See, e.g.,* A.R. Radcliffe-Brown's statement that "in advanced society religion becomes more individual; such individual religion comes under [the] head of psychology and not of sociology." George W. Stocking, Jr. (ed.), *Dr. Durkheim and Mr. Brown: Comparative Sociology at Cambridge in 1910, in* Functionalism Historicized, *supra* note 2, at 106, 124.

Conclusion

❧

OUTLOOK AND RECOMMENDATIONS

The organizing thesis of this volume has been that the relationship between anthropology and law is profitably evaluated against the standard of balanced reciprocity. When interacting within a relationship of balanced reciprocity, law and anthropology relate as true intellectual peers, with neither discipline consistently occupying a place of privilege over the other. Both anthropology and law have something essential to contribute to the larger project of understanding ourselves and our world, and of acting effectively therein. The contributions they make toward these ends are commensurate. Further, we have aimed to show the bases upon which this reciprocity could be built in terms of what each needs from, and offers to, the other.

Although the balanced reciprocity we envision may not describe the current relationship between the two disciplines, we can say that we are closer to this ideal than we have been in the recent past. We have already described the close ties between law and anthropology that prevailed at the time of anthropology's founding as an independent discipline. Thereafter, the two experienced a parting of the ways. Only recently have law and anthropology rediscovered one another.

The Intermediate Period of Degeneracy

One perspective on the undulating relationship between law and anthropology is afforded through the law reviews. Law reviews are the primary vehicle for the presentation of legal scholarship. Although they

---

strike scholars in other fields as peculiar for having student editors, lacking peer review, and allowing (even expecting) simultaneous submissions to multiple journals, the reviews and journals published by the law schools carry enormous prestige within the legal subculture. To be nominated to the editorial board of a school's primary law review is the highest academic honor a law student can achieve. In the past, important anthropological pieces by influential anthropologists were first seen within the pages of these law reviews. It is less surprising that the law reviews might welcome such works than that the anthropologists would consider the reviews an appropriate outlet for their work. Until recently, anthropologists have not regularly written for the law reviews.

An indication of an earlier cordial relationship between anthropology and law, which then deteriorated, is the ease with which articles of significant and primary anthropological importance appeared within the pages of flagship law reviews. The *Yale Law Journal* has historically been especially open to this kind of disciplinary exchange.

As one might expect, those with law degrees—Max Gluckman[1] and Robert Redfield,[2] for example—appear to have accessed this publication venue most readily. E. Adamson Hoebel, whose work among the Cheyenne has already been mentioned, published at least twice in law reviews.[3] Two "giants" in the field also have law review articles to their credit. "[A]lmost the last words written for publication"[4] by Bronislaw Malinowski appeared in the *Yale Law Journal*.[5] Radcliffe-Brown's "Patrilineal and Matrilineal Succession" ran in *The Iowa Law Review*.[6]

After this initial success, the appearances of anthropologists in law reviews dropped off. For the decade of 1970-79, no article was published that contained anthropological credits in the author's biographical footnote. Only one article in that period was published with the word "culture" in the title.[7] The next decade, 1980-89, showed a slight increase: nineteen author credits referring to anthropology, and sixty-one titles containing "culture."

One possible explanation for this lack of interest from anthropologists in law reviews as a publishing venue looks to institutional status. In the introduction, we described how law shifted its formal emphasis from liberal arts education to professional training. We suspect that this change has diminished the stature of the law school in the estimation of the other sectors of the university.[8] This lessened esteem combines with the special features of law reviews (such as their having student editors and no peer-review) to perhaps make them undesirable publication outlets for tenure-track anthropology academics. When reviewing a recent submission by one of us to a traditional academic peer-reviewed journal, the anonymous reviewer objected to the article's citation to publications from law reviews. The implication was that that kind of publication did not really "count" among "real" academics, and thus citation to those sources did not satisfy the need to document claims through reference to prior (serious) literature. Publication in a law review might be better than not publishing at all, however, for untenured faculty members still laboring under the dictum "Publish or perish" (especially, one might suppose, if the member's university supports its own law school. Consistency would lead one to hope that the university does not, on the one hand, maintain and support its fleet of law publications, yet then penalize its faculty in other departments for publishing in them). We therefore believe that more anthropologists do not avail themselves of this publication venue because of its perceived low stature in the eyes of other anthropologists.

We should not, however, put the blame for this degeneration from former intimacy wholly upon the shoulders of the anthropologists. Again, the divide emerges as a consequence of the aspirational shift in legal education toward strictly professional preparation. A law review member was recently heard to complain that the article he was editing was "all about science, but no law." In an earlier time, the more broadly educated lawyer would have appreciated that everything beneficial for a lawyer to know was not always limited to codes and court opinions. From the other side, then, perhaps the problem isn't necessarily that anthropologists avoid submitting their work to law reviews, but rather that law reviews have ceased to see the merit in such work, and therefore reject it.

Prospects for the Future

These same data, however, indicate that the divorce between anthropology and law is coming to an end. Indeed, the two appear to be reintegrating at an amazingly fast pace. The decade of 1990-99 turned up 146 biographical references for law review authors that referred to anthropology in some way. "Culture" appears as a title term in five hundred articles. These figures represent a yearly average over this range of 14.6 author references and 50 titles. Those yearly averages are useful to compare with the first three years of the decade, 2000-2002. This span has produced 79 author biographies and 250 titles, for yearly averages of 26 authors and 83 titles with an anthropological focus. Clearly a trend emerges that shows anthropologists appearing in law reviews with increasing frequency.

Although these figures indicate that anthropological authors now consider law reviews worthy outlets for their professional writing, and law reviews in turn again consider anthropological perspectives germane to legal audiences, some differences remain that distinguish this renewed interaction with the original period of the founding of anthropology. For example, comparatively fewer of these articles appear to be by an *éminence grise* of the discipline, such as Clifford Geertz, Marvin Harris, or Napoleon Chagnon. Whereas in the early days of anthropology the likes of Malinowski, Redfield, Gluckman, and Radcliffe-Brown wrote for the law reviews, today the articles seem predominantly to be by narrow subject specialists or junior members of the profession.

Due to excessive topical specialization, few anthropologists today achieve the general importance and influence as did Boas or Malinowski. Instead, contemporary researchers are more likely to be well-known within their particularly specialties (names familiar to law and anthropology readers would include Laura Nader, Alison Dundes Renteln, Lawrence Rosen, and William O'Barr and John Conley), but unrecognized and underappreciated beyond those borders. There are, in other words, fewer *grises* available to write such articles, so any then-versus-now comparison would necessarily suffer.

Still, the mutual rediscovery of law and anthropology is cause for satisfaction that at least we are moving in the right direction toward balanced reciprocity. Further improvement could result if the achievement of balanced reciprocity became an explicit rather than an intuitive goal. We need, therefore, to clarify the sense in which balanced reciprocity has been posited as the "ideal." By this we do not mean that it would be "nice"—a manifestation of mere collegial camaraderie. While this is certainly true, the same could be said for any pair of university departments selected at random. Were that all we intended, the gap could be bridged by relatively easy solutions: a class or two in the other subject within the formal curricula of the home discipline; the welcome admission of the other into one's professional organizations with the requisite subsectional forums sponsoring special training sessions and discussion seminars; a few well-placed statements by preeminent personalities. In other words, any effort raising the visibility and prestige of the one discipline within the confines of the other, as well as modest efforts to acquaint practitioners with the basic premises of the allied discipline, would suffice. The rising numbers of articles authored by anthropologists within law reviews would satisfy this lower standard. In order to conclude that this trend satisfied the higher standard of a balanced reciprocity, a more detailed content analysis of the articles, as well as the impact of those articles upon the actual practice of law, would be necessary.

By that higher standard we mean that a balanced reciprocity must obtain if law and anthropology are each to attain their self-appointed goals. Law cannot achieve law's purported aims absent a grounding in social facts provided by anthropology. Anthropology cannot complete one of its own most fundamental objectives—the ethnographic capture of lifeways of other peoples in all their subtle permutations—without a sophisticated command of the institution of law.

Experts in both fields may be guilty of assuming that what the other does is so obvious that no special training is required to adequately allow for it. The fieldworking anthropologist assumes he or she knows well enough what "law" is to devote entire chapters of a final work-product to it, needing no deliberate exposure to what legal specialists have to say. Contrarily, judges and legislators make decisions and pass laws believing themselves to be in full command of the social implications of their actions based almost entirely upon only their own experiences as culture participants. While useful to generate initial hypotheses or well-founded opinions, these assumptions can never provide the rigorous bases for the transmutation of the hypothesis into a "fact," or the opinion into "knowledge."

For each field to take this final step in its own intellectual development will require a much more intimate grappling with the other discipline than what suffices to establish simple collegiality. We recommend three changes to make possible the end condition of balanced reciprocity.

First, each field needs to concede the important contribution the other must make before it can fulfill its own ambitions. Academic disciplines have a history of jealously preserving their perceived intellectual boundaries.[9] Walter Goldschmidt speaks of the "natural territorialism of scholarly disciplines,"[10] with its jealously defended boundaries that few dare to cross. The earlier openness of the lawyer to the social sciences may have hardened as he saw his "territory" threatened and his status diminished:

> [T]he lawyer fears the loss of his age-old function as intellectual broker and his ultimate replacement in terms of power and prestige by the specialist and expert. The "threat theory" argues that judges view science as a threat to their power and prestige, and that people with legal training have traditionally occupied high-status positions. If the law was to become dependent on science for answers to legal questions, the role of those with legal training would be diminished and scientific techniques, alien to lawyers, might then replace the familiar dialectic of law as the basis for decisions.[11]

An original mentoring attitude became distant, and even obstructive, as a reaction to threatened prerogatives. If true, law refuses to let anthropology contribute all that it could to the solution of social problems because it sees social science as a possible usurper.

Similarly, most anthropologists probably hold one of these negative attitudes about the law: (1) to the extent that it is a necessary concept for anthropology, its meaning is self-evident; (2) to the extent that legal concepts are not self-evident, they are idiosyncratic to the original social context, and thus have no relevance to the study of other socio-cultural systems; or (3) to the extent that legal concepts are necessary—not self-evident but still relevant—their elaboration can be delegated to a few specialists whose publications are read only by others in the same small group. Both fields need to realize that the other holds critical insights that need to be mastered by everyone, not just the narrow specialists. Although it is unlikely that this interdisciplinary exchange will dissolve the boundaries between academic disciplines,[12] it must be realized that the preservation of these boundaries should *not* be the goal of the intellectual exercise. Any time the choice is between preserving disciplinary purity or arriving at the correct result, there should be no choice at all.

One can receive only what is ready to be offered. Therefore, as our second recommendation, each discipline must recognize what specific contribution the other is waiting for it to formulate, and direct energies on that project. A cynic could conclude that anthropology seems to have answers to every question *except* the ones law deals with most. Consider some of the examples we have discussed in this book. If anthropology is now capable of refuting the assumptions law has incorporated into its decision making—such as the belief that polygamy leads to despotism and is, therefore, necessarily incompatible with American democratic society—it has done so for its own reasons, and not to challenge or improve the legal position first assumed in *Reynolds*. As a result, its conclusions are neither formulated in a digestible form nor presented to the appropriate audience. More typical, we find, has been the concerns of some early readers of this work, for example, who worried that we had not accorded polyandry an equivalent status to polygamy. Our response is that polyandry is not a significant legal problem, and only barely an ethnographic phenomenon.[13] The conviction that it should receive equivalent analytic emphasis as that given polygamy is only a quest for logical symmetry. That approach minimizes the theoretical usefulness to law without yielding commensurate benefits to anthropological insight.

Similarly, neither has anthropology been concerned, as a discipline, to clarify the elements of culture that would warrant (or refute) the cogency of a "culture defense." Quite likely the law will arrive at its own answer before most anthropologists even realize that an issue exists.

On its side, the law must wrestle with its own swarm of issues upon which anthropologists depend. What, for example, is the status of cultural products as intellectual property that can be copyrighted or patented? What standards will be required for the admission of cultural expertise in trials? What is the fount of authority that charters a social institution as law?

Finally, although we speak as though the disciplines themselves are agents (e.g., "law" must do this, "anthropology" should think that), all actions, decisions, and so forth, must, of course, be executed by persons. Therefore, the third recommendation that would facilitate the condition of balanced reciprocity addresses the level of personal development. Balanced reciprocity presumes the exercise of interdisciplinary scholarship. The cooperative alliance between practitioners of each field (of which the long-running research collaboration between lawyer John M. Conley and anthropologist William M. O'Barr is a prime example) is but a first, if necessary step on the way to the kind of interdisciplinary perspective that balanced reciprocity will require.

Ideally, the disciplines should meet and inform one another not in the discourse between specialized individuals, but within the mind of a single person. It is not simply that the courtroom should become more receptive to the presentation of social scientific information. "Judges should acquire more knowledge of the social sciences to enable them to fulfil their policy-making function of using law as a means to the ends of serving society wisely and to its good."[14] Balanced reciprocity is best achieved when the intellectual content of each discipline can interact with the other within the mind of one individual. This position leads to the conclusion that neither field should consider itself healthy unless it has a cadre of persons formally trained in both[15] (i.e., holds both a J.D. and a Ph.D.: the aforementioned John M. Conley is only one such dual-degreed practitioner exercising his expertise in both fields simultaneously) who can move easily between each, and is prepared to listen to what these persons have to say on appropriate subjects. Specialization yields nothing if it becomes synonymous with marginalization. These are the persons who would be best positioned at the boundaries between the disciplines to manage the export and import of appropriate ideas from one to the other. A computer search of the Who's Who database suggests that less than 5 percent of anthropologists satisfy this criterion of training in both disciplines. Significantly fewer than this, one can suppose, actually exercise this dual expertise.

If these three conditions are met (each knows what it needs from the other, prepares what the other needs from it, and bestows disciplinary status and prestige upon those persons specifically trained and suited to manage this exchange), then balanced reciprocity can be achieved. If that happens, then both fields will have fulfilled a necessary precondition to the attainment of their specific intellectual goals.

Notes

1. *See, for example,* Max Gluckman's *Civil War and Theories of Power in Barotse-Land: African and Medieval Analogies,* 72 Yale Law Journal 1515 (1963), and *The Role of the Barotse King in the Judicial Process,* 14 Stanford Law Review 110 (1961).
2. Robert Redfield, *Primitive Law,* 33 University of Cincinnati Law Review 1 (1964).
3. E. Adamson Hoebel's *Fundamental Legal Concepts as Applied to the Study of Criminal Law,* 51 Yale Law Journal 951 (1942), and *Three Studies in African Law,* 13 Stanford Law Review (1961).
4. George Peter Murdock, *Bronislaw Malinowski,* 51(8) Yale Law Journal 1235 (1942).
5. Bronislaw Malinowski, *A New Instrument for the Interpretation of Law—Especially Primitive,* 51 Yale Law Journal 1237 (1942).
6. A.R. Radcliffe-Brown, *Patrilineal and Matrilineal Succession,* 20 Iowa Law Review 286 (1935).
7. We take "culture" as a representative term suggesting work with a major anthropological emphasis. Other words may have served equally well.
8. For general observations about the relationship of the law school and its faculty to the wider university setting, *see* James M. Donovan, *Do Librarians Deserve Tenure? Casting an Anthropological Eye upon Role Definition within the Law School,* 88 Law Library Journal 382 (1996).
9. For instance, anthropologist Ward Goodenough writes that it is not appropriate to critique anthropological arguments with arguments from other disciplines. *See* Ward H. Goodenough, *Reply to James Donovan,* 93 American Anthropologist 691 (1991). The distinctions which "beset philosophers and theologians" do not concern him as an anthropologist.
10. Walter Goldschmidt, Comparative Functionalism: An Essay in Anthropological Theory 3 (1966).
11. Rosemary J. Erickson & Rita J. Simon, The Use of Social Science Data in Supreme Court Decisions 15 (1998).
12. From some perspectives the dissolution of the largely arbitrary distinctions between disciplines might be a good thing. If E.O. Wilson is correct, it may even be inevitable as all knowledge converges onto relatively few organizing principles. *See generally* Edward O. Wilson, Consilience: the Unity of Knowledge (1998). *See also* Karl N. Llewellyn, *A Realistic Jurisprudence,* 30 Columbia Law Review 431(1930), *reprinted in* Jurisprudence: Text and Readings on the Philosophy of Law 875, 904 (George C. Christie & Patrick H. Martin eds., 2d ed., 1995)("As to the overlapping of the field [of law] as thus sketched with that of other social sciences, I should be sorry if no overlapping were observable. The social sciences are not staked out like real estate. Even in law the sanctions for harmless trespass are not heavy.").
13. Whereas the majority of the world's cultures are polygamous, "only 0.5 percent of all societies permit a woman to take several husbands simultaneously." Helen E. Fisher, Anatomy of Love: The Natural History of Monogamy, Adultery, and Divorce 69 (1992).
14. John Minor Wisdom, *Random Remarks on the Role of Social Sciences in the Judicial Decision-Making Process in School Desegregation Cases,* 39 Law and Contemporary Problems 134, 148 (1975).
15. *See* Peter Lawrence, *Law and Anthropology: The Need for Collaboration,* 1 Melanesian Law Journal 40, 49 (1970) ("The immediate reaction might be to promote collaboration between the two disciplines by having legal scholars and social anthropologists working together in the field. This, no doubt, will happen. ... I believe that if we are to take this type of study seriously, we should try to have scholars who understand and can use both disciplines, having been trained in both.").

SELECTED BIBLIOGRAPHY

Aborampah, Osei-Mensah. *Plural Marriage and Fertility Differentials: A Study of the Yoruba of Western Nigeria.* 46(1) HUMAN ORGANIZATION 29-38 (1987).

Altman, Irwin, and Joseph Ginat. POLYGAMOUS FAMILIES IN CONTEMPORARY SOCIETY. New York: Cambridge University Press, 1996.

Anechiarico, Frank, and James B. Jacobs. THE PURSUIT OF ABSOLUTE INTEGRITY: HOW CORRUPTION CONTROL MAKES GOVERNMENT INEFFECTIVE. Chicago: University of Chicago Press, 1996.

Ariès, Philippe. THE HOUR OF OUR DEATH. Translated by Helen Weaver. New York: Knopf, 1981.

Asad, Talal. *Anthropological Conceptions of Religion: Reflections on Geertz.* 18 MAN 237-259 (1983).

Bagemihl, Bruce. BIOLOGICAL EXUBERANCE: ANIMAL HOMOSEXUALITY AND THE NATURAL WORLD. New York: St. Martin's Press, 1998.

Barrett, Stanley R. ANTHROPOLOGY: A STUDENT'S GUIDE TO THEORY AND METHOD. Toronto: University of Toronto Press, 1996.

Barry, Herbert, III. *Description and Uses of the Human Relations Area File. In* HANDBOOK OF CROSS-CULTURAL PSYCHOLOGY, vol. 2, edited by Harry C. Triandis and John W. Berry, 445-478. Boston: Allyn and Bacon, 1980.

Bary, Wm. Theodore de. ASIAN VALUES AND HUMAN RIGHTS. Cambridge, MA: Harvard University Press, 1998.

Bauman, Zygmunt. MORTALITY, IMMORTALITY & OTHER LIFE STRATEGIES. Stanford, CA: Stanford University Press, 1992.

Bean, L.L., and G.P. Mineau. *The Polygyny-Fertility Hypothesis: A Re-evaluation.* 40 POPULATION STUDIES 67-81 (1986).

Becker, Ernest. THE DENIAL OF DEATH. New York: Free Press, 1973.

Beckstrom, John H. SOCIOBIOLOGY AND THE LAW. Urbana: University of Illinois Press, 1985.

Benedict, Ruth. THE CHRYSANTHEMUM AND THE SWORD. New York: Meridian, 1946.

Berger, Peter L. THE SACRED CANOPY: ELEMENTS OF A SOCIOLOGICAL THEORY OF RELIGION. New York: Anchor Press, 1967.

_____. *Some Second Thoughts on Substantive versus Functional Definitions of Religion.* 13(2) JOURNAL FOR THE SCIENTIFIC STUDY OF RELIGION 125 (1974).

Betzig, Laura L. DESPOTISM AND DIFFERENTIAL REPRODUCTION: A DARWINIAN VIEW OF HISTORY. New York: Aldine, 1986.

Boas, Franz. THE MIND OF PRIMITIVE MAN. New York: Macmillan, 1916.

Bogus, Carl T. *The Death of an Honorable Profession.* 71 INDIANA LAW JOURNAL 911-947 (1996).

Bretschneider, Peter. POLYGYNY: A CROSS-CULTURAL STUDY. Uppsala, Sweden: Acta Universitatis Upsaliensis, 1995.

Brown, Michael F. *Can Culture Be Copyrighted?* 39(2) CURRENT ANTHROPOLOGY 193-222 (1998).

Bushman, Claudia L. MORMON DOMESTIC LIFE IN THE 1870s: PANDEMONIUM OR ARCADIA? Logan: Utah State University Press, 1999.

Buss, David M. THE EVOLUTION OF DESIRE. New York: Basic Books, 1994.

Candland, Douglas Keith. FERAL CHILDREN & CLEVER ANIMALS: REFLECTIONS ON HUMAN NATURE. New York: Oxford University Press, 1993.

Capaldi, N. *Hume's Rejection of "Ought" as a Moral Category.* 63 JOURNAL OF PHILOSOPHY 126-137 (1966).

Casino, Bruce J. *"I Know It When I See It": Mail-Order Ministry Tax Fraud and the Problem of a Constitutionally Acceptable Definition of Religion.* 25 AMERICAN CRIMINAL LAW REVIEW 113-164 (1987).

Chisholm, James S., and Victoria K. Burbank. *Monogamy and Polygyny in Southeast Arnhem Land: Male Coercion and Female Choice.* 12 ETHOLOGY AND SOCIOBIOLOGY 291-313 (1991).

Choper, Jesse H. *Defining "Religion" in the First Amendment.* 1982 UNIVERSITY OF ILLINOIS LAW REVIEW 579-613.

_____. SECURING RELIGIOUS LIBERTY. Chicago: University of Chicago Press, 1995.

Clark, Walter Houston. *How do Social Scientists Define Religion?* 47(1) JOURNAL OF SOCIAL PSYCHOLOGY 143-147 (1958).

Cochran, Robert F., Jr., and Teresa S. Collett. THE RULES OF THE LEGAL PROFESSION. St. Paul, MN: West, 1996.

Collier, Steven D. *Beyond* Seeger/Welsh: *Redefining Religion under the Constitution.* 31 EMORY LAW JOURNAL 973-1013 (1982).

Conley, John M., and William M. O'Barr. *Legal Anthropology Comes Home: A Brief History of the Ethnographic Study of Law.* 27 LOYOLA OF LOS ANGELES LAW REVIEW 41-64 (1993).

_____. JUST WORDS: LAW, LANGUAGE, AND POWER. Chicago: University of Chicago Press, 1998.

Constantine, Larry L., and Joan M. Constantine. GROUP MARRIAGE. New York: Macmillan, 1973.

Coriden, James A. AN INTRODUCTION TO CANON LAW. New York: Paulist Press, 1991.

Craven, J. Braxton. *The Impact of Social Science Evidence on the Judge: A Personal Comment.* 39(1) LAW AND CONTEMPORARY PROBLEMS 150-156 (1975).

Davis, Ray Jay. *Plural Marriage and Religious Freedom: The Impact of* Reynolds v. United States. 15 ARIZONA LAW REVIEW 287-306 (1973).

Diamond, Jared M. THE THIRD CHIMPANZEE. New York: Harperperennial, 1993.

Dobyns, Henry F. *Taking the Witness Stand. In* APPLIED ANTHROPOLOGY IN AMERICA, 2d ed., edited by Elizabeth M. Edy and William L. Partridge, 366-380. New York: Columbia University Press, 1987.

Donnelly, Jack. INTERNATIONAL HUMAN RIGHTS. Boulder, CO: Westview Press, 1993.

Donovan, James M. *A Philosophical Ground for Gays' Rights: "We Must Learn What Is True in Order to Do What Is Right."* 4 GEORGE MASON UNIVERSITY CIVIL RIGHTS LAW JOURNAL 1-40 (1993-94).

_____. Defining "Religion": Death and Anxiety in an Afro-Brazilian Cult. Ph.D. diss., Tulane University, 1994.

_____. *God Is As God Does: Law, Anthropology, and the Definition of "Religion."* 6(1) SETON HALL CONSTITUTIONAL LAW JOURNAL 23-99 (1995).

_____. *Restoring Free Exercise Protections by Limiting Them: Preventing a Repeat of* Smith. 17(1) NORTHERN ILLINOIS UNIVERSITY LAW REVIEW 1-49 (1996).

_____. *DOMA: An Unconstitutional Establishment of Fundamentalist Christianity.* 4(2) MICHIGAN JOURNAL OF GENDER & LAW 335-373 (1997).

_____. *Espying the Limits of Human Knowledge.* 38(3) ANTHROPOLOGY NEWSLETTER 16 (March 1997).

_____. Reconciling Arguments regarding a Self-Preserving Soul with Evolutionary Theory. M.A. thesis, Louisiana State University, 2000.

_____. *Implicit Religion and the Curvilinear Relationship between Religion and Death Anxiety.* 5 IMPLICIT RELIGION 17-28 (2002).

_____. *Rock-Salting the Slippery Slope: Why Same-Sex Marriage Is Not a Commitment to Polygamous Marriage.* 29(3) NORTHERN KENTUCKY LAW REVIEW 521-590 (2002).

Douglas, Mary. PURITY AND DANGER: AN ANALYSIS OF THE CONCEPTS OF POLLUTION AND TABOO. 1966. Reprint, London: Ark, 1984.

Downey, Roger. RIDDLE OF THE BONES: POLITICS, SCIENCE, RACE, AND THE STORY OF KENNEWICK MAN. New York: Copernicus, 2000.

Doyle, William E. *Can Social Science Data Be Used in Judicial Decisionmaking?* 6(1) JOURNAL OF LAW & EDUCATION 13-21 (1977).

Driessen, Patrick A. *The Wedding of Social Science and the Courts: Is the Marriage Working?* 64 SOCIAL SCIENCE QUARTERLY 476-493 (1983).

Drummond, Lee. *Who Wants to Be an Anthropologist?* 41(8) ANTHROPOLOGY NEWSLETTER 6-7 (November 2000).

Dunfey, Julia. *"Living the Principle" of Plural Marriage: Mormon Women, Utopia, and Female Sexuality in the Nineteenth Century.* 10(3) FEMINIST STUDIES 523 (1984).

Durham, William H. COEVOLUTION: GENES, CULTURE AND HUMAN DIVERSITY. Stanford, CA: Stanford University Press, 1991.

Durkheim, Emile. THE ELEMENTARY FORMS OF THE RELIGIOUS LIFE. 1915. Reprint, New York: Free Press, 1965.

Dyer, Robert G. *The Evolution of Social and Judicial Attitudes Towards Polygamy.* 5(1-3) UTAH BAR JOURNAL 35-45 (1977).

Engels, Frederick. THE ORIGIN OF THE FAMILY, PRIVATE PROPERTY AND THE STATE. 1884. Reprint, New York: International Publishers, 1972.

Erickson, Rosemary J., and Rita J. Simon. THE USE OF SOCIAL SCIENCE DATA IN SUPREME COURT DECISIONS. Urbana: University of Illinois Press, 1998.

Evans-Pritchard, Deirdre, and Alison Dundes Renteln. *The Interpretation and Distortion of Culture: A Hmong "Marriage by Capture" Case in Fresno, California.* 4(1) SOUTHERN CALIFORNIA INTERDISCIPLINARY LAW JOURNAL 1-48 (1994).

Faigman, David L. LEGAL ALCHEMY: THE USE AND MISUSE OF SCIENCE IN THE LAW. New York: W.H. Freeman, 1999.

Feinberg, Joel. SOCIAL PHILOSOPHY. Englewood Cliffs, NJ: Prentice-Hall, 1973.

Fienberg, Stephen E., ed. THE EVOLVING ROLE OF STATISTICAL ASSESSMENTS AS EVIDENCE IN THE COURTS. New York: Springer-Verlag, 1989.

Finnis, John. NATURAL LAW AND NATURAL RIGHTS. Oxford: Clarendon Press, 1980.

Firmage, Edwin B. *Religion & the Law: The Mormon Experience in the Nineteenth Century.* 12 CARDOZO LAW REVIEW 765-803 (1991).

Fisher, Helen E. ANATOMY OF LOVE: THE NATURAL HISTORY OF MONOGAMY, ADULTERY, AND DIVORCE. New York: W.W. Norton, 1992.

Fitzpatrick, Peter. MODERNISM AND THE GROUNDS OF LAW. Cambridge: Cambridge University Press, 2001.

Foster, Kenneth R., and Peter W. Huber. JUDGING SCIENCE: SCIENTIFIC KNOWLEDGE AND THE FEDERAL COURTS. Cambridge, MA: MIT Press, 1999.

Freeman, Derek. MARGARET MEAD AND SAMOA: THE MAKING AND UNMAKING OF AN ANTHROPOLOGICAL MYTH. Cambridge, MA: Harvard University Press, 1983.

Freeman, Michael. *The Philosophical Foundations of Human Rights.* 16 HUMAN RIGHTS QUARTERLY 491 (1994).

Freeman, Michael, and Helen Reece, eds. SCIENCE IN COURT. (Brookfield, VT: Ashgate/Dartmouth, 1998).

Freud, Sigmund. THE FUTURE OF AN ILLUSION. 1927. Reprint, New York: W.W. Norton, 1961.

———. CIVILIZATION AND ITS DISCONTENTS. 1930 Reprint, New York: W.W. Norton, 1961.

Fromm, Erich. PSYCHOANALYSIS AND RELIGION. New York: Bantam, 1950.

Gaffney, Edward McGlynn. *Governmental Definition of Religion: The Rise and Fall of the IRS Regulations on an "Integrated Auxiliary of a Church."* 25 VALPARAISO UNIVERSITY LAW REVIEW 203-247 (1991).

Garenne, Michael, and Etienne van de Walle. *Polygyny and Fertility among the Sereer of Senegal.* 43 POPULATION STUDIES 267-283 (1989).

Geertz, Clifford. *Religion: Anthropological Study.* In INTERNATIONAL ENCYCLOPEDIA OF THE SOCIAL SCIENCES, vol. 13, 398-406. New York: Macmillan, 1968.

———. THE INTERPRETATION OF CULTURES. New York: Basic Books, 1973.

Gellner, Anthony. ANTHROPOLOGY AND POLITICS. Cambridge: Blackwell, 1995.

Glazer, Nathan. THE LIMITS OF SOCIAL POLICY. Cambridge, MA: Harvard University Press, 1988.

214 Bibliography

Glock, Charles Y., and Rodney Stark. RELIGIONS AND SOCIETY IN TENSION. Chicago: Rand McNally, 1965.
Goldschmidt, Walter. COMPARATIVE FUNCTIONALISM: AN ESSAY IN ANTHROPOLOGICAL THEORY. Berkeley: University of California Press, 1966.
Goldsmith, Timothy H. THE BIOLOGICAL ROOTS OF HUMAN NATURE. New York: Oxford University Press, 1991.
Goldstein, Taryn F. *Cultural Conflicts in Court: Should the American Criminal Justice System Formally Recognize a "Cultural Defense"?* 99 DICKINSON LAW REVIEW 141-168 (1994).
Gottesman, Michael H. *Admissibility of Expert Testimony after* Daubert: *The "Prestige" Factor.* 43 EMORY LAW JOURNAL 867-884 (1994).
Gray, Richard L. *Eliminating the (Absurd) Distinction between* Malum in Se *and* Malum Prohibitum *Crimes.* 73 WASHINGTON UNIVERSITY LAW QUARTERLY 1369 (1995).
Greeley, Andrew. *Debunking the Role of Social Scientists in Court.* 7(1) HUMAN RIGHTS 34-36 (1978).
Greenawalt, Kent. *Religion as a Concept in Constitutional Law.* 72 CALIFORNIA LAW REVIEW 753-816 (1984).
_____. *Legal Enforcement of Morality.* 85(3) JOURNAL OF CRIMINAL LAW & CRIMINOLOGY 710-725 (1995).
Gross, Paul R., and Norman Levitt. HIGHER SUPERSTITION: THE ACADEMIC LEFT AND ITS QUARRELS WITH SCIENCE. Baltimore, MD: Johns Hopkins University Press, 1994.
Harris, Marvin. THE RISE OF ANTHROPOLOGICAL THEORY. New York: Harper & Row, 1968.
_____. COWS, PIGS, WARS AND WITCHES. New York: Vintage, 1974.
_____. THEORIES OF CULTURE IN POSTMODERN TIMES. Lanham, MD: Rowman & Littlefield, 1999.
Heidegger, Martin. BEING AND TIME. 1927. Reprint, New York: Harper & Row, 1962.
Helfer, Laurence R. *Forum Shopping for Human Rights.* 148 UNIVERSITY OF PENNSYLVANIA LAW REVIEW 285 (1999).
Herbrechtsmeier, William. *Buddhism and the Definition of Religion: One More Time.* 32 JOURNAL FOR THE SCIENTIFIC STUDY OF RELIGION 1-18 (1993).
Herek, Gregory M. *Myths about Sexual Orientation: A Lawyer's Guide to Social Science Research.* 1 LAW & SEXUALITY 133-172 (1991).
Hern, Warren M. *Polygyny and Fertility among the Shipibo of the Peruvian Amazon.* 46(1) POPULATION STUDIES 53 (1992).
Herskovits, Melville J. MAN AND HIS WORKS. New York: Knopf, 1948.
Herz, Michael. *Rediscovering Francis Lieber: An Afterword and Introduction.* 16(6) CARDOZO LAW REVIEW 2107 (1995).
Hohfeld, Wesley Newcomb. *Some Fundamental Legal Conceptions as Applied in Judicial Reasoning.* 23 YALE LAW JOURNAL 16-59 (1913).
Hood, Ralph W., et al. THE PSYCHOLOGY OF RELIGION. New York: Guilford Press, 1996.

Hopper, Kim. *Research Findings as Testimony: A Note on the Ethnographer as Expert Witness*. 49(2) HUMAN ORGANIZATION 110-113 (1990).

Hume, David. A TREATISE OF HUMAN NATURE. 1739-40. Reprint, edited by L.A. Selby-Bigge, Oxford: Clarendon Press, 1888.

Hunsinger, George. KIERKEGAARD, HEIDEGGER, AND THE CONCEPT OF DEATH. Stanford, CA: Stanford University Press, 1969.

Ingold, Tim, ed. WHAT IS AN ANIMAL? London: Routledge, 1994.

Iversen, Joan Smyth. *Feminist Implications of Mormon Polygyny*. 10(3) FEMINIST STUDIES 505-536 (1984)

_____. *A Debate on the American Home: The Antipolygamy Controversy, 1880-1890*. 1(4) JOURNAL OF THE HISTORY OF SEXUALITY 585-602 (1991).

James, William. THE VARIETIES OF RELIGIOUS EXPERIENCE. 1902. Reprint, New York: Longmans, Green, 1916.

Johnson, Nan E., and A.M. Elm. *Polygamy and Fertility in Somalia*. 21 JOURNAL OF BIOSOCIAL SCIENCE 127-134 (1989).

Jones, Robert Alun. *Robertson Smith and James Frazer on Religion. In* FUNCTIONALISM HISTORICIZED: ESSAYS ON BRITISH SOCIAL ANTHROPOLOGY, edited by George W. Stocking, Jr., 31-58. Madison: University of Wisconsin Press, 1984.

Josephson, Steven C. *Status, Reproductive Success, and Marrying Polygynously*. 14 ETHOLOGY AND SOCIOBIOLOGY 391-396 (1993).

Kastenbaum, Robert, and Paul T. Costa. *Psychological Perspectives on Death*. 28 ANNUAL REVIEW OF PSYCHOLOGY 225-249 (1977).

Kierkegaard, Søren. THE SICKNESS UNTO DEATH. 1849. Reprint, translated by Howard V. Hong and Edna H. Hong, Princeton, NJ: Princeton University Press, 1980.

Kilbride, Philip L. PLURAL MARRIAGE FOR OUR TIMES: A REINVENTED OPTION? Westport, CT: Bergin & Garvey, 1994.

King, Thomas F. CULTURAL RESOURCE LAWS & PRACTICE: AN INTRODUCTORY GUIDE. Walnut Creek, CA: AltaMira Press, 1998.

Kluckhohn, Clyde. MIRROR FOR MAN: THE RELATION OF ANTHROPOLOGY TO MODERN LIFE. Tucson: University of Arizona Press, 1985.

Koepping, Klaus-Peter. ADOLF BASTIAN AND THE PSYCHIC UNITY OF MANKIND. St. Lucia: University of Queensland Press, 1983.

Kuhn, Thomas. THE STRUCTURE OF SCIENTIFIC REVOLUTIONS. Chicago: University of Chicago Press, 1970.

Kuznar, Lawrence A. RECLAIMING A SCIENTIFIC ANTHROPOLOGY. Walnut Creek, CA: AltaMira Press, 1997.

Labov, William. *Objectivity and Commitment in Linguistic Science: The Case of the Black English Trial in Ann Arbor*. 11 LANGUAGE IN SOCIETY 165-201 (1982).

Laner, Mary Riege. *Unpleasant, Aggressive, and Abusive Activities in Courtship: A Comparison of Mormon and NonMormon College Students*. 6 DEVIANT BEHAVIOUR 145-168 (1985).

Lawrence, Peter. *Law and Anthropology: The Need for Collaboration*. 1 MELANESIAN LAW JOURNAL 40-50 (1970).

Leach, Edmund. Claude Lévi-Strauss. New York: Viking Press, 1970.

Leaf, Murray J. Man, Mind, and Science: A History of Anthropology. New York: Columbia University Press, 1979.

Lett, James. Science, Reason and Anthropology. Lanham, MD: Rowman & Littlefield, 1997.

Lieber, Francis. *The Mormons: Shall Utah Be Admitted into the Union?* 5(27) Putnam's Monthly 225-236 (1855).

_____. Legal and Political Hermeneutics. 1860. Reprinted as 16 Cardozo Law Review 1879-2105 (1995).

_____. Manual of Political Ethics, Designed Chiefly for the Use of Colleges and Students at Law. 2d ed. Philadelphia: J.B. Lippincott, 1876.

Lindholm, Charles. *Logical and Moral Dilemmas of Postmodernism.* 3 Journal of the Royal Anthropological Institute 747-760 (1997).

Linford, Orma. *The Mormons and the Law: The Polygamy Cases.* Part 1. 9 Utah Law Review 308-370 (1964).

_____. *The Mormons and the Law: The Polygamy Cases.* Part 2. 9 Utah Law Review 543-591 (1965).

Llewellyn, Karl N., and E. Adamson Hoebel. The Cheyenne Way: Conflict and Case Law in Primitive Jurisprudence. Norman: University of Oklahoma Press, 1941.

Lonetto, Richard, and Donald I. Templer. Death Anxiety. Washington, D.C.: Hemisphere Publishing, 1986.

McGrew, W.C., L.F. Marchant, S.E. Scott, and C.E.G. Tutin. *Intergroup Differences in a Social Custom of Wild Chimpanzees: The Grooming Hand-Clasp of the Mahale Mountains.* 42 Current Anthropology 148-153 (2001).

Maine, Sir Henry Sumner. Ancient Law: Its Connection with the Early History of Society and Its Relation to Modern Ideas. 1861. Reprint, New York: Dorset Press, 1986.

Malinowski, Bronislaw. Crime and Custom in Savage Society. London: Routledge & Kegan Paul, 1926.

_____. Magic, Science and Religion and Other Essays. Garden City, NY: Doubleday, 1948.

Manderson, Desmond, ed. Courting Death: The Law of Mortality. London: Pluto Press, 1999.

May, Dean L. *People on the Mormon Frontier: Kanab's Families of 1874.* 1(2) Journal of Family History 169-192 (1976).

Mead, Margaret. Coming of Age in Samoa. New York: William Morrow, 1928.

_____. Male and Female. New York: Dell, 1949.

Meissner, W.W. Psychoanalysis and Religious Experience. New Haven, CT: Yale University Press, 1984.

Mill, John Stuart. The Subjection of Women. 1869. Reprint, Cambridge, MA: MIT Press, 1970.

Miller, Jeremy M. *A Critique of the Reynolds Decision.* 11 Western State University Law Review 165-198 (1984).

Mithen, Steven. Prehistory of the Mind. New York: Thames and Hudson, 1996.

Monahan, John and Laurens Walker. *Social Authority: Obtaining, Evaluating, and Establishing Social Science in Law.* 134(3) UNIVERSITY OF PENNSYLVANIA LAW REVIEW 477-517 (1986).

Morgan, Lewis H. ANCIENT SOCIETY. New York: Henry Holt & Co., 1877.

Morse, Allison. *Social Science in the Courtroom: Expert Testimony and Battered Women.* 21 HAMLINE LAW REVIEW 287-321 (1998).

Morse, Stephen J. *The Misbegotten Marriage of Soft Psychology and Bad Law.* 14(6) LAW AND HUMAN BEHAVIOR 595-618 (1990).

Mulder, Monique Borgerhoff. *Marital Status and Reproductive Performance in Kipsigis Women: Re-evaluating the Polygyny-Fertility Hypothesis.* 43 POPULATION STUDIES 285-304 (1989).

Murphy, Michael. GOLF IN THE KINGDOM. New York: Penguin, 1972.

Nader, Laura, ed. LAW IN CULTURE AND SOCIETY. Berkeley: University of California Press, 1969.

Nedrow, G. Keith. *Polygamy and the Right to Marry: New Life for an Old Lifestyle.* 11(3) MEMPHIS STATE UNIVERSITY LAW REVIEW 303-349 (1981).

Nelson, Caleb. *Stare Decisis and Demonstrably Erroneous Precedents.* 87(1) VIRGINIA LAW REVIEW 1-84 (2001).

Nelson, William E. *MARBURY V. MADISON*: THE ORIGINS AND LEGACY OF JUDICIAL REVIEW. Lawrence: University Press of Kansas, 2000.

Noble, William, and Iain Davidson. HUMAN EVOLUTION, LANGUAGE AND MIND. Cambridge: Cambridge University Press, 1996.

Ottenheimer, Martin. FORBIDDEN RELATIVES: THE AMERICAN MYTH OF COUSIN MARRIAGE. Urbana: University of Illinois Press, 1996.

Otto, Rudolph. THE IDEA OF THE HOLY. 1917. Reprint, 2d ed., London: Oxford University Press, 1950.

Overton, Thomas W. *Lawyers, Light Bulbs, and Dead Snakes: The Lawyer Joke as Societal Text.* 42 UCLA LAW REVIEW 1069-1114 (1995).

Paden, William E. RELIGIOUS WORLDS: THE COMPARATIVE STUDY OF RELIGION. Boston: Beacon Press, 1988.

Pardun, John T. *Good Samaritan Laws: A Global Perspective.* 20 LOYOLA OF LOS ANGELES INTERNATIONAL AND COMPARATIVE LAW JOURNAL 591-613 (1998).

Patzer, Gordon L. THE PHYSICAL ATTRACTIVENESS PHENOMENA. New York: Plenum Press, 1985.

Peoples, James, and Garrick Bailey. HUMANITY: AN INTRODUCTION TO CULTURAL ANTHROPOLOGY. 2d ed. St. Paul, Minn.: West, 1991.

Popper, Karl. CONJECTURES AND REFUTATIONS: THE GROWTH OF SCIENTIFIC KNOWLEDGE. New York: Harper & Row, 1965.

Premack, David. *Language and Intelligence in Ape and Man.* 64(6) AMERICAN SCIENTIST 674 (1976).

Price, H. Marcus. DISPUTING THE DEAD: U.S. LAW ON ABORIGINAL REMAINS AND GRAVE GOODS. Columbia: University of Missouri Press, 1991.

Quinn, D. Michael. SAME-SEX DYNAMICS AMONG NINETEENTH-CENTURY AMERICANS: A MORMON EXAMPLE. Urbana: University of Illinois Press, 1996.

Radcliffe-Brown, A.R. STRUCTURE AND FUNCTION IN PRIMITIVE SOCIETY. New York: Free Press, 1952.

Rappaport, Roy A. Pigs for the Ancestors: Ritual in the Ecology of a New Guinea People. New Haven, CT: Yale University Press, 1984.

Redfield, Robert. *Primitive Law*. 33 University of Cincinnati Law Review 1-22 (1964).

Renteln, Alison Dundes. International Human Rights: Universalism versus Relativism. Newbury Park, CA: Sage, 1990.

_____. *A Justification of the Cultural Defense as Partial Excuse*. 2 Review of Law and Women's Studies 437-526 (1993).

Renteln, Alison Dundes, and Alan Dundes, eds. Folk Law: Essays in the Theory and Practice of Lex non Scripta. Madison: University of Wisconsin Press, 1994.

Rhéaume, Jean. *Human Rights and Human Nature*. 28 Revue Générale de Droit 523-534 (1997).

Riley, Mary, and Katy Moran, eds. *Culture as Commodity: Intellectual Property Rights*. 24(4) Cultural Survival Quarterly 1-57 (2001).

Rosen, Lawrence. *The Anthropologist as Expert Witness*. 79 American Anthropologist 555-578 (1977).

Sack, Peter, and Jonathan Aleck, eds. Law and Anthropology. New York: New York University Press, 1992.

Salisbury, Joyce E. *Human Beasts and Bestial Humans in the Middle Ages*. In Animal Acts: Configuring the Human in Western History, edited by Jennifer Ham and Matthew Senior, 9-21. New York: Routledge, 1997.

Saltzman, Penelope W. Potter v. Murray City: *Another Interpretation of Polygamy and the First Amendment*. 1986 Utah Law Review 345-371.

Schusky, Ernest L. Manual for Kinship Analysis. 2d ed. Lanham, MD: University Press of American, 1983.

Searle, John R. *How to Derive "Ought" from "Is."* 73(1) Philosophical Review 43-58 (1964).

Shaikh, Kashem, K.M.A. Aziz, and A.I. Chowdhury. *Differentials of Fertility between Polygynous and Monogamous Marriages in Rural Bangladesh*. 19 Journal of Biosocial Science 49-56 (1987).

Shell-Duncan, Bettina, and Ylva Hernlund, eds. Female Circumcision in Africa: Culture, Controversy, and Change. Boulder, CO: Lynne Rienner, 2000.

Shuman, Daniel W., and Bruce D. Sales. *The Impact of Daubert and Its Progeny on the Admissibility of Behavioral and Social Science Evidence*. 5(1) Psychology, Public Policy, and Law 3-15 (1999).

Siegel, Adam J. *Setting Limits on Judicial Scientific, Technical, and Other Specialized Fact-Finding in the New Millennium*. 86 Cornell Law Review 167-214 (2000).

Sieghart, Paul. The Lawful Rights of Mankind. Oxford: Oxford University Press, 1985.

Simpson, George Gaylord. The Meaning of Evolution. New Haven, CT: Yale University Press, 1950.

Sinha, S. Prakash *Why and How Human Rights*. 10(6) International Journal of Legal Information 308-319 (1982).

Slovenko, Ralph. *The De Facto Decriminalization of Bigamy.* 17 JOURNAL OF FAMILY LAW 297-308 (1978-79).

Smith, John E. QUASI-RELIGIONS: HUMANISM, MARXISM, AND NATIONALISM. New York: St. Martin's Press, 1994.

Smith, William Robertson. THE RELIGION OF THE SEMITES. New York: Meridian Books, 1889.

Spiro, Melford. CULTURE AND HUMAN NATURE. Chicago: University of Chicago Press, 1987.

Stark, Rodney. *Must All Religions be Supernatural? In* THE SOCIAL IMPACT OF NEW RELIGIOUS MOVEMENTS, edited by Bryan Wilson, 159-177. New York: The Rose of Sharon Press, 1981.

Stetter, Roger A., ed. IN OUR OWN WORDS: REFLECTIONS ON PROFESSIONALISM IN THE LAW. New Orleans: Louisiana Bar Foundation, 1998.

Stocking, George W., Jr. *Functionalism Historicized. In* FUNCTIONALISM HISTORICIZED: ESSAYS ON BRITISH SOCIAL ANTHROPOLOGY, edited by George W. Stocking, Jr., 3-9. Madison: University of Wisconsin Press, 1984.

Stone, Gregory B. *The Philosophical Beast: On Boccaccio's Tale of Cimone. In* ANIMAL ACTS: CONFIGURING THE HUMAN IN WESTERN HISTORY, edited by Jennifer Ham and Matthew Senior, 23-42. New York: Routledge, 1997.

Stone, Lawrence. THE FAMILY, SEX AND MARRIAGE IN ENGLAND, 1500-1800. New York: Harper & Row, 1979.

Strasser, Mark. LEGALLY WED: SAME-SEX MARRIAGE AND THE CONSTITUTION. Ithaca, NY: Cornell University Press, 1997.

Tenopyr, Mary L. *A Scientist-Practitioner's Viewpoint of the Admissibility of Behavioral and Social Scientific Information.* 5(1) PSYCHOLOGY, PUBLIC POLICY, AND LAW 194-202 (1999).

Thomson, Judith Jarvis. THE REALM OF RIGHTS. Cambridge, MA: Harvard University Press, 1990.

Tillich, Paul. THE ESSENTIAL TILLICH. Edited by F. Forrester Church. New York: Collier Books, 1987.

Turnbull, Colin. THE FOREST PEOPLE. New York: Simon and Schuster, 1962.

Volpp, Leti. *Blaming Culture for Bad Behavior.* 12 YALE JOURNAL OF LAW & THE HUMANITIES 89-116 (2000).

Waal, Frans de. GOOD NATURED: THE ORIGINS OF RIGHT AND WRONG IN HUMANS AND OTHER ANIMALS. Cambridge, MA: Harvard University Press, 1996.

_____. THE APE AND THE SUSHI MASTER. New York: Basic Books, 2001.

Wafer, Jim. THE TASTE OF BLOOD: SPIRIT POSSESSION IN BRAZILIAN CANDOMBLÉ. Philadelphia: University of Pennsylvania Press, 1991.

Wanderer, Nancy A., and Catherine R. Connors. *Culture and Crime: Kargar and the Existing Framework for a Cultural Defense.* 47 BUFFALO LAW REVIEW 829-873 (1999).

Weigert, Andrew J. *Whose Invisible Religion? Luckmann Revisited.* 35 SOCIOLOGICAL ANALYSIS 181-188 (1974).

Wengle, John L. ETHNOGRAPHERS IN THE FIELD. Tuscaloosa: University of Alabama Press, 1988.

Whiten, Andrew, and Christophe Boesch. *The Cultures of Chimpanzees.* 284(1) Scientific American 61-67 (January 2001).

Wilson, Edward. O. *The Biological Basis of Morality.* 281(4) Atlantic Monthly 53-70 (1998).

_____. Consilience: The Unity of Knowledge. New York: Alfred A. Knopf, 1998.

Wiredu, Kwasi. Cultural Universals and Particulars: An African Perspective. Bloomington: Indiana University Press, 1996.

Wisdom, John Minor. *Random Remarks on the Role of Social Sciences in the Judicial Decision-Making Process in School Desegregation Cases.* 39(1) Law and Contemporary Problems 134-149 (1975).

Wrightsman, L.S. Assumptions about Human Nature. 2d ed. Newbury Park, CA: Sage, 1992.

de Zengotita, Thomas. *The Functional Reduction of Kinship in the Social Thought of John Locke. In* Functionalism Historicized: Essays on British Social Anthropology, edited by George W. Stocking, Jr., 10-30. Madison: University of Wisconsin Press, 1984.

INDEX

ANTHROPOLOGY & MASS COMMUNICATION
Media and Myth in the New Millennium

Mark Allan Peterson
Assistant Professor of Anthropology and International Studies,
Miami University, Oxford, OH

Anthropological interest in mass communication and media has exploded in the last two decades, engaging and challenging the work on media in mass communications, cultural studies, sociology and other disciplines.

This is the first book to offer a systematic overview of the themes, topics and methodologies in the emerging dialogue between anthropologists studying mass communication and media analysts turning to ethnography and cultural analysis. Drawing on dozens of semiotic, ethnographic and cross-cultural studies of mass media, this study offers new insights into the analysis of media texts as well as models for the ethnographic study of media production and consumption, and suggests approaches for understanding media in the modern world system.

Placing the anthropological study of mass media into historical and interdisciplinary perspectives, this book examines how work in cultural studies, sociology, mass communication and other disciplines has helped shape the re-emerging interest in media by anthropologists.

From the Contents: Mass Mediations; Whatever Happened to the Anthropology of Media?; Media Texts; The Power of the Text; Media as Myth; The Ethnography of Audiences; The Ethnography of Media Production; Cottage Culture Industries; Mapping the Mediascape; Mediated Worlds

© 2003, *ca.* 336 pages
ISBN 1-57181-277-6 hardback, ISBN 1-57181-278-4 paperback

www.ingramcontent.com/pod-product-compliance
Lightning Source LLC
Chambersburg PA
CBHW072103020426
42334CB00017B/1612